The Ultimate PIPE BOOK

by

Richard Carleton Hacker

SOUVENIR PRESS

To S. Holmes, who first introduced me to the "spirit" of the pipe . . . and to Joan, who so graciously puts up with my devotion to this most noble of pastimes.

First published in the U.S.A. by
Autumngold Publishing

First British Edition published 1988 by
Souvenir Press Ltd., 43 Great Russell Street London WC1B 3PA

ISBN 0 285 62869 0

Photoset by Rowland Phototypesetting Ltd
Bury St Edmunds, Suffolk
Printed in Great Britain by
Mackays of Chatham plc, Chatham, Kent

". . . the moment a man takes to a pipe he becomes a philosopher. It's the poor man's friend; it calms the mind, soothes the temper, and makes a man patient under difficulties. It has made more good men, good husbands, kind masters, indulgent fathers, than any other thing on this blessed earth."

– from Sam Slick, the Clockmaker
by Thomas Chandler Haliburton, 1836

Table of Contents

Foreword

To paraphrase that venerable American corncob connoisseur, Mark Twain, "Everybody wants to smoke a pipe but nobody knows much about it." That is how this book got started.

I was first lured to the pipe while still in college, well over two decades ago. The complete recounting of these exploits (or as much of it as I felt the reader could endure) will be stumbled over occasionally as we wind our way along the course of the pages beyond. But suffice to say, nobody ever *taught* me how to smoke a pipe. Like many of the most important lessons in life, I had to learn for myself and was all the worse for it. Ah, had I only had a mentor! Unfortunately, there were no readily available books on the subject back then. My only encounters with any pipe smokers that I knew on a regular basis were Sherlock Holmes in novels and a few characters in the comic strips. Still, I persisted in my eager pursuit of the briar, learning as I went, making new discoveries and, in time, meeting others of the pipe smoking coterie, an opportunity which enabled me to share not only friendships, but information as well. I soon learned that the pipe smoking world was omnipresent and in many cases served as a common bond that linked a humanitarian cohesiveness between individuals, ideologies and international borders. So ubiquitous has the pipe become, yet how often it is ignored; how little importance do we actually place upon it in the overall scheme of things. This situation must be changed, if pipe smoking is to endure beyond our time. There is a danger of losing anything that we take for granted and our hobby is already under fire by those who wish to dictate the way in which we live. And so, I felt that now was the time for this book to be written.

Of course, no book so all-encompassing as ***The Ultimate Pipe Book*** can be the work of any one person. An author can do only so much with words and a typewriter. In an endeavor such as this, he needs facts to back him up, to verify his findings, and to shed new light down dimly-lit ancient corridors of misinformation. I could not have completed this book without the help of many who are listed within its pages. Fortunately, much of the pipe industry's history is recent enough that in many cases, I was able to go directly to the sources of information for a first-hand recounting of the facts. Additionally, my personal acquaintances with individuals of the world's leading pipe companies enabled me to open doors that have been previously shut and for this kindness, I am forever grateful; their cooperation has resulted in both the dispelling of myths and the enhancing of truths, and that was one of the reasons for which this book was written.

Since the beginning of the First Puff, there has always been an aura of informal camaraderie among pipe smokers, even though one may not know what brand of pipe or blend of tobacco the other is smoking. It can best be likened to an informal linking of souls between individuals who may have nothing more in common other than the fact that they share an enriched appreciation of life, and all that goes with it. Perhaps that is why so many gave so freely and unselfishly of their vast knowledge in order to help make this book as complete and factual as possible. While many are mentioned elsewhere within these pages, others should be acknowledged here, lest their own penchant for modesty hide them from the reader forever. First and foremost is Ben Rapaport, the dean of Antiquarian Tobacciana and one of the world's foremost experts on antique pipes, who fervently sent me bulging packages of his vast reference material, including originals of irreplaceable documents for me to review, copy and catalogue, as I saw fit. His dedication to the preservation of the pipe must be publicly applauded.

Additionally, one of America's most knowledgeable Dunhill and estate pipe dealers, Hugh Getzenberg of the Century City Pipe Shoppe in West Los Angeles, California, openly shared his invaluable knowledge and enthusiasm on high grade briars, asking only for a cup of coffee in payment. Other U.S. collectors, such as the late Mark Kaufman, Fred Janusek, Basil Sullivan, Frank Burla, and Dave Braddock supplied information that helped fill in many gaps while others, too numerous to mention, all helped add notes to my research and in many cases, inspired a new thought that caused me to explore another path that eventually led out of the fog of mystery that has surrounded so many of the old pipes. Of course, my warmest corporate thanks must go to the Tinder Box International, Ltd., the U.S. tobacco chain which not only gave me complete access to their valuable antique pipe collection for photography and study, but which also made their library of rare volumes of tobacciana available to me, thereby permitting a firsthand look into historical texts that few authors have ever seen.

Over on the British side of the Atlantic, the pipe industry itself personified the very product that it manufactures, being not only responsive and cooperative in my requests for information, but in many cases, extremely supportive. Of particular note are two of the "giants" of the industry, Dunhill Pipes Ltd. and Cadogan Investments. We are not only speaking of companies, we are also speaking of the *people.* Aubrey Styles and Ken Hillson made me feel more than welcome on my many visits to the home of the White Spot. And spending long-awaited time with Ian McOmish was almost as climactic as my visit to the Dunhill Archives themselves. Likewise, the unselfish time and enthusiasm generously given me by John Adler enabled me to verify numerous facts concerning Comoy's, GBD's and BBB's. Another organization that must be saluted is The British Pipesmokers' Council and their dedicated cooperation on my behalf, which only makes me wish we had such an organization in my own country. Also of note is John Barber of John Barber Pipes Ltd., who rallied forth with requested items time and again, even when surprised by an impromptu trunk call necessitated by an incomplete paragraph stuck in my typewriter. And who better than the gracious Alfred Sasieni himself to help verify my findings on the history of his legendary pipes? Likewise, I must light a bowl in honor of friend Jacques Cole, for his knowledge and dedication to an industry of which he is so much a part. There are others to thank, but by continuing to name them, I only increase the risk of leaving someone out, although you will find many of them listed in this book.

The one person who deserves a paragraph all to herself is my wife, Joan. Her support of ***The Ultimate Pipe Book*** has never waned from its first inception, many, many years ago. Through clouds of Latakia, Burley and Perique, she endured, not only in her support of the effort, but in the sheer physical and emotional energy of typing out and editing my rough-typed manuscript, and sacrificing times when other couples were "just being together." Now at last, we can read these pages "together." While I smoke a pipe, of course.

To be sure, there were some hardships connected with the completion of the final pages you now hold before you. On one occasion, I had all my pipes cleaned and polished for a photographic session, and upon finishing writing a chapter at 2 a.m. one night (or is that really morning?) and wishing to smoke a bowlful before retiring, I could not find a single briar that had not been scheduled for photography. Thus, rather than risk tarnishing my props, I smoked a clay for the next month and a half. Also, because I took most of these photographs myself, our home began to look like a tobacco warehouse and one of the neighbors finally suggested that we hold an auction during the next harvest season. Finally, in testing many of the tobaccos, I invariably emptied the leftover portions of some of the packets into a humidor that I kept just for this purpose. One day a friend came over and, as was his custom, invariably helped himself to a bowlful of my multi-mixture in the humidor.

"Wow!" he exclaimed upon taking his first puff. "This

stuff is great. You're the expert (sic) writing the pipe book . . . what is this super blend?"

For the life of me, I could not tell him.

I doubt if I could have written this same type of book about cigarettes or cigars, for once they are smoked, they are gone forever. But a pipe stays with you always, like a fond memory. It is not just an inanimate hollowed-out object which we fill with tobacco. The pipe is a unique invention of Man that has combined his creativity with the elements of nature: fire, earth, water and smoke, all of which co-mingle with the sky. There is a certain mystique to it all, and, perhaps that is why, when you see someone smoking a pipe, you cannot help but think he knows something you do not. But perhaps that mystique should now be dissipated and left for others, not to reverent pipe smokers such as we. For, my main goal and fervent hope is that reading this book will at least give you as much inner pleasure and enlightenment as a bowlful of your favorite tobacco in your most treasured briar, and that these pages that you now hold in your hands may somehow make that first puff before a crackling fire on a cold evening just a little bit more enjoyable.

After all, that was why this book was written.

RICHARD CARLETON HACKER

South American stone pipe and Indian effigy pipe from the Iroquois nation of North American Indians.

Chapter One

The Origins of Pipe Smoking

"In wreaths of smoke, blown waywardwise,
Faces of olden days uprise."

– In Wreaths of Smoke –
by Frank Newton Holman

I have no doubt that soon after God said, "Let there be light," someone else cried out, "*Give* me a light!" Pipe smoking has been with us almost that long. No one knows who the first pipe smoker actually was, but one of the oldest documented examples depicting a human being smoking a pipe is the carved statue of a Mayan priest which was discovered by archaeologists in a temple in Chiapas, Mexico. The priest, costumed in richly elaborate ceremonial dress, is puffing on a tube which is stuffed with smoldering weed. The statue has been dated as being carved sometime around the year 100 A.D. Additionally, there is evidence that as far back as the Roman Empire, smoking of some sort was going on. And I'm not just talking about Pompeii.

Because much of history is based upon hypothetical conjecture (and then facts are brought in to support the hypothesis), it is not too farfetched to assume that somewhere, somehow, someone swinging through the trees in the dim, dark jungles of man's ecological past actually may have inadvertently fashioned a pipe-like device out of a hollow reed or an animal bone, crammed it full of a nondescript plant, set fire to the whole affair and thereby established himself as the World's First Pipe Smoker. Of course, we don't know this for a prehistoric fact. What we do know is that before a pipe smoker could enjoy his craft, he would already have had to discover fire – although there are some who say that fire was discovered just so mankind could enjoy pipe smoking; after all, man had already been accustomed to eating raw meat and certainly didn't need fire for *that*. But puffing on an unlit pipe would make for a very long and frustrating evening. Thus, we can logically place the discovery of fire to lie somewhere in the same historical proximity as the smoking of tobacco. In fact, long before "civilized" countries began cautiously drifting out upon the oceans to explore their world, pipe smoking was already in vogue among the more "primitive" cultures of Mexico and Central America, where the Mayan, Toltec and Aztec nations smoked their pipe-like tubes and reeds and hollowed-out clay effigies for both medicinal and religious purposes; the use of pipe tobacco as a substance strictly for relaxation was not thought of. Elsewhere, tribes in Africa and the North American Indians incorporated the smoking of pipes and tobacco as important and symbolic elements of their various cultures. All of this was happening well before the 15th century.

The year 1492 has been branded into every U.S. citizen's brain since schooldays as the date that Columbus discovered America. But of equal importance to readers of this book is the fact that 1492 is also the date Columbus discovered tobacco. In fact, the exact date was Tuesday, November 6th, the exact place was in the Bahamas on the island of San Salvador and I believe the weather was slightly overcast.

Actually, it wasn't Columbus who first discovered tobacco, but rather two of his crew members, who were exploring the island and came across a tribe of natives busily burning "magical" tobacco leaves for incense in a religious ceremony. Unfortunately, the natives were unfamiliar with the *true* magic of tobacco, as they had never really smoked it (the honor of being the first civilization to actually *smoke* tobacco in a pipe-like device must go to the Mayans of Mexico and Central America). Still, the Spanish scouts told Columbus of their find and the famed explorer, following a practice long held in business, politics and the military, took credit for their work. Thus, Columbus became the first European to discover tobacco, although no one placed very much importance on the incident at the time, which is why every October 12th the United States celebrates Columbus Day rather than Pipe Tobacco Day.

Nonetheless, Columbus *can* lay direct claim to actually naming the strange new weed "tobacco." It was during this same celebrated search for a new sea route to Asia that his entourage came upon an island in the Caribbean where the natives used a pronged hollow-reed device they called a "tobago" for sniffing their magical smoke. Finding another Y-shaped island shaped like the Indian's tobago and noting that the same leaf-burning and smoke sniffing was going on there, Columbus simply called the new plant "Tobago,"

Woodcut of a 17th century English pipe smoker with clay.

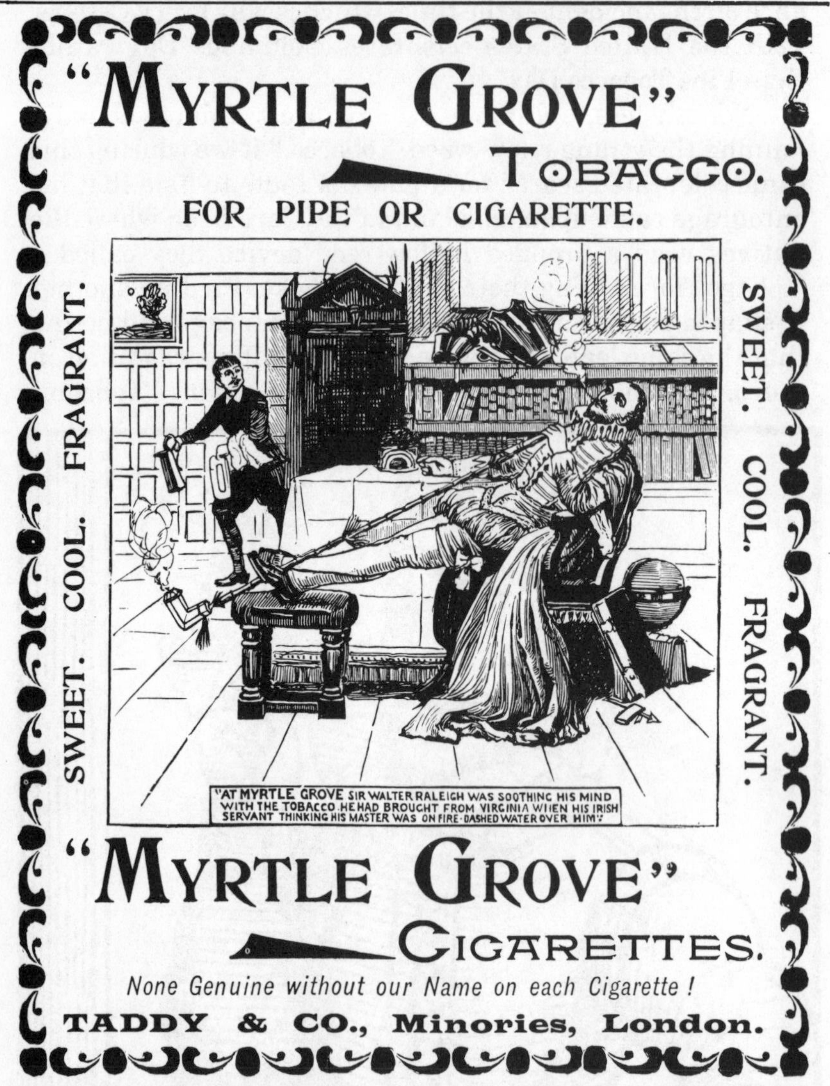

The celebrated incident of Sir Walter Raleigh's dousing with a bucket of water because his valet thought he was on fire was immortalized by this packet of cigarettes 200 years later.

which soon changed phonetically and finally emerged as the noun, Tobacco. Thus, a legend was born and although Chris sailed away without finding his famed trade route, he had unknowingly discovered something of far more esoteric value, the knowledge of pipe smoking, which he brought back to an unsuspecting world.

While Columbus' exploits as an explorer are fairly well documented, the knowledge of his discovery of tobacco lay forgotten in a long-lost manuscript for nearly three centuries, until it was finally discovered and published in 1875. This explains why earlier books on tobacco make no mention of the Spaniard's historic role in the annals of pipe smoking. Of course, Columbus had no earthly idea of the importance of his botanical discovery, the social prominence it would achieve, and the tremendous wealth it would eventually bring to all countries who engaged in its growth, sale, and use.

Although the Spaniards now knew about pipe smoking, no one did anything about it for a long time, but sporadic reports of its existence kept filtering back to Europe; in 1519 Cortez reported finding various tribes in Mexico puffing smoke from "perfumed reeds" (there is a good chance that the "perfume" Cortez wrote of was actually the aroma of the tobacco smoke itself). Seventeen years later, in 1536, French explorer Jacques Cartier, while searching for the famed Northwest Passage, found that pipe smoking was already an established ritual in Canadian Indian society.

Finally, in 1559 it was decided to import some of these "magical" tobacco leaves into Spain for use as medicinal herbs. After all, if so many cultures were doing it, there might be something to learn from the practice. The religious aspect of tobacco usage was completely ignored, although pipe smokers today pay homage to that custom by combining the heavenly flavor of their tobacco with angelic white clouds of smoke.

Just as pipe smoking had become widespread throughout the various tribes and civilizations of the Americas, it now just as quickly began to spread throughout the Mediterranean countries and Europe. In France, Jean Nicot, the Ambassador to Portugal, used ground and powdered tobacco leaves to effectively cure some of the French and other European nobility of various pains and ailments. Consequently, he was honored by having a variety of the leaf christened Nicotiana and the word Nicotine keeps his memory alive with us today.

The tobacco plant itself was finally classified by a Swedish botanist named Linnaeus as a member of the Solanaceae family, better known as "the consolers." How right he was in placing tobacco in that category, for pipe smoking has since been called "the contemplative man's relaxation." Indeed, pipe tobacco has become more than just a weed to be harvested, dried, flavored and sold; it is now a way of life, or more properly, a *part* of life itself!

However, medical practitioners and priests of the 16th century continued to look upon pipe smoking strictly in the context of its original medical connotations. It was the common man, the travellers, traders, merchants, soldiers and explorers who began to partake of Nicotiana Tabacum strictly for the pure pleasure it afforded, much as pipe smokers do today.

Although Spain can lay claim for introducing tobacco to Europe, it was the English, most notably Sir Walter Raleigh, who popularized pipe smoking for the masses by puffing a clay pipe in public. But Raleigh was not the first to do so; like Columbus, he was merely fortunate enough to have position, title, influence and the ability to communicate, all of which combined to give him far greater publicity than would have been possible otherwise. In all probability, the very *first* non-Indian pipe smokers were the seafaring merchants and explorers cruising along the shores of the Americas in the early 1500s.

In fact, as early as 1570, two English doctors had written a report which stated, "You see many sailors, and all those who come back from America, carrying little funnels made from a palm leaf or a reed, in the extreme end of which they insert the rolled and powdered leaves of this plant (tobacco)." This is probably the earliest recorded use of pipe smoking in England, although we do know that five years earlier, Sir John Hawkins actually brought some tobacco leaves back to Britain.

However, the first authenticated English smoker was a chap named Ralph Lane, whom Raleigh had appointed as the first Governor of Virginia. When Lane returned to England from the Colonies in 1586, it was recorded that ". . . he drank tobacco publicly in London and . . . the Londoners flocked from all parts to see him." From Virginia, Lane had brought an Indian pipe, which he presented to Raleigh and taught him how to smoke.

It is interesting to note that many early accounts of pipe smoking refer to the practices as "drinking" tobacco, as the smoke was actually sipped through a straw-like pipe stem and then blown out through the nose. In this way, it was generally believed to clear the nasal passages, thereby giving further credence to the medicinal benefits of pipe smoking, a belief that still survives to this day, although the benefits, I suspect, are more psychological than medicinal. But more of that later.

Raleigh's immediate infatuation with pipe smoking is legendary and under his influence, the court of Queen Elizabeth and English society in general were soon viewing pipe smoking as a very fashionable recreation. As might be expected, the creation of the now-famous English pipemaking industry was not very far behind the public discovery of tobacco and four years after Raleigh took his first public puff, the mass production of clay pipes began. There had been some earlier pipes fashioned from walnut shells, silver and pewter, but clay had the advantage of being both inexpensive and relatively fire resistant as a tobacco smoking instrument. The bowls, of course, were quite small by our present standards today, as one of the primary objections to the new-found sport of pipe smoking was the extremely high cost of tobacco. In fact, throughout pipe designing history, it is interesting to note that as tobacco gets less expensive, the bowls become bigger and a visual interpretation of how the price of pipe tobacco has fluctuated in various countries during the past 400 years can be made simply by lining up all the pipes from each period in chronological order and then observing the differing sizes of their bowls.

As it is to this day, pipe smoking was welcomed by writers, philosophers, historians and civic leaders (see Chapter Eight for more on this). It became looked upon as the thinking man's pastime and the Mermaid Tavern in London became a local smoking spot that was celebrated in both verse and song of the era. By 1602 pipe smoking had made its way throughout most of Europe, as well as India and even into the isolated realms of China and Japan, where it was said special smoking societies had been established.

A very few countries, such as Austria, tried to outlaw tobacco, but without much success.

Of course, smoking a pipe in those early years was not without its pitfalls. Although popular, it was still a strange new custom to many who were not used to seeing others "drink smoke." Our Leader himself, Sir Walter Raleigh, tells us of two unpleasant pipe predicaments that befell him in the 1580s, during pipe smoking's infancy. On one occasion, he was calmly smoking his clay pipe at a public gathering when, no doubt due to the strong, raw tobacco he was using, Raleigh suddenly found himself quite devoid of female companionship; in fact, all of the ladies in the room left *en masse* until he had finished consuming his bowlful, a situation that I (out of respect for history) sometimes reenact today when smoking a particularly strong English blend that I favor. However, I have never encountered Sir Walter's second experience, in which his valet threw a bucket of water upon his master, thinking the famous pipe smoker was on fire because he was blowing smoke through his mouth!

Although Queen Elizabeth frowned upon pipe smoking, she put up with it, largely because of Raleigh's charm. He once bet her that he could actually weigh the smoke from his pipe. She accepted the bet and Raleigh won by first weighing his fully-packed pipe, then smoking it until it was empty, and weighing it again. The difference between the two weights, he claimed, was the weight of the smoke! To her credit, the Queen paid the wager while stating, "Many alchemists have . . . turned gold into smoke, but Raleigh is the first who has turned smoke into gold!"

These happy-go-lucky days of introductory pipe smoking were soon to end, however, as tobacco also had its enemies, among whom were King James, King Charles and Cromwell. James was the first to make his anti-smoking wrath felt when, in 1603, he issued his infamous (to pipe smokers of then and now) "Counterblaste to Tobacco," in which he cursed all non-medicinal use of the weed in language that sought to send every pipe smoker down into the depths of hell. The king was so prejudiced against pipe smoking that if James I were alive today, he would no doubt put the smoking section of airlines on the runway rather than in the rear of the aircraft.

The King James "Counterblaste" was the first anti-smoking campaign in history and like U.S. Prohibition three centuries later, it had just the opposite effect of its intended purpose. In order to make his views known, James had his anti-tobacco propaganda carried throughout the British Isles. As a consequence, Englishmen in even the remotest parts of the Kingdom who had not yet heard of "drinking smoke" began to wonder just what was it about this strange new weed that caused royalty to be making such a fuss. Therefore, thousands were compelled to try it out of curiosity. To their pleasant surprise, they liked it and pipe smoking caught on with the sudden intensity of a bone dry bowlful of Burley lit with a blowtorch in the Sahara Desert.

The King was appalled; how dare his subjects overrule his wishes? He raised the import duty on tobacco and sales boomed! Moreover, tradesmen began importing other varieties of tobacco from Portugal and Spain. Finally, in an effort to divert some of the taxation in the Colonies, John Rolfe began the first commercially grown crop of tobacco in North America in 1612, and the first shipment of American-grown West Indian tobacco was made to England one year later, starting an industry that helped bring prosperity to the fledgling Colonies which later became the same States that produce practically all of the "English made" pipe tobacco today. It is a shame that most history books only refer to Rolfe as the husband of Pocahontas, rather than as the man who started the tobacco industry in America.

In spite of the royal displeasure it incurred, by 1615 a London historian wrote that ". . . tobacco shops are now as ordinary as tap-houses and taverns." Clearly, pipe smoking was *the* thing to do in England, even though Cambridge students were threatened with expulsion if caught with a pipe in their mouths. But for Sir Walter, the penalty was even more severe, for while pipe smoking can sometimes make one giddy, it caused him to completely lose his head in the Tower of London. Before the executioner's axe blade fell, Raleigh's last act was to smoke a bowl of tobacco. One would assume that he chose a pipe with an extraordinarily large bowl and had what was probably the longest smoke in his life. The date of his execution was October 28, 1618, an event marked in London each year by the presenting of pipes and tobacco to the Chelsea Pensioners at the Royal Hospital. Such is England's homage to their rightful place in pipe smoking history.

Yet, Raleigh did not die in vain; one year later King James begrudgingly signed the charter incorporating all British pipemakers, an act he must have enjoyed as much as

This early woodcut shows a typical English pub smoking scene from the 1600s. It was said that by lighting two pipes from a single candle, a friendship or bargain would be sealed.

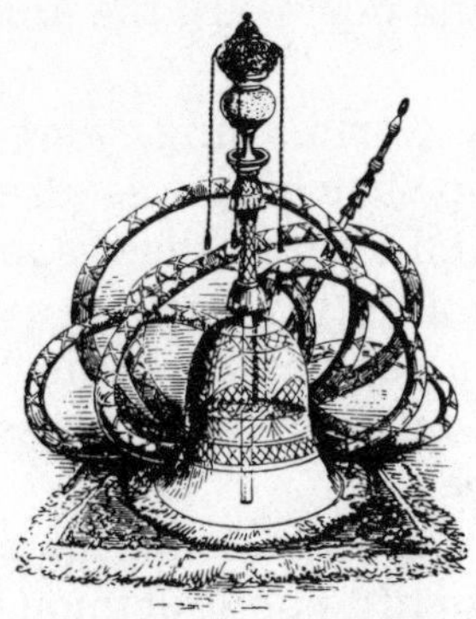

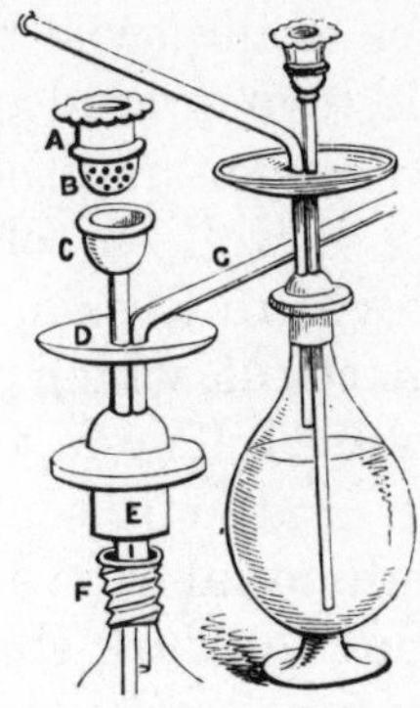

The hookah or water pipe, and its various parts.

An early Dutch smoker with a 17th century porcelain pipe designed for smoking outside the house while the smoker remained inside!

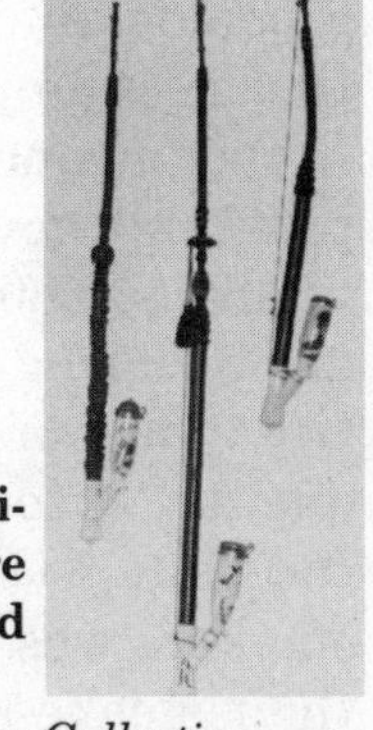

Germanic regimental pipes are decorative and historic.
Credit: Erik Nørding Collection

pipe smoking itself. But public opinion and the taxation laws ruled against him. James responded by banning from England all tobacco other than that which was shipped to the Mother Country from the Colonies, and limiting even that amount to 100 pounds per year per planter. The Jesuit priests countered by stating publicly that tobacco was an aid to both health and morals and such a paltry amount to be imported would not be enough to save Mankind. In 1633 King James lashed out at pipe smoking again by requiring that all tobacconists be licensed. Although intended as punishment by taxation, the new law officially recognized the profession for the first time, thereby giving the tobacco shop a new stature in society. It seemed that every time King

James would twist the pipe smoking dog's tail, the animal would turn around and bite him.

However, in other parts of the world, things were not going so well for tobaccophiles. Pipe smoking was already outlawed in Russia, Switzerland and even in the Colony of Connecticut, which passed a law prohibiting smoking a pipe in public. In Persia, the penalty for pipe smoking was instant death, and to this day it is still the only sure way to prevent an individual from enjoying his pipe.

But the dark shadows that had been tainting the pure white pipe smoke were beginning to lift; public opinion was gradually winning out, especially in those countries where the leaders had partaken of the clay pipe themselves. In France, King Louis XIII took a pinch of snuff in 1637 (his first, it is believed) and enjoyed it so much he immediately repealed all of France's anti-tobacco laws, thereby opening the doors for pipe smokers to come out of the French closets. In fact, France quickly turned the growing of tobacco into a profitable government monopoly which, by 1771 was yielding $5,500,000 to the treasury; by 1917 that amount would grow to over $90,000,000. Meanwhile, in Russia, Peter the Great not only learned how to smoke a pipe, but consequently encouraged all Russians to do likewise. In Persia, the Shah was now smoking a pipe and the death threat for smokers was lifted, enabling thousands of citizens to leave their smoke-filled tents and puff freely in the fresh desert air.

By now England was the undisputed pipe smoking capital of the civilized world, in spite of the fact that it had many restrictive laws against the practice. By the mid-1600s coffee houses were providing an assortment of clay pipes and various tobaccos for periodic use by guests. Pipe smoking was even looked upon as a deterrent to crime, as a publicized complaint by a hangman stated that there was not enough work for him to do because people were too busy growing, harvesting and smoking pipe tobacco to have any time left over for breaking laws.

In addition to the social bonds and relaxing moments it afforded, pipe smoking was widely viewed as a general cure for practically every known physical ailment of the 16th century, including headaches, hoarseness, stomach disorders, toothaches and even the gout. Pipe smoking was believed to be especially healthful during the months spelled without an R, although through dedicated experimentation, I have found my pipe to be equally rewarding the other eight months of the year as well. However, the real test of pipe smoking as a healthful disinfectant occurred during England's plague years of 1644–66. In fact, during the Great Plague of 1665, as it is commonly referred to, tobacco achieved an unbelievable boost in popularity when it was discovered that very few tobacconists or their pipe smoking customers were affected by the wide-spread pestilence. Soon, physicians were seen attending the "dead carts" and the sick while smoking clay pipes, a professional endorsement which increased pipe sales all the more. In the northern end of the islands, an Irishman wrote of his twenty-four-year-old friend who lay dying in bed. His doctor had forbidden him to smoke his pipe until he recovered, but feeling he would soon be buried in the clay before he could ever again enjoy the pleasures of the clay, he began smoking the pipe daily. Within a week he had recovered. Such stories are commonplace among both early and present-day accounts of pipe smokers and while pipe tobacco is no longer listed as a medicine, we do know that smoke itself is a great preservative, which no doubt explains why so many pipe smokers look and feel so young!

The ascension of William III to the throne of England in 1697 was a long-awaited blessing to pipe smokers throughout the realm. A pipe smoker himself, William of Orange brought with him the large Dutch clays of his homeland. English society was quick to pick up the fashion, and England's clay pipemakers immediately began increasing the size of their bowls. This of course, resulted in a greater consumption of tobacco per sitting, which in turn placed greater demand upon the tobacconists. It also gave the pipe smoker a longer, more rewarding session with his clay.

By the 1700s pipe smoking had become commonplace in the Colonies to such an extent that pipe tobacco was used as a form of barter to purchase land, rifles and even the service of ministers. In fact, in 1724 Pope Benedict XIII discovered the peaceful rewards of pipe smoking and promptly absolved all users of the weed from any wrongdoing. Another convert (a word that is most respectfully used in this case) had been won over to pipe smoking.

Unfortunately for Europe, the pipe had temporarily gone out of style by the late 1700s, being replaced with the more aloof habit of snuff. But by now pipe smoking was very much in vogue in the "revolutionary" United States. So much was tobacco a part of young America's culture that Thomas Jefferson had tobacco leaves designed as part of the decoration of the new nation's capital building. Tobacco leaves are also found adorning the columns outside the Supreme Court. The fact that many prominent leaders, such as George Washington, were also prominent tobacco growers no doubt helped start our country's burning love affair with Ms. Nicotiana.

Like mini-skirts and narrow ties of a later age, social customs can be a fickle thing and by 1837, when Queen Victoria took the throne in Great Britain, pipe smoking was once again in fashion throughout Europe, where the clay pipe was making a strong public re-appearance, most notably in the ale houses and private clubs of England. This was somewhat ironic, for Queen Victoria was opposed to all forms of tobacco. Perhaps that explains why pipe smoking underwent an unusual transformation during the Victorian era.

Previously, pipe smoking had been a social endeavor, with pipes very much in evidence in public and polite society. But gradually, pipe smoking was being transformed into a strictly private affair, to be conducted only in a special "smoking room" of the house or within the hallowed halls of private smoking clubs, in which men of fashion gathered to sit, smoke, and share the pleasantries of meaningful conversation if the opportunity presented itself. Moreover, this turn of events spawned a new style of fashion: the smoking jacket and cap, to better protect the male pipe smoker from the odor of his own tobacco. Of course, the less affluent smoker who possessed neither smoking chamber nor smoking jacket could always smoke in the main room of the house, providing he kept his smoke out of polite society by judiciously blowing it into the blazing hearth of the fireplace and up the chimney, a practice your humble author still follows to this day, at least whenever the hay fever season is in bloom for my charming wife and some of her non-aromatic-sniffing friends. So closely was pipe smoking associated with the home that with the advent of the automobile, many tobacconists feared that the new-fangled contraption would lure men from their houses and pipe smoking would fade away like so much tobacco smoke.

Like the pipe smoker, the pipe itself has undergone a number of changes since it was first devised by Man unknown centuries ago. In the beginning, it was a crude tube filled with tobacco. Later, these tobacco holding devices were decorated with symbols or carved into shapes representing magical or mythical beliefs. Many of these early pipes were designed in the shapes of birds, animals, men or geometric designs, all of which had a preordained meaning that related to the specific reason the pipe was being smoked. Perhaps the crudest pipe, if it can be called that, was devised by the Indians of the American Northwest, who simply dug a hole in the ground, filled it with tobacco, set fire to the earthbound clump of weed and sucked the smoke up through a hollow reed stuck into the hole. I suspect they had very little pipe cleaning problems with this arrangement.

Other Indians made their pipes from a variety of materials, including jasper, marble and stone. However, with tobacco's introduction to European civilization, the clay pipe was born, the longest reigning design, for it is still with us to this day (see Chapter Three).

Starting out as rather plain and small-bowled in design, clay pipes underwent a transformation all their own. Probably the oldest of these pipes was first conceived in the British Isles and became known as the diminutive-bowled "Fairy Pipe" (sometimes confusingly called the "Dutch Pipe") of Ireland. In Scotland, these tiny clays are referred to as "Elfin pipes" or "Celtic pipes." The Irish and Scots have traditionally smoked clays with shorter stems (usually around three inches long), called dundeens or Cutty Pipes, the word "cutty" meaning "short." Some of the early clays even had flat-bottomed bowls so that they could stand upright, a style reappearing today, especially by many of the custom briar pipe-makers of the world (see Chapter Two).

The Elizabethan clays of Sir Walter Raleigh's time were very graceful affairs, with thin bowls and elongated narrow stems. When the Dutch got hold of this design, they enlarged the bowl and lengthened the stem to about 14 to 16 inches on average, although variations are always found. This style became known as the Alderman, and was "officially" introduced by William II around 1700. Later, the Alderman was adopted by the English, who put a graceful curve to the stem and called it their "Yard of Clay," or Churchwarden, as it is more commonly known today. The purpose of the elongated stem was to allow the smoker to rest his hand and bowl on the arm of his chair as he dreamily puffed away. The tiny knob on the bottom of the bowl was originally put there to keep the hot clay from touching, and consequently burning, the arm of the chair. Later, this nodule simply became a design element on shorter pipes. By 1815, Churchwarden clays were all the rage among the elite, although the common man was often relegated to the shorter-stemmed clays, made even shorter each time the tip of the stem was snapped off in order to fully detach oneself from all physical contact with the pipe's previous smoker, as many of these clays were community property at the various ale houses that dotted every English village.

Although the earliest clays had very small bowls, these were gradually enlarged to about two inches in height to allow for greater consumption of tobacco, a welcomed Dutch influence. In addition to being able to procure clay pipes of different bowl sizes and stem lengths, by the 1800s it was possible to find pipes with a variety of designs cast into their bowls, ranging from a simple maker's mark, such as found on early North American fur-trade era pipes, to elaborate Victorian scrollwork, romping animals, and even the personages of famous individuals. Because they were so inexpensive, the clay was popular with all classes of smokers. The tips of some of the better made clays were often glazed or covered with wax in order to keep the clay from sticking to the smoker's lips (and not, as some erroneously believe, as a health measure). In fact, for a while, clay pipes that were

The solace of the pipe became a favorite subject for early illustrators, such as this 1888 depiction of a gentleman with his churchwarden, sketched by John Wallace.

completely glazed and sometimes colored were quite the fashion and I have in my collection a glazed clay sporting a small round clay loop cast under the bowl; when one places his eye very near this loop and looks through it, a line drawing of the St. Louis Exhibition can be seen. The pipe was obviously made during that time to commemorate the event and as well made as it is, I have often wondered why nobody ever smoked it.

Clay pipes are still being manufactured, and literally millions of clays are sold each year to pipe smokers as well as pipe collectors. Although it remained unchallenged as the most popular smoking instrument for the first 250 years of recorded pipe history, the time-honored clay began to lose ground in the 1850s, with the introduction of briar.

Up to and including the present day, there has been a never-ending search among pipe smokers and pipemakers to find the ultimate material for the fashioning of pipes. Everything from seashells to metal to space-age synthetics has been used, with varying degrees of success. (From about 1790 to 1820 pipes were even made of glass, most notably around Bristol and Nailsea; fortunately they were used for trade signs, not for smoking.) Yet to date, nothing has ever surpassed the smoking qualities of briar, a hardened, dense wooden burl that is found within the root system (which is why it is sometimes called briar-root) of the white heath tree (known as Erica Arborea for you Latin-speaking pipeologists), a plant that originated in France and Corsica.

It is the French who can, in all probability, lay claim for bringing the briar pipe to fruition. For years, in the small valley-enclosed village of Saint-Claude, pipemakers have been practicing their trade and as early as 1800 were experimenting with pipes made out of beechwood and boxwood. Most of these finely carved pipes were created for French nobility, including the elite officer's corps of Napoleon's army, an ironic fact, inasmuch as the emperor himself did not approve of pipe smoking, a prejudice derived from a liquor-laced evening which was climaxed by Napoleon gagging on a bad lot of ragweed. Perhaps inspired by this, Prussian General Gebhard von Blücher insisted on raising

An extremely fine example of an antique Chinese water pipe with cloisonne inlays. The brush and spade were used to clean out the thin tubular metal bowl.

Courtesy: Tinder Box Collection

Primitive African (Basutoland) tribal effigy pipe made of wood with flanged mouthpiece.

Courtesy: Wells Collection of Tobacco Antiquities, Bristol, England

his pipe in the air as he led his troops into battle, which included Waterloo, of course.

Nonetheless, it was around 1840 when a pipemaker named Francois Comoy (who, in 1825, started the first full-time pipe factory in Saint-Claude) began carving pipes out of France's native bruyère (which has subsequently been called brier and finally briar). The briar pipes smoked amazingly well, without the adverse effect of hot smoke and occasional tongue bite that the clay pipe exhibited. In addition, the briar pipe provided a cooler smoke, enabling the puffer to hold the bowl in his hand (smokers of the thin-walled clays must always hold their pipes by the stem or else they run the risk of burning their hands). Moreover, the briar pipe seemed to "breathe," and consequently kept the embers of the tobacco lit for a greater period of time. It also

A variety of European and American Tomahawk pipes used for trade and ceremonial purposes.

seemed to provide a more flavorful smoke. Thus, an industry was born and today, France, along with England and Italy, has become one of the top briar pipe producing countries in the world; Saint-Claude is often called the "pipe-making capital," and the Comoy pipe, although now made in London, is still carved from the briar-root of the French heath tree.

The first briar pipes were introduced in England around 1854 and that historic nation of pipe smokers found immediate favor with the unique wood, discovering that its beautiful grain, cool smoking qualities and, of course, durability, all far outclassed the old clay. By 1859 briar was firmly established as *the* serious smoker's pipe. At first, only "straights" were produced in briars, with mouthpieces of amber, vulcanite or horn. Sometime around 1885, the first briar "bent," or curved pipe was introduced and today, trivia buffs can take great pleasure in discrediting certain period films that are set in years prior to 1880 which depict a character smoking a *bent* briar pipe.

Next to briar, the second most highly desirable pipemaking material among both pipe smokers and collectors is meerschaum, which is a German word meaning "sea-foam." The substance itself is comprised of the fossilized remains of prehistoric, microscopic sea creatures, and is composed of silica, magnesia, carbonic acid and water. It is only found in one area of Turkey, where it occurs in clumps found deep underground (see Chapter Two for more information on the mining of meerschaum). In its rawest form it can be soaked in water to produce a lather and early Turkish and Mongolian tribes used it for washing their linens. Today meerschaum has a much more highly prized value among pipe smokers.

The material itself is relatively soft, lightweight, and porous. Properly treated, it is very easy to carve and meerschaum pipes have been transformed into images of animals, people, gods and freeform designs, all of which are carved by a relatively small coterie of Turkish craftsmen whose skill ranges from crude to exquisite, and it is the quality of the carving as well as the quality and size of the meerschaum pipe itself that determines the price of the object. Early meerschaum pipes of the Victorian era were often decorated and inlaid with jewels and precious metals, but this is rarely done nowadays, with the importers relying mainly on the characteristics of the various artisans who do their carvings for them.

A meerschaum pipe starts out as being pure white in color, but as it is smoked, it gradually (over a period of months) starts to change into a light tan, then a darker tan and finally it transcends into the brown realms, as the material is gradually permeated with years of tobacco juices, tars and smoke. Eventually, if the person keeps at it long enough, a meerschaum pipe will acquire a deep reddish brown patina that is highly prized by both smoker and collector alike.

So desirable was the look of a "truly aged" meerschaum that in the 1880s and 90s, many of these finely carved (and some not so finely carved) pipes were sold as "artificially aged." Yet even today, over 100 years later, with over a century of *real* aging upon them, they do not have the same look, depth and color to the trained eye. In pipes, as in life itself, nothing can equal the genuine article. It is interesting to note that these "pseudo-smoked" antique meerschaums now have a collector's value of their own, but they do not equal the value of a similar meerschaum pipe which has been genuinely smoked through the years to achieve its deep, inwardly glowing brown color. Even today there are artificially colored waxes formulated to speed up the coloring process, but they have yet to approximate the real thing.

The first meerschaum pipe of record was created in 1723 and was the result of the whim of an Austrian Count named Andrassy. While visiting Turkey, Count Andrassy had been given a large block of meerschaum as a product unique to that area. Impressed by its light weight and remarking how similar the texture of the meerschaum was to his clay pipes, Andrassy commissioned a local pipemaker named Karl-Kowates to carve a pipe out of this unusual material. Kowates was resourceful on two counts: first, he carved not one but two pipes – one for Andrassy and one for himself. Second, because he was aware that very few pipe carvers ever get rich (even back then!), he also was a shoemaker, in an entrepreneurial attempt to make ends meet.

We have no record of how Count Andrassy's pipe fared, but we do know something of the shoemaker's meerschaum smoking adventures. As he puffed on his new pipe over a period of months, he noticed that the bowl, where it was constantly held, was gradually turning a rich tannish brown color. After analyzing the situation, the cobbler deduced that it was the shoe wax from his hands that was heating up as he smoked the pipe and was somehow responsible for the coloring. He then set about purposefully waxing the entire bowl and eventually, through a lengthy period of smoking the pipe, day after day, saw his creation start to turn a rich chestnut brown. Thus, the legendary meerschaum pipe was born.

Although briar and meerschaum are by far the most popular pipes today (with briar outselling meerschaum by a substantial margin), there are other equally historic pipes in smoking geneology which should be chronicled, especially since many of them are still popular with various segments of the world.

For example, long before the acceptance of briar as a pipemaking material, the Germans were experimenting with various types of wood, and ended up literally carving a place in pipemaking history for themselves as they fashioned elongated pipes with tall, slender bowls which reflected various aspects of Germanic history and folklore. Forest scenes, wild stags, running boars, beautiful maidens and stoic military portraits were just a few of the many designs that decorated the large Teutonic bowls, which were made of material that ranged from oak to porcelain. The designs were carved into the wooden bowls, but the porcelain variety had their scenes meticulously handpainted with the same loving care that an artist might lavish on a much larger canvas. Later, some of the less expensive versions of these porcelain pipes merely used colored transfers to achieve this same visual effect. Tyrolean pipes were normally constructed in three parts: the stem (often made from cherrywood), a hollowed out bottom bowl which was used as a handle and also served both to cool the smoke and to act as a depository for moisture from the tobacco, and the tobacco bowl itself, which sometimes featured a hinged lid to keep wind and rain away from the bowl as well as to keep burning ashes from falling out of the pipe and onto the floor. In fact, during the 1800s, some European establishments actually had laws requiring all pipes smoked within their premises to be equipped with these "fireproof" lids.

These Germanic pipes, in all their various forms, are often referred to as Swiss, Bavarian or Tyrolean in design and are quite picturesque and particularly charming when displayed in groups of three or more, hanging on a wall. They are still made today although they are more readily available in Europe than in the United States. If you want to obtain this particular design of pipe for smoking (as opposed to using it only as a decorator item or a collectible), care must be taken to purchase the best you can buy from a reputable dealer, as there are many cheaper versions that are sold strictly as souveniors and are not ideally suited to smoking.

The Germans were not the only pipemakers to utilize porcelain. As noted previously, the English and especially the French created some exquisitely decorated bowls featuring glazed enamel portraits and pastoral scenes. During the 1850s the French also experimented with lining the bowls of their various wooden pipes with clay or porcelain to keep the smoking tobacco from burning through the sides. These lined bowls met with a certain degree of success (some are still being made today) but it is their development of the briar pipe for which we owe the French a debt of smoking gratitude.

Perhaps one of the most cumbersome yet enjoyable and fascinating pipes is the hookah, or water pipe. Invented by the Persians and made popular long before the 1600s, the hookah has been a popular smoking instrument in practically every European country, including Russia and Germany as well as in Asia and Africa. Water pipes have been fashioned of everything from copper to coconuts and in Africa I even saw one made from an eland's horn. In the United States, the hookah is still considered a novelty, even though it does provide an exceptionally cool smoke. Going through a bowlful of Turkish tobacco can be quite pleasurable if one doesn't mind sounding like the kitchen sink every time one takes a bubbly puff.

Basically, the hookah is constructed like a jar, which is filled one-half to three-quarters full with water. The narrow neck of the jar is sealed with a stopper, through which two hollow tubes are inserted. One tube is connected to the pipe bowl and is long enough to almost touch the bottom of the water-filled jar. The other tube ends above the waterline, extends out through the stopper and is connected to a long, flexible woven tube, to which is fitted a mouthpiece. When the pipe is puffed, the smoke is drawn down into the water, which acts as a filter. The cooled and cleansed smoke then bubbles up to the surface, where it is drawn out through the mouthpiece. Because the outgoing tube is above the waterline, only the smoke is puffed, not the water (which takes on the pungent smell of nicotine almost immediately and should be emptied after each smoke). Sometimes "flavoring agents" such as brandy are used instead of water but because of the large capacity of the hookah, be sure to use a very *cheap* brandy, as you most definitely will not want to drink it

An early 17th century European smoking scene. Note the small clay bowls and the pipe "accessories" lying on the table.

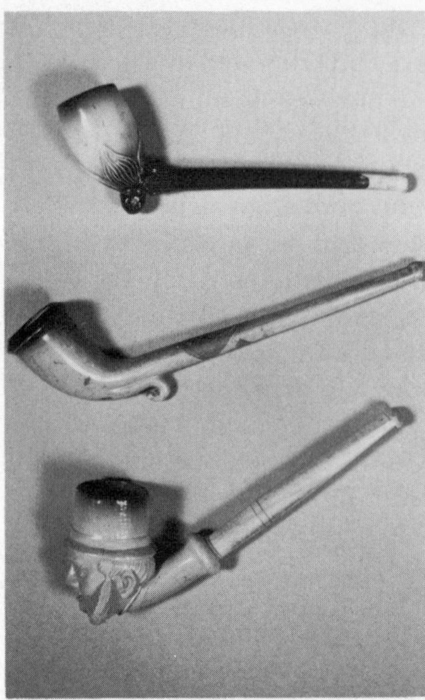

Three different styles of 19th century glazed clay pipes manufactured with tonal coloring to give them a "smoked" look. The nodule underneath the bowl of the top pipe contains a miniature view of the St. Louis Exhibition and was probably sold to commemorate that event. The middle pipe still has its original "goedewaagen pijp – Gouda, Holland" label affixed to it. The bottom pipe features a wooden stem as a separate piece.

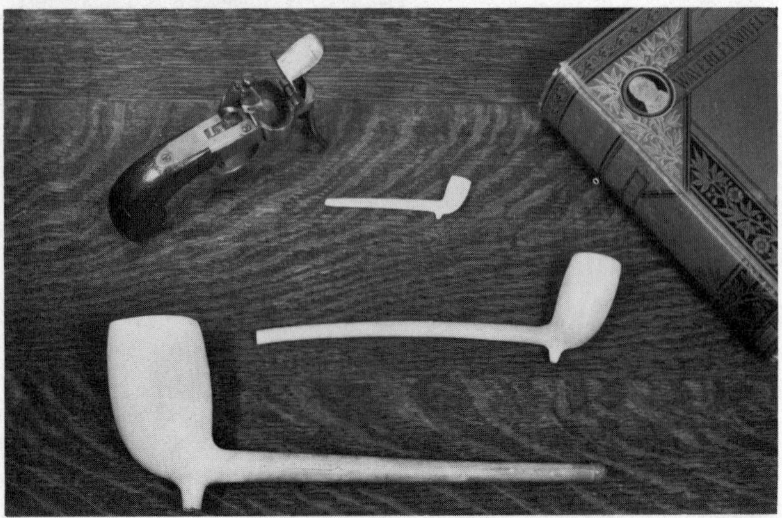

Three sizes of 18th century clay pipes. The small elfin pipe on top is unmarked; center broken churchwarden is stamped ES and was made by goedewaagen, Holland. The unusually large clay on the bottom was made by W. White, Glasgow, Scotland, and is so marked. The late 17th century tinder lighter is English and is the forerunner of the modern match.

British Staffordshire Ware coil clay, c. 1808, was more decorative than practical. *Courtesy: Dunhill Collection*

An early 1850s Germanic "dry bowl" pipe. Some individual pipe-makers are re-introducing this "screw-in" bowl style today; although the stylings are substantially different, the idea is not new.

During the 1840 fur trade era of the Mountain Man in the American West, the buckskin "gage d'amour" was a favored way for frontiersmen to carry pipe and tobacco.

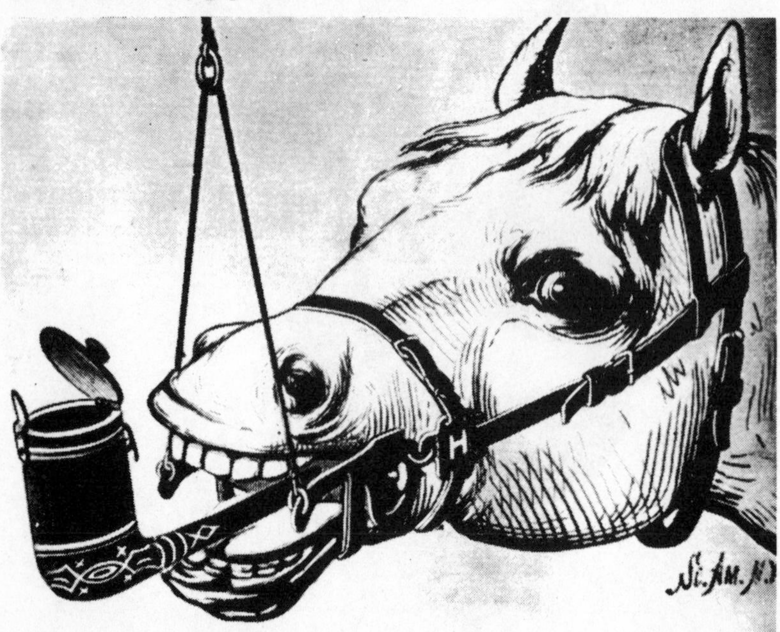

By the late 19th century, the popularity of the pipe convinced many people that its pleasures should be shared by all creatures, as evidenced by this unique invention that was proposed, but thankfully, never put into production.

A late 19th century studio portrait of an American Plains Indian in full ceremonial dress with brass-beaded "Peace Pipe."

Many American western frontiersmen considered a pipe as part of their regular attire. This early photo is of Mose Milner, better known as "California Joe," who scouted for General George A. Custer and was rarely seen without a pipe in his mouth. Milner was one of the few who elected not to ride with Custer to the Little Big Horn, as he was out of tobacco and did not want to make the trip without his pipe! It was a decision that enabled him to enjoy many more bowlfuls in later years.

Credit: Herb Peck Collection

after a bowlful of Nicotiana Tabacum has been filtered through it. Hookahs can be very plain or extremely ornate, and are usually made of glass, brass, porcelain or cut crystal. The Orientals created some extremely ornate and colorful lacquered water pipes which are smaller than the Turkish design. But normally, a water pipe is not the sort of thing you would carry with you to the next Managing Directors meeting unless you happen to own the company; it is better adapted for relaxing at home while watching Soccer matches on TV. The hookah is a unique and pleasant method of obtaining one of the "purest smokes" possible, as long as you don't mind the gurgling of the pipe with each puff, although I suspect the sound of the hookah might have a soporific effect on pet goldfish.

Today, after West Germany and England, the United States is the third largest pipe smoking country in the world. Thus, the next two pipes we will examine are distinctly American and represent a spectrum as diverse as the many nationalities that reside in that great nation.

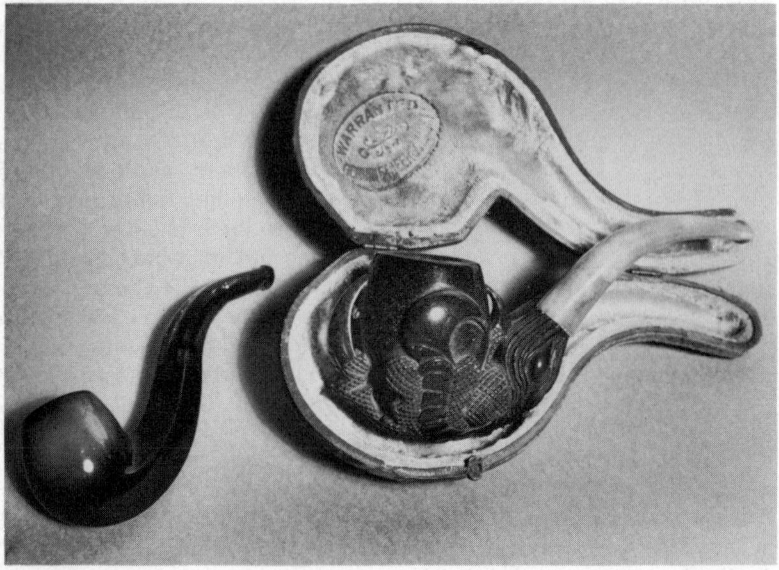

Two examples of pre-colored meerschaums. The pipe on the left is from the early 1900s while the eagle-claw pipe dates from the late 19th century.

The first, and rarest, of these pipes is the Indian Calumet, or peace pipe. Already established as an integral part of North American Indian culture by the time the first white explorers ventured into the uncharted regions of the Far West, the peace pipe served as a powerful and binding contract among the various tribes. It was normally kept in the possession of the tribal chieftain and a great and solemn ritual was attached not only to smoking the pipe, but also to whom you smoked it with. The bowl was normally made of wood or clay and the long wooden stem was often decorated with strips of animal hide, beads, trade wool and in later years, after 1820, with brass tacks. The pipe was smoked with a "spiritual" mixture of tobacco and bark or special herbs, depending on the tribe.

In an effort to make this pipe book as complete as possible, I am now going to relate a passage from the 1850 American Western classic, *Wah-To-Yah and The Taos Trail*, which actually tells you how to smoke a peace pipe. To my knowledge, this is the first time such information has been disseminated to the 20th century pipe smoker and I trust it will make for interesting conversation at your next cocktail party. In his 19th century pipe smoking observations among the Cheyenne Indians, the author, Lewis Garrard wrote:

> ". . . Religion they (the Cheyenne) have none, if, indeed, we except the respect paid to the pipe; nor do we see any signs or vestiges of spiritual worship; but, one remarkable thing – in offering the pipe, before every fresh filling, to the sky, the earth, and the winds, the motion made in so doing, describes the form of a cross; and in blowing the first four whiffs, the smoke is invariably sent the same four directions."

It is interesting to note how pipe smoking creates a common bond among all men, no matter how diverse their backgrounds, for in reading through the rest of his book, Garrard writes frequently of the evenings at camp after long, hard and dangerous days in the saddle, in which the most relaxing moments were spent in the solemn company of a trusty and well-smoked clay pipe. Relating his personal exploits with the mountain men and explorers of that era, he writes, "... the lonely trapper who, in momentary danger of losing his scalp, builds his fire, cooks his meat and smokes the pleasant tobacco, (but) not without first offering, to the towering crests, the mouth of his pipe, and the freely given homage of the first and most honorable puff."

It was shortly after this time, in fact the year was 1868, that the second uniquely American pipe got its start and has been with us ever since, growing in popularity every year, it seems, no doubt due to its extremely low cost when compared to other forms of smoking. It is the historic corncob, a pipe immortalized by such diverse personages as General Douglas MacArthur and Popeye. The corncob deserves a lot more credit than we are apt to give it, for it was also smoked by Mark Twain, Herbert Hoover, Carl Sandburg and Thomas Hart Benton to name a few (for other famous American corncob smokers, be sure to see Chapter Eight). So much was the corncob a part of early American culture that during World War I the U.S. government ordered four million corncobs shipped to U.S. "doughboys" overseas.

The corncob pipe was the invention of a Dutch settler named Henry Tibbe, who founded the cob pipemaking firm of H. Tibbe & Son in 1868 and later changed the company's name to The Missouri Meerschaum Company, which is still in business today and is the only large-scale producer of corncob pipes in the world. The pipes are still made by hand, one at a time, in the same brick building that has housed the firm for over a century.

Pipes made from hollowed out corncobs had been a practice among American frontiersmen and Indians long before Tibbe came on the scene. The problem with these early home-made affairs was that they quickly burned out and were extremely porous, giving a hot, wet smoke that was unpleasant to say the least. But Tibbe was a woodcarver by trade and being aware of the popularity of the inexpensive corncob pipes, thought he could make them a little bit better. He had the local chemist mix up a special plaster-of-paris paste, which he soaked into the cobs in order to seal off the porousness. He then sanded the cobs to a smooth finish, giving them a more polished look and feel. Cutting some hollow reeds from the banks of the nearby Missouri River and pounding them into holes drilled in the sides of his cob pipe bowls, Tibbe put his first batch of "improved" corncobs in his workshop window and sold every one for a nickel apiece on the first day. The rest, as they say, is corncob history. Today, Missouri Meerschaum turns out more than 35,000 pipes a year and completely dominates the industry; its only other competitor is the small firm of Buescher Industries, located one block away! To keep up with the demand and the quality of its world-famous corncobs (in addition to their extensive U.S. sales, corncob pipes are popular in Europe as symbols of the Old West), a special hybrid corn has been grown since 1946 to create larger and stronger cobs in addition to the standard designs (for more information on corncob pipemaking, see Chapter Two). It is a unique market, for corncobs, being corncobs, do not last as long as briar pipes and therefore must be constantly replaced, thereby insuring a perpetual place for themselves by continuously self-destructing. Their claim to fame is that they are inexpensive, picturesque, and uniquely American.

Throughout the 20th century, the pipe has waxed and waned as a barometer of mankind's smoking habits. In England the first "tobacconists" started out by selling nothing but the weed. By the turn of the century, however, they had added not only pipes, but smoking accessories of all descriptions, including walking sticks, which were popular items and could be fashioned to carry pipes in the handles. Many times these tobacco shops also offered additional services, such as selling newspapers or providing haircuts! Thus, the pipe shop in Great Britain had become very much a part of everyday life.

By contrast, in America there were no pipe shops as such until around 1910. Prior to that, there were only cigar stores and general merchandise shops which also happened to sell pipes. One of the oldest continuously operating pipe stores in the U.S. is Iwan Reis, which first opened its doors as Hoffman's Cigars in 1857. Other than those found in historical recreations and tourist parks, there are very few pre-World War I pipe shops left to see in America and, consequently, it is always refreshing for U.S. pipe smokers to visit London and see notices such as "since 1880" on Sullivan & Powell's window or "Est. 1862" on Astley's brochure.

Extremely popular up until World War I, pipe smoking took a nosedive in the U.S. when tobacco and imported pipes became difficult to obtain. But the "War To End All Wars" could not defeat the pipe in Great Britain. One of the most notable examples was the special "Christmas 1914" packaged tin created by Princess Mary and distributed to His Majesty's Expeditionary Forces. The tin, of course, contained tobacco, among other things. And the venerable firm of Dunhill produced a special, economically priced Campaign Pipe; although it did not sport a white dot, it surely proved to be a comforting companion for troops under fire. Even before the smoke from the great conflict had cleared, pipes were again being lit up with renewed fervor, as if to make up for precious lost hours of smoking pleasure. In America, nationalism prevailed as homespun brands like Yellowbowl, Kaywoodie, Medico and William DeMuth took hold. The better known British pipes, such as Dunhill, Comoy and GBD were more expensive, but were usually favored by the more sophisticated smoker. By the 1930s many U.S. briars were equipped with filtration or "condensor" systems (snidely referred to as "plumbing" by non-users) and even Charatan with its Underbore and Comoy with its Grand Slam were not immune to this phenomenon (which is largely frowned upon by U.S. pipe smokers today, but is currently quite popular in West Germany). In 1933 Dr. Lewish Linkman perfected the pre-caked pipe, which was marketed under the name of Dr. Grabow. Pipe smoking had taken on a new look of specialization.

World War II caused a great many soldiers to switch to cigarettes when that was all they could find in their rations. After the war, the British brands remained the same but the U.S. pipe smoker was rewarded with new names, such as Savinelli and Castello. Although in short supply due to wartime efforts, at least the pipe was back. Besides, with newfound knowledge of the atomic bomb, the world had become a more sobering place to live, and man began searching for remnants of the old values. By the 1950s the briar pipe had become the natural embodiment of civilized warmth and security. It began to appear in advertisements and motion pictures and wherever a symbol of strength and reliability was needed.

Today, with over 1.5 million pipe smokers in England alone, the symbol of the pipe still provides an image of stability and in fact is stronger than ever before due to a constant closing in and fear of the technological world around us. The pipe remains standing as a bastion of individuality and security. With the advent of computers, laser beams, and dehumanizing robots and words like "artificial intelligence," "petrodollars," and "megapollution," mankind's natural instinct is to seek solace and retain a sense of self-esteem by returning to the very basics of life. The pipe provides much of this. It is a trusted friend, a "working" companion and a symbol of all that is right and orderly in the world. Likewise, the pipe smoker is viewed as a thoughtful, intelligent individual, reflecting the early 19th century connotations when bards such as Thackeray, Byron and Tennyson partook of clays. But there have been some changes: no longer is the pipe thought of in strictly the male gender, for over the years women have been gradually entering its ranks. And cigarette smokers who never touched a briar are now turning to the pipe in their quest for better health, a topic hotly disputed by non-smokers but rarely denied by pipe smokers, who would seem to be more qualified to speak on the subject.

One notable pipe smoker is David Boska, M.D., a physician whose clientele encompasses many well-known entertainment, sports and government individuals, including John F. Kennedy while he was President.

"I've used a pipe to get people off smoking cigarettes," Dr. Boska relates, "and I've been more successful than just having them go cold turkey. It's hard to get someone to smoke cigarettes in moderation. Most people just can't do that. But with a pipe it's different.

"For one thing," he continues, "you're getting better tobacco." According to the doctor, when cigarette smokers switch over to a pipe, they tend to slow down and relax. On the same note, a recent study by two doctors from St. Vincent's Hospital in Dublin revealed that pipe smokers had the same mortality rate as ex-smokers and non-smokers. And many U.S. life assurance companies medically classify pipe smokers as non-smokers.

That is why the U.S. Surgeon General's report has completely missed the mark after repeatedly issuing highly publicized reports, most notably in 1968 and in 1982. These messages were unsuccessful in meeting their goals because they were delivered with threatening negativism rather than constructive positivism. As we will discover in Chapter Four, the secret of successful pipe smoking lies in a combination of moderation, an understanding of proper smoking techniques, and an intelligent appreciation of tobacco usage. With that philosophy as our guide, the history of pipe smoking can best be defined as the constant quest by mankind to derive the utmost in personal satisfaction and relaxation out of the few mortal years we are allocated here on Earth.

David Boska, M.D., is a prominent California physician who believes that pipe smoking can be a positive force in today's world, and has successfully prescribed the pipe as a means for relaxation, as well as to help his patients break the cigarette habit.

The tremendous popularity of the pipe during the first part of the 20th century is evidenced by these greeting cards.

This American tobacco store in New York City dates from around 1909. Note the wooden cigar store Indian, which makes an interesting parallel to the Scottish Highlander seen around many old snuff shops. Both are rarities today. *Credit: Herb Peck Collection*

Because of its nostalgic link with the past plus its favorable health aspects, much media attention is now being focused on the pipe smoker.

Today, pipe smoking is literally a compilation of everything it – and we – have been in the past. It is both revered and feared, depending on whether you are talking to a pipe smoker or a militant non-smoker. A gracious hostess may implore you to "light up," realizing that her guests might enjoy the fragrance of your tobacco as much as you appreciate its flavor (pipe smokers cannot smell the aroma of their own pipes, a curse, I suspect, put upon us by King James). On the other hand, most airlines have completely forbidden pipe smoking (except on British Airways' Concorde, for some reason), although the cigarette is still permitted to permeate the air. New laws are constantly threatening to interfere with a constructive working environment by outlawing pipes from office buildings. Even some restaurants have frowned upon the pipe, oblivious to the fact that tobacco both stimulates the appetite and settles the stomach. Nonetheless, pro-pipe organizations in countries such as Denmark, Holland, and England's own Pipesmoker's Council have recently mounted national campaigns to popularize the positive aspects of our noble pastime. Thus, it is in our private lives that freedom still survives for the late 20th century pipe smoker. At home, on a walk, engaging in a hobby, the pipe is with us, a true friend, a constant companion, in essence, a part of our very being. And that is something that no person, no government and no law can ever take away from us, for the existence and use of the pipe is itself an integral part of Man's history.

Chapter Two

PIPEMAKING TODAY

. . . and here combined – why it must be the
birth of some enchanted sea,
Shaped to immortal form, the type
and very Venus of a pipe.

– poem by James Russell Lowell –

Although there is much talk of "the modern pipe" and "modern pipemaking methods," the plain fact is that pipemaking today has changed very little during the past 100 years, which is as it should be for one of the most personal and individualistic possessions of mankind. In earlier times, pipes were fashioned from natural elements and were used basically as nature had made them. As we noted in Chapter One, tobacco has been smoked in everything from gourds to hollow reeds to seashells and there is even a documented case in the 19th century of an East African tribe of warriors who smoked tobacco from the barrels of captured English trade muskets (presumably the guns were unloaded, or the first puff might have gone on record as being the most powerful light-up in history).

However, to paraphrase an old saying, good pipes are made, not born; as Man became more sophisticated and smoking became more popular, inventive craftsmen soon began to fashion the basic pipe that we know today, a simple device whose primary design and function has changed little in over 400 years of pipe smoking history. No matter how inexpensive or how costly they may be, all pipes are made with a varying degree of hand labor, which may run the gamut from a single worker designing and carving the entire smoking piece from a block of wood, to an individual merely fitting a pre-moulded stem on a machine-made pipe. The more handwork involved, the more expensive the pipe becomes. By the very nature of their construction, pipes remain one of the few man-made items in the world whose manufacture can never become fully automated, a fact that only enhances their appeal for many smokers.

By far the most popular pipemaking material today is briar; it is the one substance that combines beauty, durability, and exceptional smoking qualities. Most briar for today's pipes comes from Italy, France, Greece, Corsica and Spain. Albania and Algeria at one time were sources for premium briar, but various international situations have now rendered these sources impractical, if not outright dangerous. Briar also exists in other countries, but it is not the best quality for pipemaking.

As far as the briar pipe is concerned, it is one instance where we actually *do* find good things growing on trees! The heath tree to be exact, a scrawly bush ranging from 15 to 25 feet in height and normally found along the rugged, rocky coast of the Mediterranean. It is not the tree itself that is used for pipemaking, but rather the hardened briar burl that is formed under the root system. It takes a briar burl a minimum of fifteen years to mature, but the best smoking pipes are made from wood that is much older. Before World War II, it was possible to purchase a high grade, top quality pipe that was often made from 250-year-old briar. Then, as pipe smoking grew in popularity and more of the older wood was used up, high grade pipes were made from 100-year-old briar. Today, the number of pipe smokers continues to grow far beyond the natural ability of the briar bush to produce burls of suitable density and grain for pipemaking. The premium briar situation is further compounded by the fact that it is increasingly difficult to find workers who are willing to crawl along the hot, precarious and often inaccessible rocks just to dig for dirty clumps of burl. More money and less danger can be found in city jobs. In addition, like any plant, briar is continuously subject to the ravages of nature, such as forest fires and insect damage, not to mention the inadvertent destruction of the heath tree itself by the over-zealous actions of the harvesters who often destroy whole bushes just to get at the precious base root. Ideally, these trees should be left standing so that they can continue to reproduce their valuable by-product for future generations of pipe smokers. Yet, as today's pipe smokers become more sophisticated, they are demanding the higher-grade wood for their pipes. All of this places an increasingly heavy drain upon a product that is not easily replaceable. After all, no matter how far man has advanced technologically, it still takes nature 250 years to produce a 250-year-old piece of briar.

Today, the best smoking pipes are normally made from briar that is from 50 to 75 years old, although there are occasional rarities that have been made from briar that has been in the ground for a century or more. Only the cheapest "drugstore pipe" (a common U.S. term for any low-quality inexpensive pipe, usually found with a lacquered finish to hide its flaws) is made from briar less than 50 years old.

Why is the age of the wood so important to a pipe smoker? The answer becomes evident when we realize that briar has no annual rings – instead, it has a grain pattern to show how tumultuous a life it has had. The longer the burl remains in the ground, subjected to the hot, dry, windy environment of the Mediterranean coast, the denser and more pronounced its grain becomes and grain pattern is what enables a briar pipe to breathe as well as giving it a distinctive visual character. It is this combination of wood density, porosity and grain pattern that makes aged briar so desirable for the pipemaker and so superb for the pipe smoker.

Basically, there are two styles of grain patterns found on a high grade pipe: 1) a straight grain and 2) burl or bird's eye (close knit swirls that are actually the ends of a straight grain). We shall go into greater detail on these when discussing what to look for in a pipe (Chapter Three). It is the desire of many pipe smokers to have a "first," a perfectly flawless full-grained pipe that exhibits absolutely no imperfections in the wood. These pipes always command premium prices, as they offer an added value in the rarity and beauty of the briar. It should be remembered that the pattern of the grain does not affect the smoking qualities of a pipe; it is purely cosmetic, which is why a medium priced briar may smoke just as well as a high grade costing hundreds of pounds more (as long as both pipes are made from a piece of briar that has been properly treated and carved) and the bowl has total – but not necessarily symmetrical – grain coverage. That is why a pipe with a sand pit, grain disruption, or other minor visual imperfection (called "rejects" in the U.K. and "seconds" in the U.S.) can represent exquisite bargains for the knowledgeable pipe smoker, as we shall discover in the next chapter. It should be pointed out that in this book I am using the classification of a "first" in the purest pipemaking sense of the term. Anything with a flaw in it is a "second" and a pipe with so many imperfections that it must be physically doctored up with synthetic putty "fills" is a "third," a pipe which I consider barely suitable for smoking, unless you like to smoke putty instead of briar. I mention all this because there is a growing trend in the pipemaking industry, due to the increasing difficulty in obtaining fine quality briar, to call a superbly-figured straight grain pipe a "first" even if it has a minor sandpit. Thus, this nomenclature that has been traditionally reserved for a flawless piece of briar is now being redefined to refer only to a superior briar density and grain pattern, and not visual or aesthetic purity. In that case, what shall we call a *flawless* first . . . a "*first*-first?" Moreover, there are still some pipe firms, such as Dunhill and Upshall, which simply *do not produce seconds*; any pipe found on their workbenches with an imperfection, no matter how trivial, is discarded. Such is the dilemma facing the pipe smoker today and it is important to realize that if you want to smoke a *true* "first-first" that boasts superb graining and aged, flawless wood, you will have to pay for the privilege, whereas if you smoke a high-grade "second-first" that offers superb wood but may exhibit one or two tiny visual flaws, you must *still* pay a premium for the privilege. But for now, we need only to be aware of the basic differences between "firsts" and "rejects" in order to fully appreciate the pipemaking process.

Once the briar root has been extracted from the base of the heath tree, it is cleaned by hand and visually inspected for areas that have been affected by rot and bug damage. These useless pieces of waste are trimmed and cut away and very often, only a 10 to 15 pound chunk of potentially usable briar is all that a single root has produced. As soon as each worker has dug out enough briar burls to constitute a manageable load, he takes his harvest to a pre-arranged gathering spot, where the burls are kept moist (to prevent them from cracking) and covered until they can be shipped to one of the many sawmills in the area which specialize in cutting the briar chunks into "ebauchons" (pronounced eh-ob-showns), which are thick, roughly shaped slices of briar from which one or two pipes will eventually be carved. It is during this sawing process of briar burl into the ebauchons that many hidden flaws are discovered within the wood, a recurring malady that will continue to plague every pipemaker – from an army of workers in the largest factory to the individual custom craftsman at his home workbench – until the pipe is finally finished. Tiny grains of sand, worm holes, a disruption of the burl's grain, a split in the wood itself – in short, anything that can visually mar the appearance of a completed pipe, often lurks hidden beneath the surface of the wood like some mischievous gremlin, waiting for the chance to jump into view during some stage of the pipe's creation, whether it be in the cutting, carving or sanding processes prior to the pipe's completion. Imagine the frustration of a pipemaker, upon creating a perfectly flawless straight-grained "first," as he gives his prize one final sanding and a sandpit suddenly appears on the bowl. Now he has a "second." That is why firsts are so desirable and costly.

Sawing out the ebauchons often produces a great deal of waste, which has the effect of adding to the total cost of making a pipe. The briar ebauchons are then graded according to wood color, grain pattern and size. Next, the briar is "cured," which is just another term for aging and drying the wood, a process that takes anywhere from three months to three years, depending upon the manufacturer. During this aging process, the briar is kept in ventilated sheds and periodically moistened to keep it from cracking.

Years ago, briar was cured naturally by letting it sit in the sun for two or three summers, and wetting it periodically. In this way all of the saps and resins were eventually disseminated from the wood. Today, some briar merchants use mechanical sprinklers to keep the briar moist and have devised ways to artificially speed up the drying process. Although I am an advocate of doing things the old way, I should mention that many quality pipemakers employ some of these newer techniques and even though I smoke pipes that have been made by using both the old and the new curing processes, I find there is absolutely no difference in the smoking qualities of a high grade pipe made in the 1980s as compared to one made in the 1930s. The secret lies in having an aged piece of briar to start with, properly drying it (no matter what the length of time may actually be) and then using the utmost skill and care in creating the pipe. As further proof of this statement, I can point out that Mauro Armellini is one of the few pipemakers left who still dries his briar in the old fashioned way, leaving it stacked up against the sunny side of his house in Italy over a period of seasons. Conversely, Erik Nørding, who makes some of the finest quality high grades to come out of Denmark, invented his own drying machine which he uses to artificially cure all of his wood. Both of these craftsmen produce pipes that are superb smoking instruments, and which are eagerly sought after by experienced smokers. The irony is that Armellini, with his old fashioned curing process, uses modern machinery to make many of his pipes while Nørding, with his modern briar heating vats, literally hand-carves his high grade pipes in the Old World tradition. Such is the paradox of pipemaking!

No matter how they are dried, once fully cured, the ebauchons are again inspected and wood that has cracked or otherwise failed the curing process is discarded, further diminishing the total briar supply (it has been estimated by some pipemakers that it takes the burls from fifty different heath trees just to find a single flawless piece of briar suitable for a high grade pipe and it takes over a hundred pieces to produce one "first"). Finally, the ebauchons are sorted in groups and are given letter and numeric designations according to their quality and size. The lowest briar designation is Standard, which is used for pipes that are filled with putty, lacquered to hide their flaws or covered with leather or fur, which may make them visually attractive to the uneducated and totally unsmokable for everyone. Next in grading comes Premium, then Extra and finally Double Extra Quality. Most pipes on today's market are made from Premium Quality wood, which usually yields two or three "firsts" per thousand pipes. The best (and most costly) of the high grades come from Extra Quality plateau briar, the plateau being the outermost portion of the burl; it is the "choice cut" of briar and is normally only found on older pieces of wood. Extra Quality plateau ebauchons are specially hand picked and assembled in relatively small groups at substantially higher prices than the other ebauchons. Usually a pipemaker dedicated to producing high grades will be able to obtain half as many pieces of briar for about twice the price. Often, interested buyers will blanch off a tiny slice of briar from the plateau to try and get an indication of what aesthetic treasures the wood may hold within, but this is a rather nebulous practice, as only by actually carving the pipe can you determine what it finally will look like. Of course, not everyone is intent upon buying only high grade wood and there are many companies who make nothing but seconds, and buy their briar accordingly.

Finally, a given number of ebauchons, grouped together by grading and size, are placed in burlap bags and sold to the buyers of the various pipemaking companies around the world, most notably in England, Denmark and France. The larger pipemakers, such as GBD, Comoy's and Butz-Choquin, for example, buy enough briar to insure that they will have a far better chance of creating a profitable supply of "firsts" over a year's time. However, for many of the smaller companies and individual custom pipe carvers, premium prices must be paid for premium briar, and there is never a guarantee that a perfect "first" will be in the batch. I used to wonder why a pipemaker simply did not X-ray his ebauchons to determine what secrets the wood contained before he started carving, but I have since been told by more than one pipemaker that good briar has now become so expensive, the realities of the business dictate that they simply buy the wood and take their chances; most can ill-afford to let a single usable piece slip by unfulfilled towards its final destiny as a pipe.

As an example of how the briar situation has changed over the years, in 1970 a sack of briar could realistically be expected to yield 5% of top quality "firsts." Another 15% would become "firsts" that were suitable for sandblasting, a technique where tiny beads of glass, metal or sand are shot under tremendous pressure at a briar bowl, wearing away the softer wood and producing a hardened pipe bowl with a durable ridged or mottled effect. Many top quality high grades are sandblasted, a technique that requires a fine grain in order to produce an attractive pattern. Then the bag might yield a number of pipes suitable for "deluxe seconds," which would create a pipe that was on the borderline between a first and a "second." In those days, the balance of the briar, for a high grade company at least, would be considered worthless for any future pipemaking and the wood was simply discarded. It was a luxury in quality because back then, briar was extremely inexpensive. Today, however, due to the all-too-familiar spectres of inflation, rising labor costs, plus the fact that few workers wish to "lower" themselves to the dirty, sweaty job of digging for briar-root, prices have soared and pipemakers, in order to stay in business, find it an economical necessity to try and squeeze an extra 5% of "firsts" out of the same basic burlap sack they were using ten years ago. Thus, the emergence of the "second-first" has become a reality, although I have found numerous pipes by some lesser-known makers and private in-store brands that had perfect bowls even though they were priced substantially below the more recognizable brands. For the adventurer who likes to search the racks of his favorite tobacco shop, these pipes can be one of the most affordable bargains in the pipe world today.

Having a marketing and manufacturing creed of "Firsts Forever – no seconds!" is both commendable and costly and can only be achieved in one of three ways: burn all the seconds, keep carving past the flaw until you either get a "first" or whittle the pipe away to infinity, or develop a textured finish that relies more on premium wood and superb carving techniques rather than grain.

In light of the rising costs and scarcity of briar, I find it interesting to note that many high grade pipe firms not only continue to buy the very best of the plateau briar, but are also ready markets for Grade A and AA bowls that are occasionally encountered by other pipemakers. Additionally, it is an unacknowledged fact and up until now has been a carefully guarded secret, that many companies often turn out bowls for each other. Personally, I cannot see how this matters one bit, as long as the end product is representative of the company's image and the customer gets the quality he is paying for.

Once the ebauchons are selected and purchased by the various buyers, they are delivered to their respective pipemaking facilities. Here they are usually sawn into L-shaped blocks, the first step of the long pipemaking process, a procedure that can involve as many as 80 to 120 different steps. However, the basics of carving a pipe are shown photographically in this chapter and for those who would like to try it themselves, there are a number of pipemaking kits on the market which can be acquired from your tobacconist. In addition, pre-cured briar sources are listed in Chapter Ten and if you really want to start from scratch and have lots of time on your hands, you could even grow your own heath tree!

A pipe is fashioned into one of a number of basic and some not-so-basic shapes, much of which depends upon the design characteristics of the individual pipemaker as well as the shape of the briar block. English and French companies normally tend to create "traditional" shapes while the Danish and many U.S. custom carvers seem to lean towards the "freehand" styles. The most popular of these designs are shown in the next chapter as an aid to pipe selection. However, no matter how it is shaped, there are only three basic textures for any briar pipe: 1) smooth, 2) sandblast, and 3) carved. A pipe may be finished in one or in any combination of these three textures.

A smooth finish is just what the name implies and is usually found on pipes in which the grain of the wood plays an important part of the overall design. A smooth finished pipe can be oil-cured and left in a natural shade or can be stained any color, from a light tan all the way to a deep brown or a reddish black, depending on the wood and the whim of

Parts of the Pipe

(Alternative terms given in parenthesis)

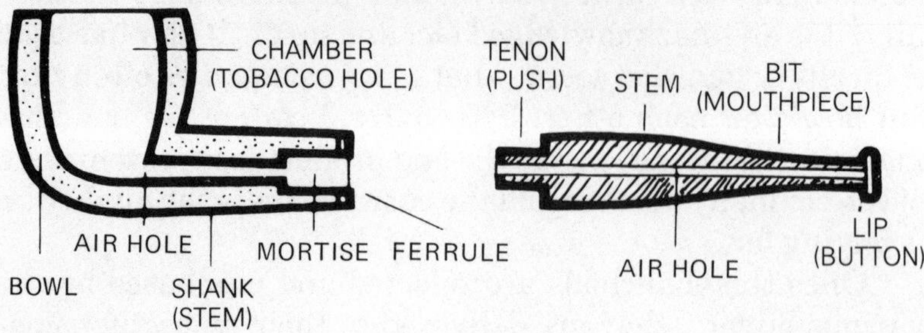

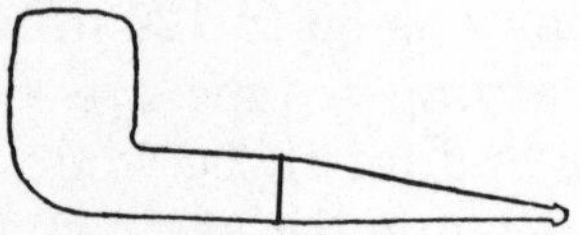

Billiard

Freehand
(sometimes called "Freeform" in the U.K.)

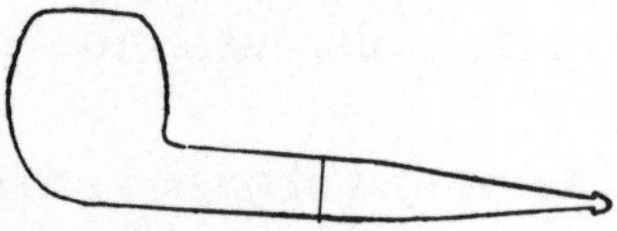

Apple

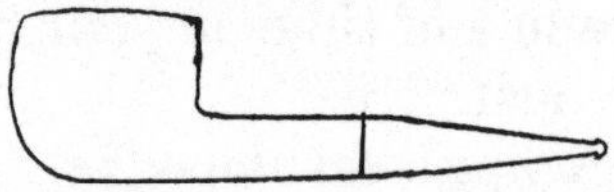

Pot

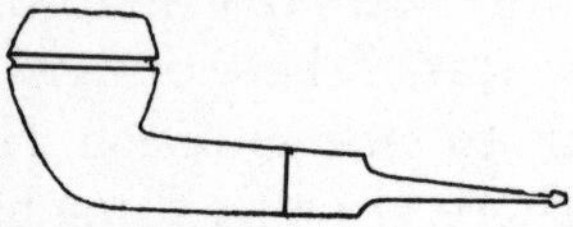

Bulldog

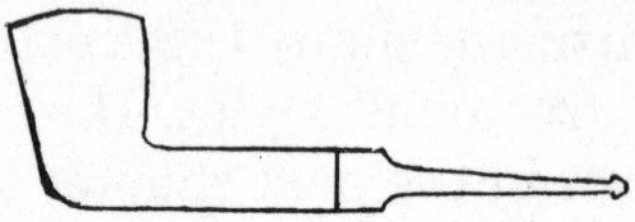

Dublin

Canadian

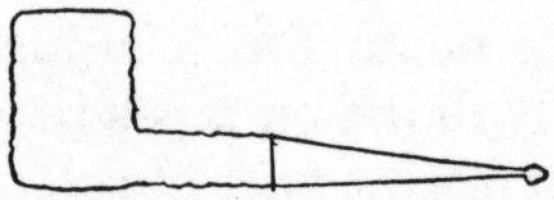

Poker

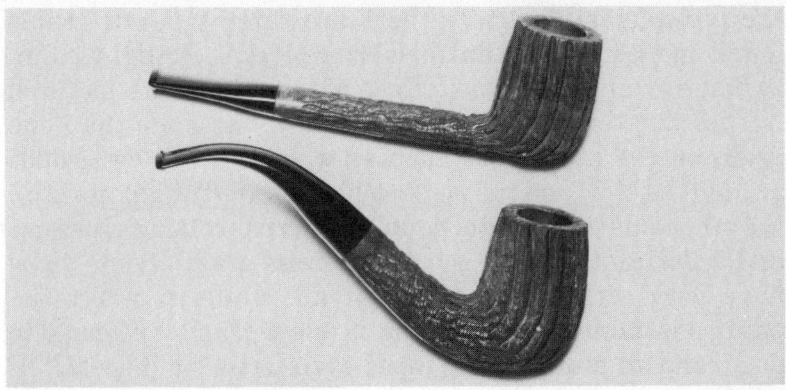

The two basic styles of pipes

(top) straight (bottom) bent

The three basic briar pipe finishes: (top to bottom) smooth, sand-blast, carved (this partially carved bent also shows a nice bird's eye pattern on the smooth part).

the pipemaker. Basically there are three types of grains found on most smooth finished briar pipes: 1) straight grain, 2) flame grain, and 3) burl. Each of these types are pictured in this chapter. It is not uncommon to find more than one grain on the same pipe, such as when a bird's eye swirls around the bowl and turns into a horizontal straight grain on the other side (this type of double pattern is called a cross-cut and a horizontal grain is called a cross-grain). Some pipes have very little visible grain at all, while in others the pattern is more pronounced but is uneven, and is referred to as a random grain. Many pipes even have "bald spots," in which the grain on the bowl is interrupted by a patch of smooth wood with little or no character. A flame grain is simply a straight grain pattern that angles either in or out along the bowl, giving it the appearance of being a "flame." And a burl grain pattern can be quite attractive if the pattern is pronounced and uniform. It is this individuality in graining that gives each briar a personality all its own and makes one pipe more appealing to an individual than another.

Sandblasted pipes (sometimes referred to as shell, rustic, relief or thorn finishes by various manufacturers) have a ruggedly attractive characteristic that makes you want to grasp the bowl firmly in your hands, as there is no concern about marring the glossy waxed surface that is found on smooth-finished briars. Sandblasted pipes have a rough, textured finish and are somewhat lighter in weight because there is less wood on the pipe. Because there is actually more wood surface area comprising the bowl, the heat is dissipated from the burning tobacco in a sandblast pipe slightly quicker than with a smooth finished briar, but frankly, the difference is so slight I doubt if many people would notice it.

It takes a good grade of briar to create a truly fine sandblast, as it is the actual wood grain that creates the dimensional dips and ridges which make a sharply defined sandblast so desirable. Unfortunately, sandblasting is also used by many pipemakers to cover up flaws and imperfections in a briar bowl of lesser character. Because of this fact, sandblasts sometimes carry a stigma about them that is undeserved, but for that reason, sandblasts are sometimes less expensive than smooth grain pipes of the same quality.

Carved pipes include spot carving (normally employed to add a decorative touch to the bowl but more often than not, used to disguise a flaw in the wood grain), sculptured pipes and freehands. Like smooth and sandblasted pipes, carved briars can be made either by hand or by machine but by their very nature, the more complicated designs are always made by hand. Do not confuse any variation of the carved pipe with the cheap varnished varieties normally found next to the chewing gum rack in your local tourist shop. Some examples of fully and partially carved quality pipes are shown elsewhere in this chapter.

Each pipe, no matter what its form, demands a certain skill, understanding of function, and expertise in its creation. For example, the freehand style, with its gently flowing curves and graceful, sweeping lines that ebb and surge throughout the pipe, show off briar grain to the fullest, but in so doing, exposes much more surface area of the briar and therefore runs the risk of uncovering many hidden flaws within the wood. The very intricacies of the designs themselves dictate that the freehand is usually a hand-carved operation. On the other hand, a straight-stemmed billiard must have visual and actual balance between bowl and stem to make it both functional and comfortable as a smoking instrument.

Detailed, carved pipes are often done by craftsmen using miniature electronic drills and dental tools which have been honed to a razor sharpness. In Italy, "rustication" is a popular process whereby a pipe is poked and prodded intricately with a special multi-pointed tool that almost gives the pipe the appearance of a sandblast. When I first organized the National Pipe Carving Contest in America in 1976, I was amazed at the pipe craftsmanship that literally came out of the woodwork. After all these years I still find it fascinating to note the intricacies that a patient and skilled pipe carver can produce from a single block of briar, using just his hands and his imagination.

Whether carved by a single individual in his home workshop or in the factories that turn out thousands of pipes each year for the pipe smoking world, each brand has its own feel and style . . . a certain "look" about it that gives the pipe individuality and character. Likewise, I have found that every pipemaker has a definite sense of pride in his craft, whether he is working alongside hundreds of others on a lathe in a factory or carving by himself alone in a stucco-plastered room in a dusty Italian village. And practically all pipemakers of note strive to develop a certain "secret" or personal touch that will make their pipes stand out above the others. For example, noted pipemaker Bill Taylor, who ships less than 3,000 Ashton pipes a year from his shop in Essex, takes great pride in his hot oil treatment of every high grade piece of briar, which makes them exceedingly light and dry smoking. On the other hand, Les Wood's unique Ferndown pipes are usually found in a dark rusticated finish that is often set off by an elegant silver mounting, as only Les can do. And Ken Barnes has an almost uncanny knack of finding the best concentration of grain in every ebauchon, so that his Upshall pipes are always distinctive and immediately spotted in a pipe rack. But it is not just the newer pipemakers who exhibit individuality. Not satisfied with merely sandblasting their "shell" pipes, in 1986 Dunhill created a "ring grain," whereby certain pipes feature parallel rings stacked horizontally up the bowl.

Indeed, not only is briar the most smokable of all the pipemaking materials, but in terms of design and carving capabilities, it is also the most versatile.

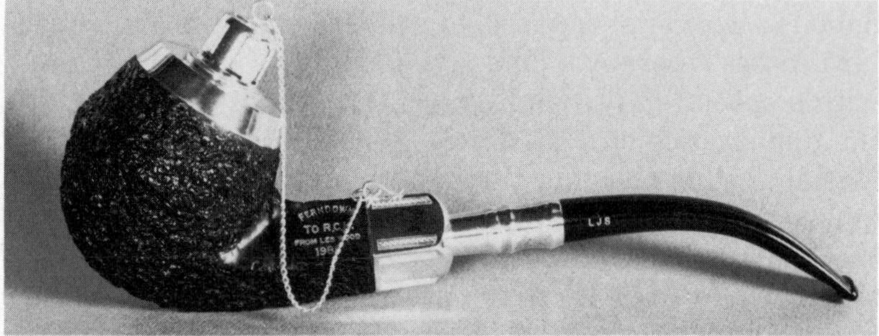

Les and Dolly Wood epitomize England's "new era" of pipemakers with their handsome creation of a specially commissioned Ferndown pipe, which combines rustication with a semi-traditional bulldog variation accented with silver mounted fittings and windcap with silver chain.

Second in popularity as both a pipemaking and a pipe smoking material is meerschaum, which has the unique ability to change color as it is smoked over a long period of time, gradually turning from white to a deep cherry brown. The best pipes are made from solid block meerschaum, which is only found in Turkey. Interestingly, meerschaum of a slightly different texture is found in other parts of the world, including the United States and Africa, although most of it is not of pipemaking quality. The meerschaum product of the Dark Continent, while not as porous as the Turkish mineral, is used for some oil-hardened and pre-colored pipes, most notably those that are fashioned in Israel and on the Isle of Man, off the west coast of England.

As a caveat to first-time meerschaum pipe purchasers, it should be pointed out that there are a number of imitation substances on the market, such as pipes made from powdered meerschaum or synthetic polymers and resins. These pipes are always cheaper than block meerschaum and at first glance may look like the real thing, but they offer none of the smoking qualities and coloring properties of the genuine article.

Although not commonly known, Turkey's entire meerschaum supply is centered within a twelve mile radius of the tiny village of Eskisehir, located just 200 miles east of Istanbul. Here, in this single pinpointed area of the world, mine shafts poke as deep as 400 feet into the earth (often far below the water table of that area) and workers risk their lives in wet, subterranean shafts just to bring the pure, porous, and precious meerschaum chunks to the surface.

When the clumps of meerschaum are first brought up into the light of day, they must be cleaned of all dirt, sand, and other debris. The meerschaum is then sawn into blocks representing an approximate pipe-like shape. Many of these blocks are of a small to medium-sized nature, but occasionally a meerschaum chunk of unusual size will be found, and these prizes demand extra attention, for with proper skill they can be turned into a true museum-quality showpiece. The basic pipe bowls are fashioned on a lathe, but one of the real attractions of meerschaum to a pipe smoker is its ability to be carved in great detail. It is during this carving stage

How to Make a Pipe

The basic pipemaking process is illustrated by this series of step-by-step photographs and captions:

(1) The basic items you will need (see text)

(2) First the block of briar is rough-cut and bored with two holes: one for the bowl and a connecting airhole through the stem.

(3) The basic pipe shape is predetermined by eye or a template pattern and is sometimes drawn on the briar with white marking chalk.

(4) The rough-cut and bored briar is then trimmed of all excess wood in order to create the basic shape the pipe will ultimately take. Note the outline of the tobacco hole.

(5) The pipe is shaped with a file and begins to take on its finished appearance. Note that the stem is fitted to the shank at this point, so that it will flow into and conform with the pipe's design.

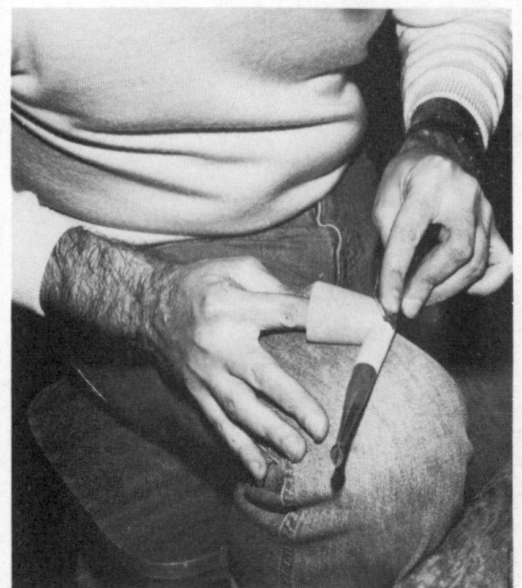

(6) Using gradually finer grits of sandpaper, the pipe's surface is smoothed of all rough finishing marks.

(7) Buffing, staining and waxing completes the pipemaking process.

Saint-Claude, France, "Pipe Carving Capital of the World."

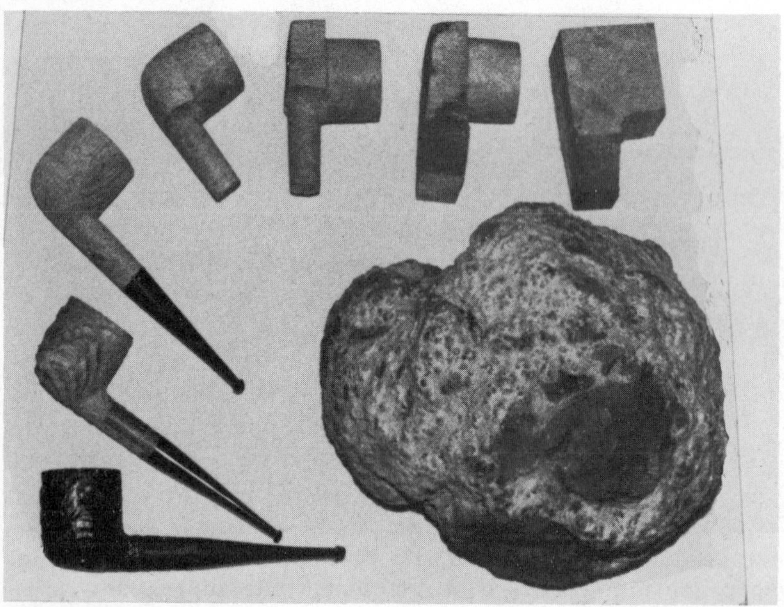

The creation of a pipe starts with the briar burl and ends with the finished product.

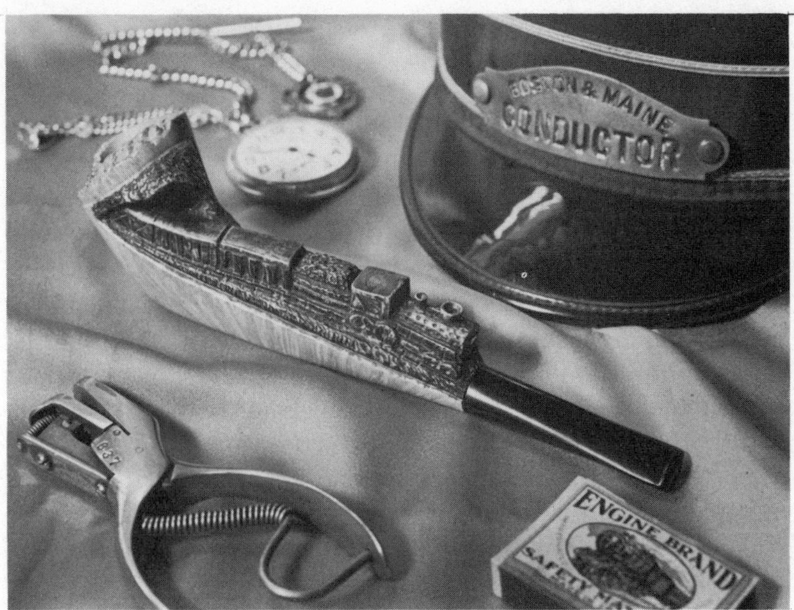

"Briar Express" by U.S. pipemaker Steve Waddell is an example of some smoking instruments that can never be mass-produced, as they are strictly one-of-a-kind pieces. When the pipe is puffed, smoke actually comes out of the funnel of the engine.

Mike Butera is a top U.S. pipemaker whose quest for perfection has made his briars very much in demand.

that an ordinary meerschaum pipe can be transformed into a true work of art. I have also seen some of these pipes whose intrinsic value had been totally destroyed by careless and unskilled butchering. Fortunately, few of these ever find their way into a quality pipe shop.

Besides the world's sole source for Turkish block meerschaum, in the area of Eskisehir also reside the men who carve and shape practically every meerschaum pipe that will eventually find its way into your local tobacconist's showcase. Some of these carvers are true artisans with enviable skills while others are simply people who happen to own a cutting tool and try to earn some extra money by attempting to whittle out a pipe or two in their spare time. In all of Turkey today, it is estimated that there are about 100 meerschaum pipe carvers of any note, of which only six are truly masterful experts, closely followed by less than two

Richard Dunhill, grandson of Alfred and spokesman for the famous London pipemaking firm.

Some pipes, such as this Upshall, are made one at a time by the old-fashioned hand-turning method.

Other factories, like Butz-Choquin, use frazing machines; with a master pattern, this worker can carve 16 bowls at once.

W. Ø. "Ole" Larsen is the fourth generation of his family to maintain the tradition of designing their pipes, all of which are made from the finest plateau briar.

The epitome of Danish pipemaking art is this W. Ø. Larsen perfect straight grain fitted with handcut amber mouthpiece.

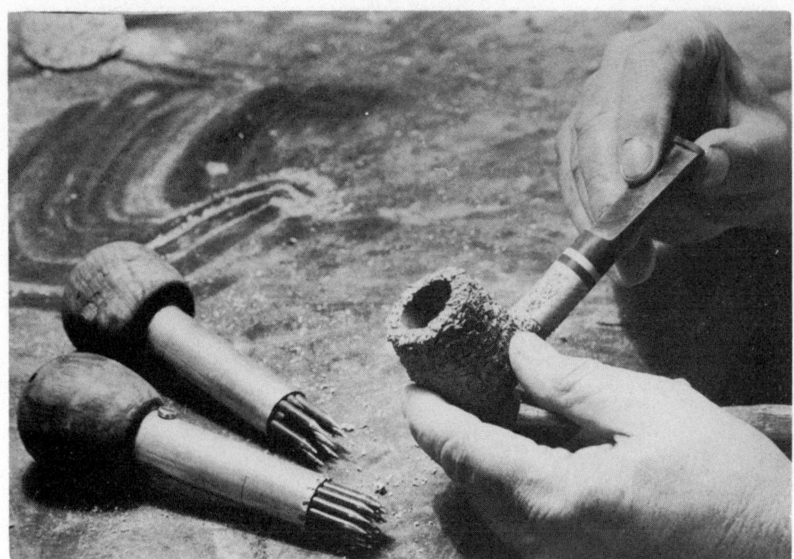

Rusticating is a finely carved finish that resembles a coarse sand-blast but is all done by hand, using special multi-pointed tools.

Silver mountings for pipes must first be formed on an exact wooden replica, such as this L & J S silver cap made for a billiard.

England is the pipemaking home of these three popular briars (top to bottom:) Loewe Original, Dr. Plumb Quintex and Kaywoodie Custom Grain.

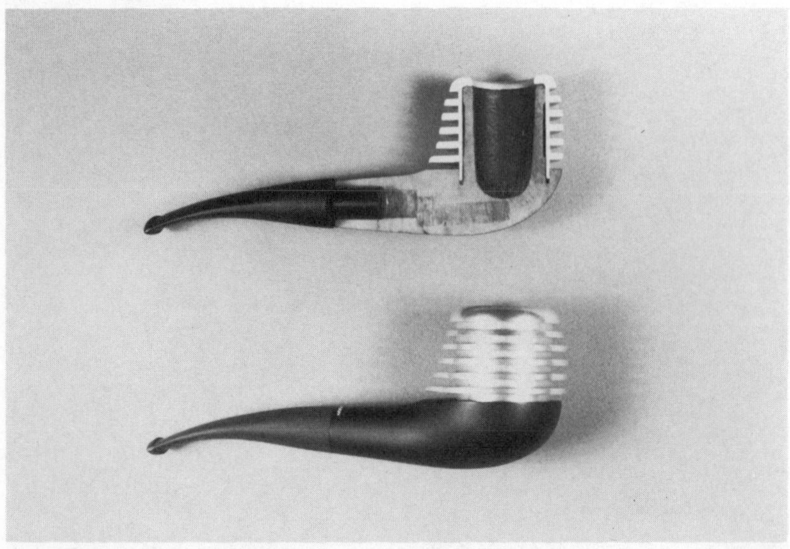

The Porsche pipe, made in West Germany, derives its aluminium-capped design from the cooling ribs of an aeroplane engine cylinder.

dozen talented apprentices. England is not without its meerschaum artisans, the most notable being London Meerschaums in South Wales. Up until the 1960s, meerschaum pipes had traditionally been carved in Austria, with Vienna's Andreas Bauer being perhaps the best-known in recent times (the Bauer firm has since changed to producing calabash pipes). When Turkish carvings began being exported in the late '60s and early '70s, the carving was not always the best quality. However, the mid-1980s have ushered in a new breed of artisans who exhibit greater refinement and skill than in the past. Today, Husseyin Yanik, Munir Aydogu, and a fellow known as "The Artist" (whose real name is Ismail Ozel) are the top pipe carvers in Turkey. It has only been recently that Yanik, Sabri, and a few others have begun to actually sign their work and most meerschaum artists rely on anonymous craftsmanship rather than the prestige of personal identity to sell their pipes, although that situation may be changing, now that the names of the carvers are known. But no matter who makes it, in a genuine block meerschaum pipe, price is determined not only by the size of the bowl, but also by the quality of the carving, and many an exquisite pipe has been fashioned by an unknown.

In spite of its rather fragile nature, meerschaum can be carved much like a briar pipe, although the delicate white "sea foam" must be kept moist, giving the material an almost cheese-like consistency, which therefore makes it much easier to work with and enables a skilled carver to create delicate facial features or intricate floral-leaf designs without chipping or otherwise destroying the material.

Once fully carved, the pipe is fitted with a stem and polished by hand with a finishing compound that smooths the surfaces. Then the meerschaum is immersed in a boiling mixture of hot beeswax which is occasionally augmented by the addition of animal oils and fats. The pipe may undergo several dippings to insure that the entire area has been completely saturated with this boiling wax mixture, for it is the soaking of beeswax into the meerschaum surface that gives it the ability to change color. The better the saturation and porousness of the meerschaum, the better the pipe will

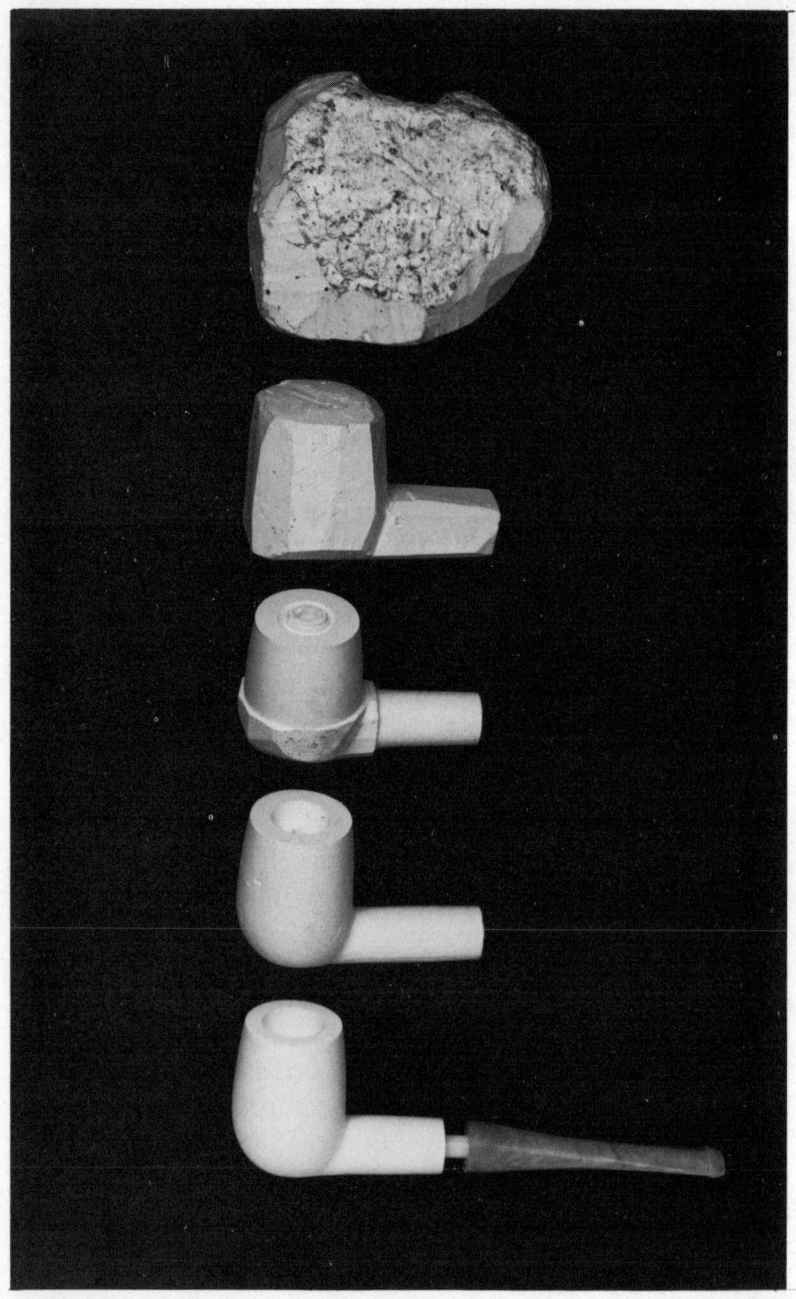

The steps of making a meerschaum pipe, starting with the raw material as it is first mined, to the finished waxed and polished pipe, ready for smoking. *Credit: SMS Meerschaums*

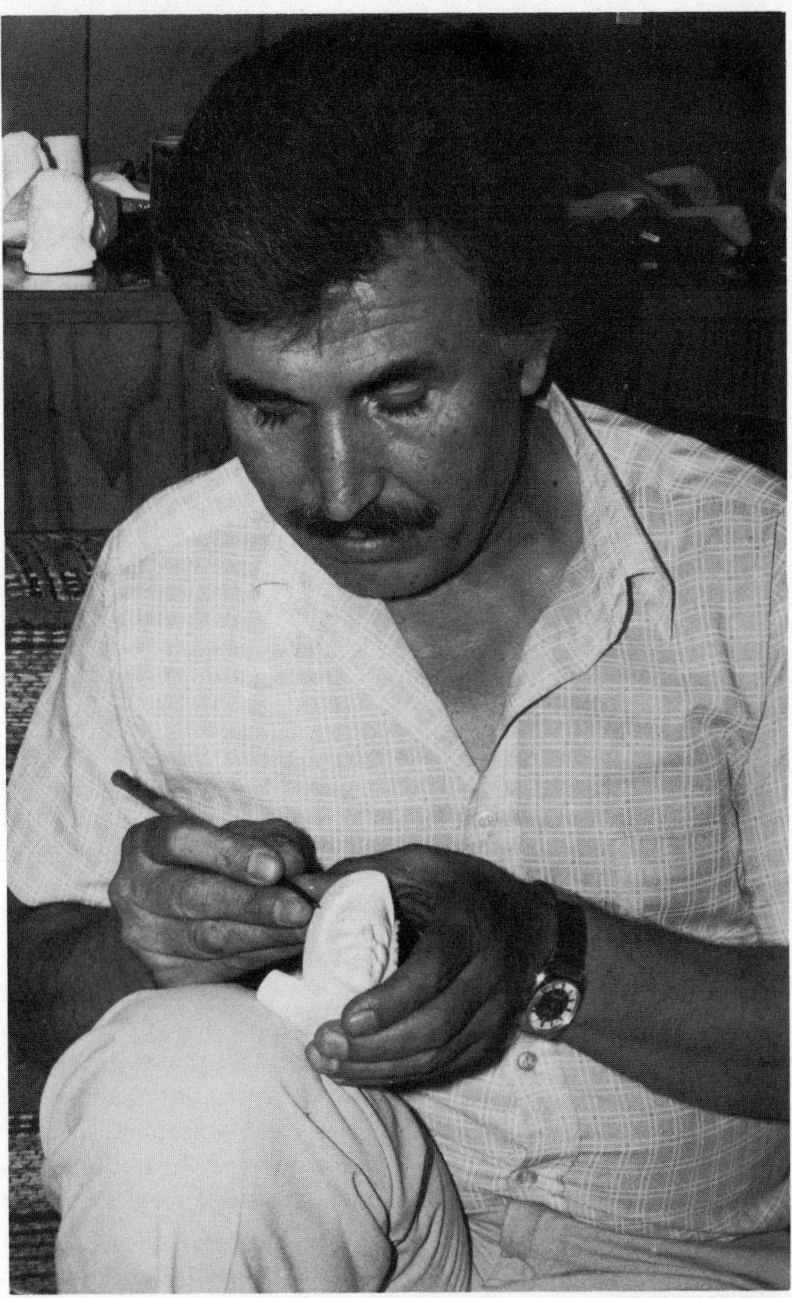

Ismet Bekler is one of Turkey's celebrated meerschaum artists. Many early carvings, which featured skulls, cavaliers and the devil, were inspired by 19th century French carved briars.

color when it is finally smoked; the nicotine and smoke from the burning tobacco seeps into the pipe, colors the wax and gradually works its way through the walls of the bowl to the outer surfaces. (That is why the thinner areas of a meerschaum pipe normally color first.) When dried, the pipe is given a final polishing.

Most meerschaum bits are made of moulded plastic of various hues, and attached with either a push-in or screw-on tennon. However, some carvers have recently reintroduced an amber bit on some of their better quality pipes and that glass-like material, once in vogue during the late 19th century, makes for a very handsome and aesthetically pleasing pipe, although it is more susceptible to breakage.

Practically all meerschaums come in their own specially-fitted cases, which not only helps protect them during shipment, but is also invaluable in storing the fragile pipes, which, due to their porousness, do not have to be kept in the bowl-down position after smoking to help drain out moisture, like briars.

When completed, the pipes are put out for the representatives from one of the many meerschaum pipe companies who periodically visit the Eskisehir area on buying trips. The buyer carefully inspects each pipe and selects those which meet his criteria for style, craftsmanship and price. Occasionally, a meerschaum buyer will work with a select group of artisans whom he knows and he can rely on, instructing them beforehand which designs he feels will sell well in the various countries that import these pipes. That explains how a craftsman in a remote village in Turkey can suddenly be compelled to create a pipe dedicated to the personages of Winston Churchill, John Wayne or Sherlock Holmes, individuals he may never even have heard of. Finally, the pipes purchased by the various importing companies are shipped to their representatives throughout the world and are then sold via national salespeople to your tobacconist, who in turn offers you a selection of one of the earth's most unique natural smoking resources, the meerschaum pipe.

Of course, no discussion of the meerschaum would be complete without an addendum regarding the calabash. The calabash pipe is most often associated with the character of Sherlock Holmes, which is ironic since that legendary detective never once smoked a calabash in any of the stories Sir Arthur Conan Doyle wrote about him (for more revelations on this elementary deduction, see Chapter Eight). Nonetheless, the calabash is still one of my favorite companions when watching the old Basil Rathbone reruns on television, or for any other form of "mysterious" at-home smoking.

Basically, the calabash is a South African gourd which has been artificially shaped during the growing process to give it a gracefully hooked neck. After harvesting, the gourd is trimmed at both ends, hollowed out and dried. It is then polished, waxed, and fitted with a solid block meerschaum bowl, although some cheaper versions resort to crushed meerschaum or clay bowls; it is the solid block versions such as those made by Andreas Bauer and even an old Parker if you can find one, which will color as nicely as anything that ever was smoked in a Victorian sitting room or on the silver screen for that matter. The pipe is then fitted with a hard rubber or a plastic carved bit to complete its well-known profile. The calabash is a large pipe and is not the sort of thing you want to cram into your coat pocket when going out to a restaurant. However, by the very nature of its construction, it is one of the few pipes in which *all* of the tobacco can be smoked right on down to the airhole in the bottom of the heel without any effort whatsoever. Furthermore, the air chamber of the inner gourd provides a cooling system that can help tame even the heaviest English blends. The calabash is truly a contemplative pipe and is best smoked at home on windy, rainy nights, when it can even turn a bad mystery book into a good one.

In dealing with the manufacture of all the popular pipes of this century, how can anyone possibly ignore the humble corncob? It has been with us long before the Iron Horse first chugged across the buffalo-covered plains of the American Far West and it still remains a favored smoke in this era of wafer-thin television sets and microwave ovens. Surely the tenacious corncob must have something going for it.

If Saint-Claude is the pipemaking capital of the world, then the tiny U.S. town of Washington, Missouri must be the corncob capital of the world, for it is here that practically every known corncob pipe is fashioned. But these historic little pipes are not created from your standard "high-as-an-elephant's-eye" grocery store variety of corn, at least not any more. In 1946, Dr. Marcus Zuber, working with the University of Missouri, developed a unique hybrid cob that was created specifically for use in pipemaking, and is now used exclusively by Missouri Meerschaum, the largest, best-known, and most prolific corncob pipe producers in the world.

The hybrid cob is larger, longer and stronger than your standard garden variety vegetable, and its fibers are so high in wood content that it takes a carbide-tipped saw to cut through them. The hybrid cob is grown by selected farmers in the rich, fertile lowlands that surround the town of Washington. The corn is grown strictly for the cobs they will produce and the small white kernels of the hybrids are regarded as a by-product (they are routinely sold off to companies who grind them up into cornmeal for tortillas). It is the thick, sturdy corncobs which provide the real income for this area. Each fall they are harvested and trucked to the same old red brick building that has been the home of Missouri Meerschaum ever since 1872. Once inside, the cobs are "de-kerneled" and piled in a ventilated storage area, where they are aged for about two years, a curing process that gradually gives them the density of fine grained hardwood. At the end of this period, the cobs are taken from the storage bins and sliced into various lengths for pipe bowls. An average cob will yield two standard sized pipes with a little left over for a miniature pipe with a one-inch bowl, which are usually sold as novelties in souvenir shops. However, it is the more practical 2-inch bowls that are favored by serious corncob smokers. Sometimes an unusually large cob will yield as many as five bowls, but these jumbo hybrids are often saved for long single-bowled pipes such as the General MacArthur style shown in this chapter.

The cut cobs are then put on a lathe and shaped with a chisel, which gives the bowl its basic external design. The next step is boring the "tobacco hole," after which the cob is drilled for a stem and coated with a Plaster of Paris mixture very much unchanged from the original brew concocted for the first corncob back in 1868. This then completes the bowl-making process for the least expensive pipes, such as the Standard model. Yes, there are highgrade corncobs! For this next step up, the bowls are hand varnished and shellacked and a tight-fitting wooden plug is hammered into the bottom of the bowl, which helps delay the burnout problem (you cannot build up a cake on a corncob). The stems used to be made out of riverbank reeds, but today the pipe stems are all fashioned from long rods of turned and drilled cobs. The one exception to this manufacturing procedure is the stem of the interestingly-christened Wanghee, which is actually the name of a variety of baby bamboo that is used to form the shank of this distinctive-looking Missouri Meerschaum. The pipe bits are moulded of either clear or black plastic, depending upon the model of the corncob. There are more than fifteen different varieties of corncobs available, ranging from freehands to the most economically-priced seven day set you will ever find in the new-pipe market. However, no matter what their size and shape, none of the corncobs are expensive. Their method of construction has remained basically unchanged for over a century, thus giving this homegrown pipe a unique niche as a piece of American history that can actually be smoked!

Throughout the world of pipemaking, history is continually repeating itself as pipemakers insist on recreating pipes made of "alternate woods," such as manzanita, mountain laurel, ebony, rosewood, olive, cherry, birch, wild lilac and hickory, just to name a few. Everything has been tried, a fact that I often try to relate to many budding pipemakers who come to me with their latest discoveries in smokable material. Unless there is a unique substance growing in the forests of Venus, I am not aware of any other wood that can match the character and long lasting qualities of briar. However, it is only proper to give a nod of recognition to the cherrywood as being the most popular non-briar wooden pipe today. Cherrywood provides a pleasant enough smoke, a little "hot" at first, but it is more absorbent than briar and stands a great chance of burning out. Consequently, it will not last as long. Cherrywood pipes are usually created in a

The Italian-made Clairmont Olivewood pipe is one of the newest variations for today's pipe smoker. The blonde wood turns matt-brown after the pipe has been smoked over a period of time.

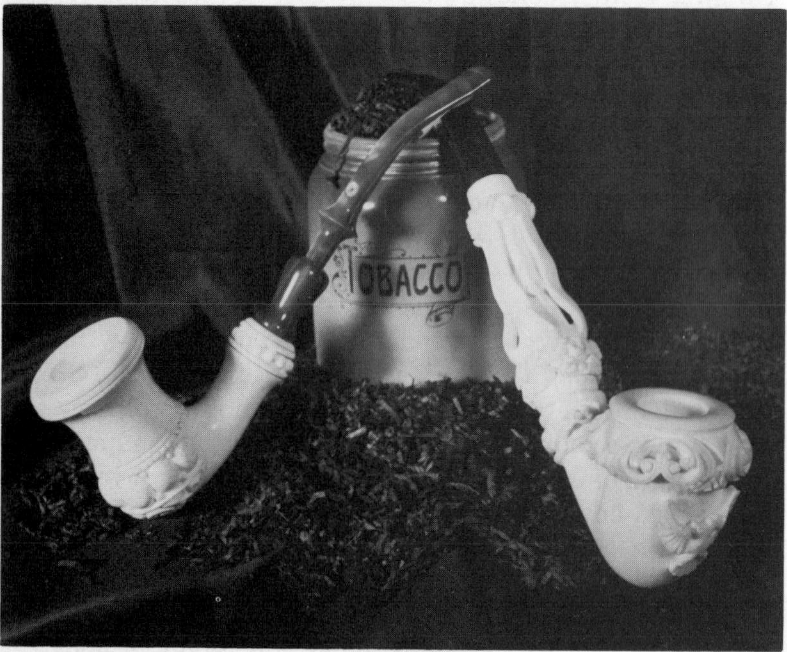

Two examples of some of Turkey's finest carvers, many of whom are now duplicating the antique carvings and designs of 100 years ago. The pipe on the left is unsigned, but the meerschaum on the right was created by Yanik.

Shaping the corncob pipe has always been a hand operation.

The Missouri Meerschaum corncob pipe selection of today includes (L. to R.) the "Mac," Mr Mizzou, Wanghee, Bulldog and Freehand.

As one of Canada's master pipecarvers, Julius Vesz gives a new dimension to briar.

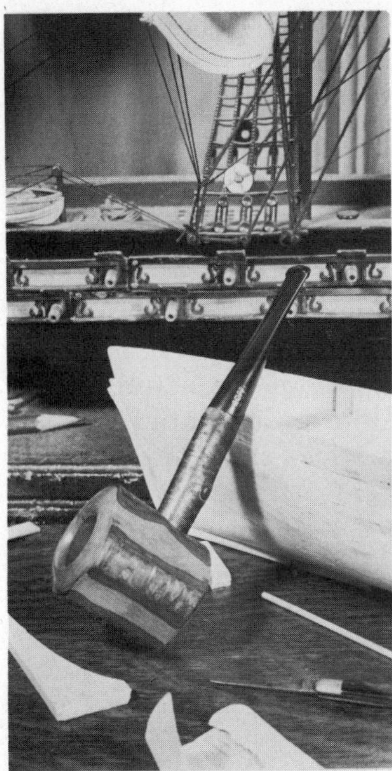

The rustic-looking cherrywood pipe.

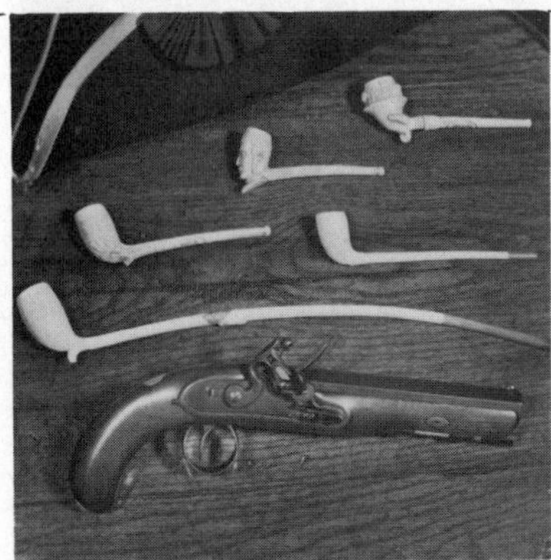

English and Dutch clays are made the same way today as they have been for centuries and offer the pipe smoker a unique way to relive history.

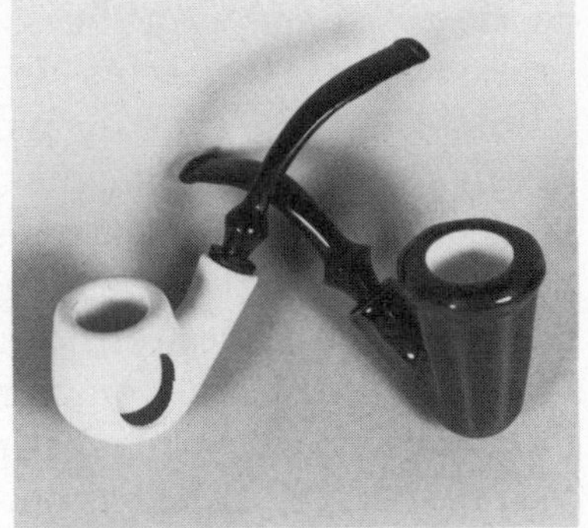

The double-walled clay, with cut-away on left showing hollow bowl cooling system.

Two examples of 20th century porcelain Tyrolean pipes of Germanic origin.

rustic pot shape with the bark left on the bowl; a primary branch often becomes the stem. Thus, smoking a cherrywood is somewhat like smoking a miniature tree.

In terms of design, the pipe bits on meerschaum and corncob pipes are pre-determined things. But there is a little more variety in the bits furnished with briar pipes. Most of these bits are made of either hard rubber (often referred to as vulcanite) or plastic (commonly called Lucite, which sounds a lot better from a marketing standpoint). Vulcanite was first used in 1878 and has become more or less a standard for many of the high grades. Because of the nature of the material, rubber can be carved into a wider variety of slimmer shapes, such as saddle bits, wide fishtail bits and even special bits for denture wearers. It is moulded in cheaper pipes but is actually handcut and shaped in the better

One of the final steps of the pipemaking process is when your tobacconist selects his store's stock at a dealer trade show.

brands. Because sulfur is a compound of rubber, vulcanite bits will eventually oxidize and turn grayish white around the mouth area and can even turn green if left under fluorescent lights for any length of time. However, it is a simple matter to have the bit cleaned and buffed to a shiny like-new blackness, a task that many tobacconists perform for their customers regularly.

Lucite is a relatively new entrant in the pipe bit field and the Italian pipemakers of the 1960s and 70s should be credited for being largely responsible for popularizing the hand-carved Lucite bit and bringing it into the world of elegant pipe fashion. Prior to the importation of their high design pipes, the plastic bit was primarily a simple moulded affair. Now, some of the best shaped pipes sport handcut Lucite bits, often colored in elegant grays, blacks and amber hues, which will not oxidize and discolor. However, unlike rubber, Lucite or acrylic bits, by the very nature of their material, are usually thicker and chunkier in design, although I find them equally as comfortable to clench between my teeth; a lot depends upon the overall pipe design, and the balance and weight of the bowl-to-bit ratio.

Of course, some pipemakers, such as England's Ashton and America's Butera, spend extraordinary efforts hand-sculpting the "button" of some of their bits; as an example, Butera's mouthpieces have *five* different angles to them. In Europe, one of the more recent trends in bit design is the blending of briar, metals and even precious jewels into a Lucite stem, thereby creating a luxurious two-tone effect. This design technique has now been picked up by other pipemakers and is sold on various models in tobacco stores throughout the world. These dressed-up pipe bits are not for everyone, however, but they can impart an elegant touch to a pipe, making it look equally at home in the pocket of a tuxedo, on board a yacht, or simply to lend a little class to a backyard barbeque.

The traditional clay is one pipe that does not require any bit and lest you think that our old friends from the 16th and 17th centuries have shattered and disappeared from the pipe-smoking scene forever, I need only point out that they are still being made in England by John Pollock & Co. as well as in Gouda, Holland (the cheese and *clay pipe* capital of the world!) by Zenith, the oldest continuously producing pipe factory known to man. Since 1749, the Zenith factory has been creating these earthenware smokables and today they turn them out at a rate of seven million pipes a year. But the world will never be overrun with clays, for it has been estimated over half of these pipes are broken annually; I personally have accounted for two of them just last year. Fortunately for environmentally concerned smokers, clay pipes are biodegradable.

Clays are still being made today in much the same manner and using many of the same moulds as when they were all the rage (in fact the *only* rage) in Europe and North America a century or so ago. The reason for their continuing popularity is partly because the cost for a clay is cheaper than the lowliest of briars and while the smoke may not be as cool and the pipe of today exhibits all of the brittleness of its centuries-old predecessors, it still retains all of the charms of yesteryear, and the recent trend of "nostalgic smoking" (not to mention the basic economy of the pipe itself) may be giving new life to the old clay. After all, how else can one experience the same sensation that Raleigh or Dickens or Tennyson may have felt in another time, or know exactly what Watson meant when he spoke of Holmes' various well-smoked clays that littered that famous sitting room at 221B? And at our house at least, it is a Christmas tradition to smoke at least a bowlful of English blend in the old blackened churchwarden on the night of the 24th, before the last embers in the fireplace have died out.

To begin with the manufacture of a clay pipe, the earthy substance is first soaked in water until it reaches a thick, dough-like stage; it is then rolled by hand into long thin tubes. After the clay has started to "set," a thin wire is pushed through the tube to form an airhole. One end of the clay tube is then pressed into a mould, which forms the shape of the pipe, into which an iron plug – or sometimes even the maker's thumb – is pressed to form the bowl. Some of the moulds have engravings or decorations on them, which are embossed onto the pipes as part of their design. The entire wire, plug and clay ensemble is then placed under pressure. When the pipes have partly dried, they are released from the moulds and a craftsman takes a knife and carefully trims away any excess clay. At that time he also determines what the length and curvature – if any – the stem will have. Sometimes a maker's mark is impressed into the bowl or the shank of the pipe. The clays are then fired in kilns, after which a lacquer or colored varnish is painted on the tips of the pipe stems as in days of yore. Then the clays are *carefully* packaged and shipped out into the pipe smoking world of the 20th century, as an enjoyable reminder of our not-so-distant pipe smoking past.

In addition to the historic single-walled clay, another variety is the double-walled ceramic pipe, first invented around 1918 (and called "Old Mokum") by the van der Want family of Zenith pipe fame. This pipe features a double-walled design with a hollow construction, somewhat on the calabash principle, except that the entire bowl is moulded of clay and then fired in a kiln, but only the outside is glazed; the inside of the bowl remains porous, so that it can absorb tar and smoke. As the pipe is puffed, the smoke circulates inside the airspace, which helps to cool it, and the double wall makes the pipe warm but not too hot to handle. The bit is a separate piece which is friction-fit into the shank. One of the unique features about the double-walled pipe is that it can be decorated with everything from "mystery" decals which only appear when the pipe is smoked, to beautiful floral designs, of which the Delft pipes are popular examples. The double-walled clay is also the only pipe which the manufacturers recommend cleaning with boiling water, but frankly, my prejudices built up over years of pipe smoking make me shudder whenever I think about this prospect. As a final note before leaving the realm of the clay pipe, it should be mentioned that the clay is one of England's great gifts to the pipe smoking world; not just on her own shores, but also in Holland, where the Dutch learned their skills from William Barantsz, a British mercenary who took up clay pipemaking as a profession and then taught others.

With all the pipemaking going on in the world today, one might wonder how these briars, meerschaums, corncobs and clays get from the worker's bench and into the pipe shop. It is the end result of the manufacturing process and should therefore be reserved for the ending of this chapter. In the U.K., locally made pipes are distributed directly to the tobacconist, but in other countries the pipes are exported and sold through a series of large and small distributing firms. In this way, many different pipes are marketed by many different firms. Some companies also use salesmen who sell their brands exclusively, while small custom pipemakers usually handle the individual marketing of their pipes themselves. However, each year massive pipe and tobacco-buying trade shows take place at various locations and at different times around the world.

In the United States the largest of these gatherings is the annual Trade Show hosted by the Retail Tobacco Dealers of America, one of the leaders of the smokeshop industry in the U.S. Because the country is so large, the four-day show moves to a different city each year, as it is not always convenient for every tobacconist to attend every year due to the great distances that must be travelled. In Great Britain, each September sees a gathering of tobacco specialists for the National Exhibition of Tobacco Retailers, which is held in Solihull, near Birmingham. This popular buying show for suppliers is sponsored by the Association of Independent Tobacco Specialists. In Europe the Frankfurt Gift Show is perhaps the largest event of its kind, and in many ways can be likened to a carnival, as virtually every pipe, tobacco and gift manufacturer is represented there in some way. Of course, numerous other pipe buying events are held at various sites in other parts of the world.

It is important to note that all of these pipe-selling conventions are for the tobacco trade only, as many products are unveiled for the first time. The public must wait until the autumn purchases come in to their local tobacconists to see what is available. Obviously, not all tobacco stores will carry the same line of pipes or even charge the same price for the same pipe, so it pays to shop around for a particular brand or style you have in mind. However, I have found it to be personally much more rewarding to have one or two pipe shops that I patronize on a regular basis. After all, pipe buying is a highly individualized activity and once your tobacconist gets to know you, your smoking preferences and what you are looking for, he should be willing to keep an eye out for pipes that might fit your particular wants and budget when he is buying pipes for his store. And if you are looking for a specific pipe, it never hurts to ask your tobacconist if he can get one for you, even if it means calling around to other stores. Most tobacconists, by the very fact that they are also pipe smokers, are friendly people and, if they are true professionals and believe in the spirit of the pipe, to say nothing of the spirit of customer service, they should be only too willing to help out a regular customer. In fact, when dealing with a well-stocked pipe shop, buying a pipe from a knowledgeable tobacconist can be one of the most rewarding ways to spend your money, if you know what to look for. And that is just what will be discussed in the next chapter.

SAFARI

Chapter Three

How to Pick the "Right" Pipe

"Pipes are occasionally of extraordinary interest. Nothing has more individuality save, perhaps, watches and bootlaces."

– Sherlock Holmes in *The Yellow Face*
by A. Conan Doyle

Buying a pipe is like selecting the clothes you wear. It has to fit your character, it has to look good, and it has to make *you* look good. These three elements are among the most subtle, yet the most important factors of pipe buying. Unless fully understood, they are all too often overlooked or completely ignored by today's pipe buyer, whether the pipe is being purchased for yourself or as a gift.

Having the luxury of choice is a benefit unique to the 20th century pipe smoker, especially in the U.S., where pipes from England, Ireland, Denmark, Italy and France all compete for equal attention. In the U.K. pipe smokers of the past have been able to choose from some of their country's greatest offerings, but today they are faced with new brands as well as newly imported pipes, most notably from Italy and Denmark. It is because of this tremendous variety that today can truly be called the Golden Age of Pipe Smoking. All of this, of course, brings the first time pipe buyer face to face with a bewildering array of smokables, most of which are touted as "excellent values," "specially priced this week only," "perfect for what you are looking for," and "a really rare piece of workmanship." The obvious question, then, is "Which pipe should I buy?"

The basic and unshakable rule is to buy the best you can afford. You can never go wrong with quality. But there is more to it than that. For example, is this to be your first pipe? If so, you may want to start out with a quality pipe in the medium price range, using it to learn the basic smoking techniques that we will be discussing in Chapter Four. Then you can upgrade even further with your next pipe purchase, although if selected wisely, a medium priced pipe will provide you with a lifetime of smoking pleasure. I still regularly smoke many of my earliest pipe purchases, as they were chosen with care, were well made, and have mellowed with me through the years to the point where they have the look and feel that is just not found on a new pipe.

On the other hand, you may already be an established pipe smoker with a number of briars in your possession, but never really gave much thought to their selection or really knew what to look for. I will never forget the time when I was on an out-of-town business trip with a fellow pipe smoker who was lamenting all during our cab ride from the airport to the hotel because he had forgotten to pack his briar. As we passed a shopping center, he suddenly ordered the driver to stop and with the meter still running, my associate jumped out of the cab, ran inside the mall and emerged less than five minutes later clenching a brand new briar in this teeth.

"How could you have bought a pipe so quickly?" I asked incredulously.

"I just ran into a tobacco shop and picked one out," the fellow answered with the same callousness as if he were talking about a stick of chewing gum.

Pipe buying, for me at least, is a pleasantly time-consuming ritual and I cannot conceive of buying a briar without spending at least half an hour searching the displays, talking to the tobacconist and examining the various waxed and buffed offerings that happen to catch my eye. After all, pipes, like ties, shirts and hats, are very personal items, which gives all the advantage to the person who is buying a briar for himself. When buying a pipe as a gift, a conscious effort must be made to take the intended recipient's personality and lifestyle into account, rather than simply picking out a pipe because you happen to think he or she will like it.

Certain people can wear certain styles of hats better than others and so it is with pipes. The shape of the face and even the person's overall physique should subtly influence the shape of the pipe that is to be purchased for him or her. For example, a thickset, portly smoker often looks better with a short curved pipe, whereas a tall, lean individual may appear more in harmony with a long-stemmed pipe and a slender bowl.

The pipe smoker's occupation is also a factor that should be taken into account when selecting a pipe. A college student with little time between classes or a factory worker who can only smoke while on break might both relish a pipe with a relatively small bowl so that shorter smokes are possible. On the other hand, an office worker or a traveling salesman who often will spend long hours sitting in one spot may prefer a pipe with a larger bowl, where a forty-five minute to one hour smoke might be the norm. And a construction worker who likes to smoke while out in the field, where the risk of pipe loss or breakage is great, might find the corncob to be practical, as it can be replaced for very little money.

A person's lifestyle is especially important to consider when selecting a pipe as a gift. Although the majority of all pipe smokers are men, it is interesting to note that a great number of all tobacco shop customers are women, which means that they are the ones who are normally buying pipes as gifts for their husbands, fathers, boyfriends, brothers or business associates. In fact, pipes continue to be one of Britain's most popular gift items, especially around Christmas, the biggest pipe-selling season of the year. Consequently, when buying a pipe for a man, it is important to consider his tastes. For example, if he lives in a chrome-and-white house and likes modern art, it is very probable that one of the finely made Danish freehands would fit his personality. On the other hand, if he wears tweed jackets and owns an Irish Setter, perhaps one of the traditional English billiards would be more to his liking.

Buying a pipe as a gift for a woman becomes slightly more critical, for women are usually more aware of style and the relationship between wardrobe and accessories. This subject is covered in greater detail in Chapter Six, but the same basic rules apply: consider her facial structure and features, what colors she prefers (light clothes could indicate a light or natural finish briar, pastels look good with a slim Danish design, etc.). Of course, all of these examples are given in the broadest of generalities and you will fare best, whether buying a pipe for yourself or as a gift, by following your own analytical inclinations along with a subtle bit of guidance from your tobacconist, being sure to buy a well-known or well-recommended brand name.

To help make the final selection when buying a pipe for yourself, you should follow the one unbreakable rule that supersedes all else: buy what you like. You will feel better about spending your money and I honestly believe the pipe will smoke better for you. Of course, prior to making your purchase, there are some very important facts about pipe selection that we should discuss.

First, practically all pipes come in one of two basic configurations, *bents* and *straights*, which is the terminology that refers to the shape of the shank and bit (a handy pipe nomenclature chart is included in Chapter Two, in case you are one of those irremediable readers who has been leap-frogging through this book by subject matter rather than by chronological order of events. Shame on you!). A bent can have its "S" shaped configuration formed in any degree of curvature, from very slight to highly exaggerated. The straight can have a stem of any length, from very short to extremely long. Normally, a bent pipe is easier for most people to hold in their mouths, as the center of gravity (i.e., the bowl) is lower and the pipe seems to "hang" better. For individuals who like to talk with a pipe in their mouths, the bent is ideal and can be quite distinctive in design. The straight is more traditional and urbane and is quite practical for me, as I often use my pipe as a pointing device when lecturing. I have been clenching straights and bents in my teeth for years with equal aplomb and the only comment I ever received regarding this practice was from my dentist, who mentioned that I have extremely well developed jaw muscles (great for cracking clams with your teeth). As a matter of observation, I find that most pipe smokers have a variety of pipes in their collections, although they usually tend to favor bents over straights by a 3 to 1 margin.

In addition to these two basic pipe configurations, there is a myriad of different pipe *shapes*, all of which come in a variety of sizes, ranging from extra small (more common in Europe than America) to extra large, with the more practical medium sizes prevailing wherever pipe smokers congregate. Sometimes it seems that any company making more than three pipes a year has to have their own name for each of these shapes and the fact that many of the larger companies issue new "shape charts" annually only compounds the problem for the neophyte pipeologist trying to get a handle on things. Although I have personally categorized over forty different pipe shapes (with many of the same shapes having more than one name, depending on how many pipe companies are making it), I have attempted to simplify things a bit by reducing this entire battalion of appellations down to eight basic styles, which you can use to help get your message across to any civilized tobacconist when he asks, "What type of pipe are you looking for?" They are:

1) Billiard: The classic pipe, always traditional with a fairly good-sized bowl. The definition of a proper billiard is "The height of the bowl equals the length of the shank."

2) Apple: A graceful pipe with a round bowl that appears to have been flattened slightly. The stems of apples can be either straight or slightly bent.

3) Bulldog: A bowl characterized by a carved band around a swelling circumference, about a third of the way down from the rim. Bulldogs usually have a diamond-shaped stem, giving them a sporty appearance. Bulldog bowls can be either squat, medium, or tall.

4) Canadian: A straight pipe with a longer-than-usual shank and a comparatively short bit. There are fewer Canadians made than the other styles, as the design requires a piece of briar that will fit the requirements of the long shank. I have always felt that Canadians were more prone to break at the mouthpiece rather than where the shank joins the bowl, but none of mine ever has.

The tobacco specialist exists in many forms, and is usually a local neighbourhood establishment . . .

. . . but it can also be part of a large internationally-known chain.

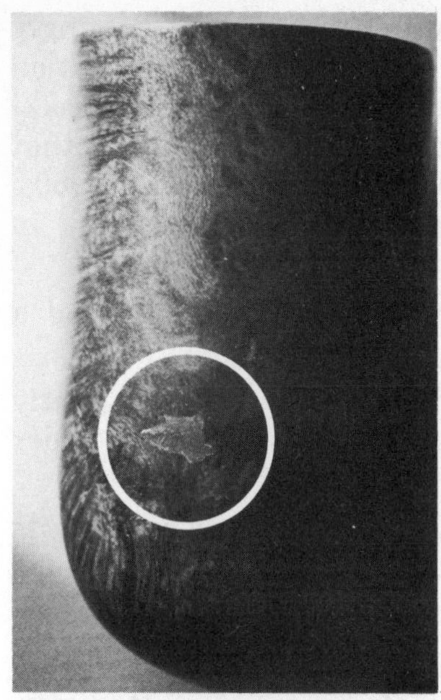
Close-up of a putty fill.

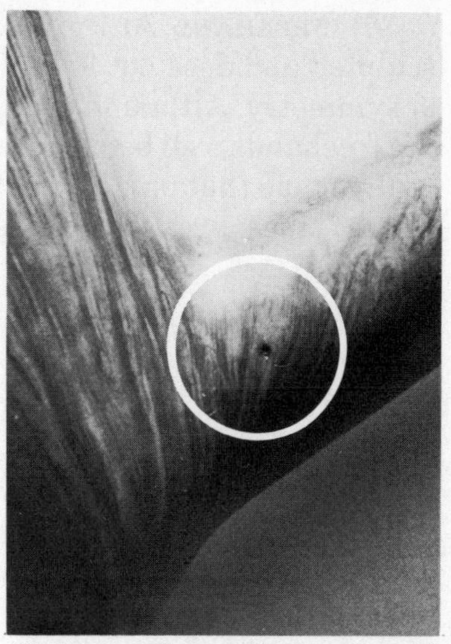
Close-up of a sand pit, although in all other respects, this pipe is a perfect flame grain.

Wood quality, styling and finishing can all affect the cost of a pipe, as shown by these two briars, both of which are made in the Comoy factory. The Lumberman Deluxe Canadian in the foreground is an excellent value, but the Spectrum "first" in the background has a better finish, comes with its own wooden case and matching tamper, and consequently sells for almost three times the price.

5) Freehand: Any pipe in which the design is seemingly sculpted and does not follow the normal bowl configuration or symmetry. Although companies like Charatan were making freehands well before World War II, it was Denmark that really made that pipe concept popular, starting in the 1960s. These pipes are sometimes referred to as *freeforms* in Europe.

6) Pot: A pipe with a short, flat-topped bowl and a rounded bottom.

7) Dublin: An old design in which the bowl gently angles up from the stem so that the top is noticeably wider than the bottom.

8) Poker: A cylindrical, self-standing pipe which has its stem slightly above the ground level of the flat-bottomed bowl.

These are the most popular styles you will encounter in any pipe shop today. Obviously, there are more categories, like the massively curved *Oom-Paul* (which always sounds like a tuba), the slabsided *Panel*, and a host of others, not to mention the sub-categories, such as the bent bulldogs, oval bowls and pipes with square shanks. Throughout this book you will find photos of most of the shapes available to the known world. If in doubt, take this book with you to your tobacconist and show him a picture that is similar to the pipe design you want.

Because the vast majority of pipes are made of briar, which is still the king of all smoking materials, let's discuss these pipes first in discovering how to select the best smoking instrument for our money. In Chapter Two we have already discovered that briar pipes can come in three different finishes: smooth, sandblast and carved. Smooth grain pipes are by far the most popular and it is through our understanding of how a pipe is made that we can select a quality pipe. Generally, smoking ability depends upon how well the briar has been cured (dried), how well it has been made (is the bowl centered and does the airhole enter the bowl from the bottom so that all of the tobacco will be smoked), and how it is finished. All good smoking briar pipes have a natural finish; that is, the bowl has not been painted or lacquered, processes that can hide flaws in the wood and which seal it, thereby preventing the pipe from breathing, a necessary ingredient in obtaining a cool smoke. Pipes sold in newsagents' and stationers' shops should be avoided. We've all seen them, stacked in a barrel alongside the counter and usually selling for less than the price of a litre of oil. While these pipes may be smokable in a literal sense of the word, few of them can give the pleasure that a true pipe person deserves. Those cheap imitations of the real thing normally have a varnished or lacquered, puttied-up finish and as a result, they produce an extremely "hot," tongue-biting smoke that is often accompanied by a gunky, wet acidic taste, caused by the heat being trapped inside the sealed walls of the bowl and further aggravated by the use of metal filters. These poorly-made pipes have no doubt been responsible for attracting many a cigarette smoker into the realms of pipedom ("Hmm, think I'll try a pipe; they're only £2 . . .") but like a cruel joke played upon the unsuspecting neophyte, they have also turned more people away from pipe smoking than a world full of King Jameses. Thus, many a would-be pipe smoker has given up the practice without ever realizing the full pleasure that could have been obtained from a properly-finished briar which would not have cost much more than the useless mass-market version. Therefore, be sure you buy only unfinished or stained briar. (These natural finishes can run the spectrum in color from light blond to tan to brown to black.)

When buying a pipe, the cardinal rule is, like everything else in this monetary world, you get what you pay for. But an interesting bonus for pipe smokers is that you can sometimes get more than you pay for in a well-stocked, aggressively merchandised tobacco shop, as very often the tobacconist will have specials on certain quality pipes, off-brands or close-outs and both the new and the experienced pipe smoker can treat himself to another briar for very little money. Of course, if you are a pipe connoisseur or a smoker who gravitates towards straight grains or cased sets, there is practically no limit to the amount you can spend. All we are establishing is the fact that quality is not expensive for the pipe smoker who has a basic knowledge of how to pick a pipe

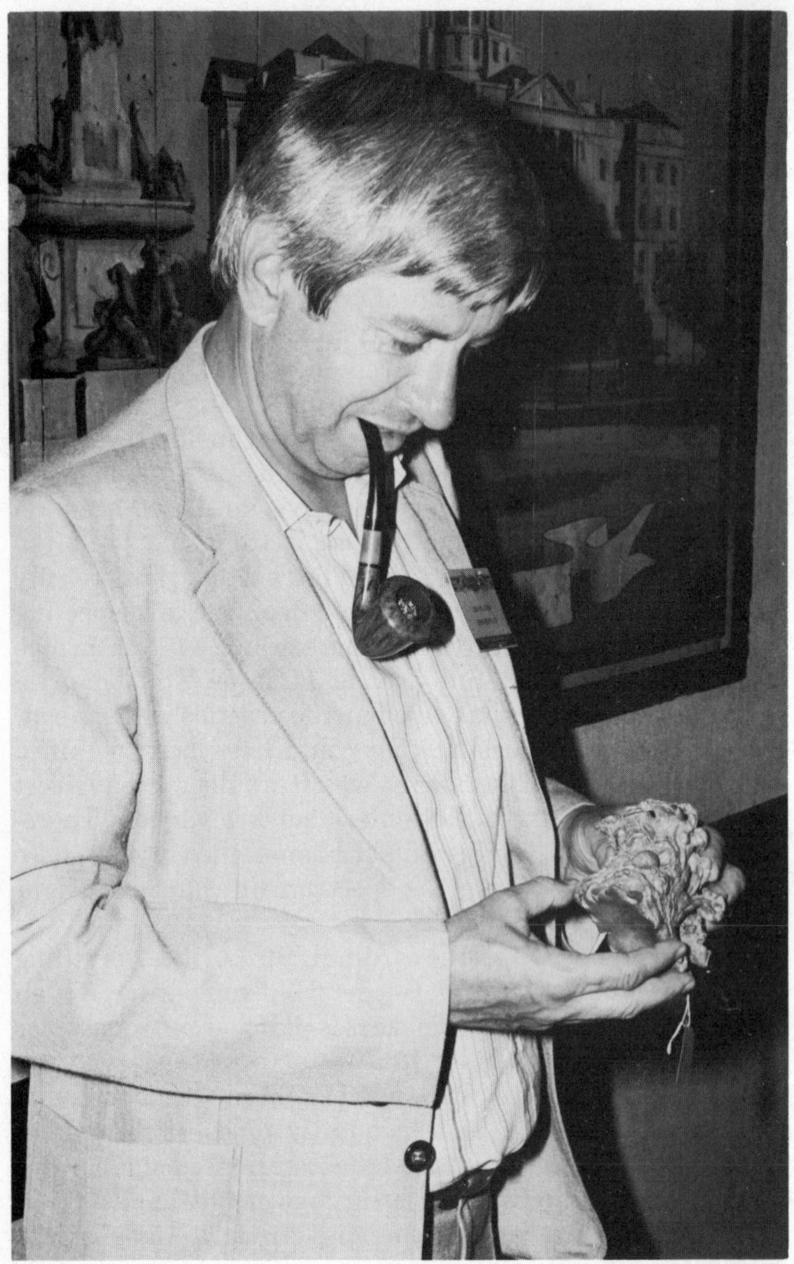

Jean-Paul Berrod, of the Butz-Choquin pipe factory in Saint-Claude in France, examines a unique creation during a pipe carving contest organized by the author. The pipe he is smoking is a Calabash Deluxe made by his company.

Dunhill has always been one of the world's premier pipemakers who only produce "firsts". So great was their reputation, that although the company used to keep a "royal drawer" for members of the royal family, the Prince of Wales often picked his pipes from regular stock. In the front row are a 1949 LB Shell, Deerstalker gold windcap, ODA bulldog, and a Shell "Duke".

James Upshall is another British pipemaker who only produces "firsts". In addition, this "new breed of British pipemaker" can re-create the old classics, like this turn-of-the-century church-warden.

Pipes are adaptable to any personality, any occupation, anywhere in the world.

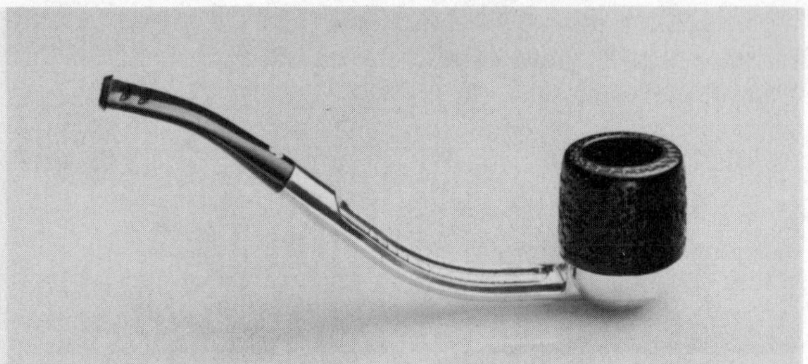

Although it originated in the U.S., the British-made Falcon, with its interchangeable bowl system, has achieved international popularity.

and who makes his purchases from a tobacco store with sufficient inventory to choose from.

Generally, the lighter a pipe weighs, the more thoroughly it has been cured and freed of resin and moisture, although be sure to take bowl size into consideration. A properly cured large billiard will naturally weigh more than a small apple design. When choosing a smooth finish briar pipe, the grain and quality of the wood is the all-important criteria. As a rule, the older the briar, the closer and more pronounced the grain pattern will become.

The relationship between quality briar and its effect upon the price of a pipe cannot be overemphasized and it is important that today's pipe smoker fully understands how it may affect his pipe buying decision. In the 1937 book, *The Odyssey of Tobacco*, U.S. author Robert Lewis Fisher stated, ". . . the cultivation of tree-heath (briar root) . . . is grown in many places on the Mediterranean in sufficient quantities to supply the present world-wide demand for briar pipes." That may have been true in 1937, but since that time, although the number of pipes has decreased, new members are joining the ranks of the briar brigade daily; in the U.S. that number has grown to greater proportions by the relatively new and popular category of pipe collector. Consequently, the demand for good quality briar grows stronger each year. Although denied by a few commercial pipemakers, most pipe manufacturers admit the growing scarcity of *old* briar. It is an established fact that at the beginning of this century, many quality briar pipes were made with 250-year-old wood. Later, just prior to World War II, the best pipes were being made with 100-year-old briar. Today we usually find 50 to 75-year-old briar being used for most top grade pipes. But it is the older wood, with its finer grain and greater density, that is most prized by collectors and many knowledgeable smokers. If artistic appreciation is to be our guideline, I can fully understand a pipe collector paying a premium for a pipe made from two-centuries-old briar. I have done so myself. But from a practical point of view, there is very little smoking difference in a pipe made from 50-year-old briar or 200-year-old briar. I have examples of both categories in my collection and smoke them regularly; although told I have a rather discerning palate, I still have a difficult time distinguishing the age of a briar pipe simply based upon its smoking characteristics. It is the *quality*, *curing*, and *workmanship* of the briar which makes the difference to a true pipe smoker. Nonetheless, collectors, or those pipe smokers concerned with more of the aesthetics of the pipe smoking art, may suggest that a real smoking difference does exist with the centuries-old wood and for them, perhaps it does. But no matter what the reasons, psychological or physical, there will always be a demand for the more ancient burl, whether it is used to make a new pipe or is found in an older briar.

Fortunately, good, well cured briar is the only type used by all of the better pipemaking firms, most of whom place a premium on grain design. The main thing to look for is symmetry of pattern. And while a perfect repetition of grain all around the bowl is always more desirable from an aesthetic point of view and because it affects the physical beauty of a pipe and often (but not always) influences the price, grain symmetry does *not* affect the smoking quality of a pipe. The main criteria for a good smoking pipe, as far as grain is concerned, is total bowl coverage.

As we stated in the last chapter, a "first" is the *ne plus ultra* of owning a briar pipe, but you must expect to pay for the privilege. In today's pipemaking world of rising labor costs and a growing scarcity of suitable briar, many pipes are being sold as "firsts" with minor pitting or surface blemishes. Only you can decide if the pipe is worth the price. Keep in mind, however, that in a few more years, pipes with even these tiny imperfections may be as rare as an unblemished "first" is today. If your budget and your personality both suggest that you smoke only "firsts," by all means do so, as they are good investments as well as being superb sources of pride. My personal recommendation is that when you get a promotion at work, when you have any birthday that ends in a "5" or a "0," when you need a boost in morale or when you are feeling especially great . . . that is the time you should buy yourself a "first."

Of course, there is absolutely nothing wrong with "seconds." They occupy the majority of spaces in most pipe racks including my own and I guarantee I will be acquiring many more "seconds" before the last match flickers over my final bowlful of Latakia. "Seconds" are notably less expensive than "firsts" and are usually made from the very same wood. The only difference is a few imperfections are present which may or may not be apparent to the casual observer and which in no way affects the quality of the smoke. Moreover, by having a good tobacconist and knowing your pipe brands, it is possible to purchase seconds that are made by some of the world's premium pipemakers. For example, Ashton pipemaker Bill Taylor makes some of England's finest high grades that sell in the three-figure price range. His perfectly cured, hand-turned briars with their excellent designs and hand-cut vulcanite stems are highly regarded by pipe connoisseurs, especially the rare smooth-finished Sovereigns. But Taylor also makes an excellent "reject" under the Briarwood name (and other brands, depending on the various pipe shops) which can be owned for substantially less money than his high grades. Comoy is another premium pipemaker (in fact, the oldest briar pipe company in the world) that carves some excellent "firsts," many of which are highly collectible and out of pocketbook reach for the majority of smokers. Yet their Everyman series is an affordable "second" that is very inexpensive, comes in a variety of shapes and provides an excellent smoke. Another example of good buys in "seconds" are the superbly figured and finished Tilshead pipes, made in the James Upshall factory, a company that was started by the late Col. Kenneth Barnes, who was managing director of Charatan for sixteen years. The company is now being run by the Colonel's son, Kennedy, who shares his father's dedication to producing fine quality pipes. All pipes stamped with the Upshall name are "firsts," but their seconds are stamped "rejects" and are sold under the Tilshead label for substantially less money to an eager market, as only plateau briar is used for any pipe coming out of the Upshall factory.

It is important for the new pipe smoker to realize that many of the top pipemaking companies have seconds that are marketed under a variety of "own brand" names. This is nothing more than an exclusive name for a pipe (in fact, they are often called "exclusives") that is reserved for a specific tobacco shop or a chain of stores. Most pipe factories will even make up a die and stamp a tobacconist's "exclusive" brand label on the stem if a sufficient quantity is purchased by the shop. Some individuals even go so far as to register their brand labels with the copyright office so that no one else can legally use the name. Other tobacconists have stamping machines that enable them to emboss their own brand label names directly on the pipes in their store.

It is a great adventure to buy and try some of the many off-brands that proliferate the market, as these briars can represent some of the best values in the pipe smoking world if your tobacconist has chanced upon an unusual find. It also pays to become familiar with some of the more respected brands in the low to medium price range. For example, Parker-Hardcastle pipes are actually made under the same roof as the famous pipes of Dunhill; they are just more economically manufactured, do not have a "white dot," and sell for far less money. If your tastes lean towards Italian styling, Savinelli is a pipemaking company that has been in existence since 1948 and their excellent smoking pipes in all price ranges, from the popular Oscar to the prestigious Autographs, are now finding favor in the U.K. Of course, there are countless other brands, and to aid you in making a selection – or to at least become familiar with some of the names – I have listed most of the better known pipemakers in the Chapter Ten Sourcebook portion of this book.

Recently, there has been a tremendous renaissance in Italian made pipes, created primarily because of the growing interest in some of the old standards such as Savinelli, Castello and Caminetto. There has also been a great deal of promotion directed towards some of the newer Italian pipemakers, resulting in an increased demand for their products. Many of them are extremely high grade pipes that exhibit excellent smoking qualities. Others are of medium quality and some are downright poor. Again, it goes back to buying a brand you know, and asking your tobacconist for advice. In the case of the Italian pipes, it is important to realize that their concept of a "first" differs from the U.S. or the British: an Italian "first" may have sand pits. It is the *quality* of the briar and the *grain* that they look at. With the exception of Savinelli, not many Italian pipes are imported into Great

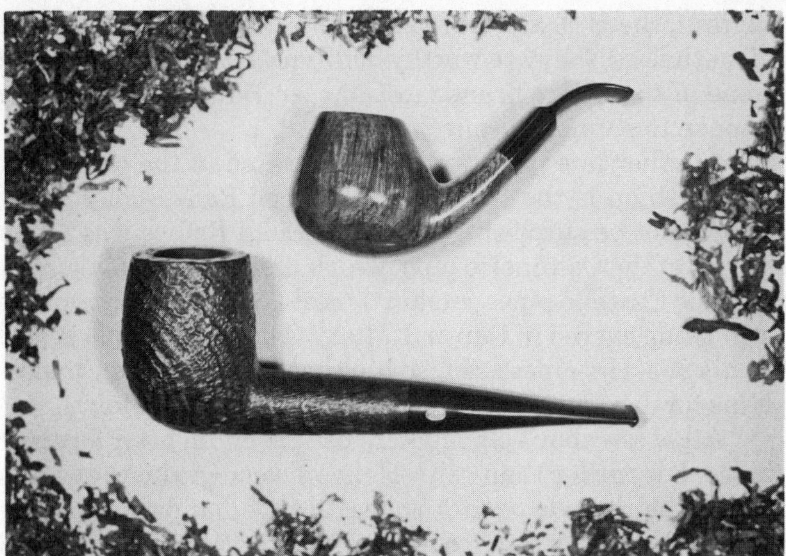

Pipes should be selected with a specific smoking purpose in mind, such as the elegant, yet easy-to-carry Nørding (top) or the large, stay-at-home GBD Kingsize Billiard (bottom).

Some of today's most sought-after Italian pipes include (back row, L to R): Caminetto New Dear, Ascorti Stack, Castello Great Line Collector Fiamatta with "U.S. diamond"; (front row, L to R): Becker bulldog, Savinelli Giubileo D'Oro, and Castello Sea Rock with European "white bar" logo.

Britain; the U.S. and Europe remain their biggest markets. Nonetheless, they are worthy of discussion and I have listed some of the better brands in Chapter Ten, just in case you happen to stumble on one.

Another fine pipe carved and smoked in the old craftsman fashion is the Radice (pronounced Rad-*ee*-chay). This should not be surprising either, as Luigi Radice was also a carver of the Caminetto pipe, which is still being made.

The Castello pipes remain a hard-to-find classic, and are still being carved in Cantu, Italy by Carlo Scotti, who is now in his 80s. His pipes are also highly collectible (see Chapter Nine for more information on this famous pipemaker).

All of the above pipemakers use premium briar for their pipes, but rather than rely solely on wood grain, they often finish their bowls with a characteristic handcarved sandblast effect (known as "rusticated") and often with a natural finish that colors to a rich tan as the pipe is smoked over the years.

Besides the Italian pipes, there are other countries, not all of which are imported in any abundance to Great Britain, which are nonetheless topics worthy of discussion among anyone interested in the existence of fine briar. Danish pipes, such as the wooden sculptured pieces from Ole Larsen, or the expensive works of art from Sven Bang, all have the ability to draw an interested glance from a pipe smoker, whether or not they approve of the style. By contrast, Danish freehand pipemaker Erik Nørding has developed a following for his classic Canadians and deep bents, especially when he dresses them up with bands of silver thick enough to serve as wedding rings! Another Danish producer of semi-classical shapes is Georg Jensen, while the respected Stanwell name has the greatest variety of pipes in Denmark. There are very few West German pipemakers, but certainly one of the best is Ingo Garbe, whose semi-traditional briars have been exhibited in art shows. Canadian pipemaker Julius Vesz is a master of metalwork, and while his plain briars are well-respected smoking instruments, his silver and gold sculptured custom pipes can best be described as spectacular; at least, you certainly would not want to bang the bowl against your boot to knock out the ashes. Finally, I must point out the tremendous number of American pipemakers who have emerged in a relatively short period of time. Too many to name, I shall merely mention that some of their representative work is scattered throughout this book and in Chapter Ten you will discover how to get a sizeable listing of this renaissance in U.S. pipemaking skill. Needless to say, all of the briars in this section are worthy of owning – and smoking.

The only briar pipes I would suggest avoiding are "thirds" – pipes made of poor quality briar and exhibiting putty "fills" – noticeable patches in the wood that literally have been filled and doctored up with coloring to try and match the wood. Putty suggests a flaw so serious in the briar that it had to be "hidden," which means you are asking for potential disappointment from the moment you start to light up. Normally, a "fill" is an indication of a weak spot in the briar and if located on the bowl, could indicate a potential danger of burnout, a situation where a hot spot of tobacco actually burns through to the outer bowl. From an aesthetic standpoint, fills are unsightly and even if stained to match the rest of the bowl, putty will not color like briar as it is smoked and will become even more noticeable as time goes on. Because a "third" is an imperfect pipe, it stands to reason that the manufacturer did not take as much time and care in making it. Thus, we go back to our basic rule for pipe buying: obtain the best you can comfortably afford.

Some briar pipes are sold with pre-carbonized bowls under the guise that they need no breaking in. Anyone who has tried such pipes knows that this is not completely true, for no amount of artificial carbonization can equal the thickness and substance of a natural cake. Following in the trail of early briar pipemakers who used to line their bowls with clay, there are a few pipes made today with meerschaum-lined bowls, the thought being that because meerschaum pipes need no breaking in, you bypass this step when lining the briar bowls with this substance. It is, at best, a compromise and for pipe smoking, the purest of the smoking arts, compromises never give complete satisfaction. For one thing, the meerschaum used is not "block," but is made up of pulverized and sometimes synthetically altered meerschaum, so the smoke does not have the porousness and coolness that one would find in a "real" meerschaum pipe. For another, the briar of these pipes is normally not of the best quality in both color and texture, and therefore does not "breathe" as a normal briar pipe would. Finally, because there is a meerschaum lining between the tobacco and the briar bowl, the pipe is not permitted to color and achieve that all-important seasoning that can only come after smoking numerous bowlfuls of tobacco in an all-briar pipe.

Besides, I look upon breaking in a briar as one of the first of many pleasures I will derive from a brand new pipe. There is a definite sense of excitement in knowing I am the very first to load the bowl, tamp the tobacco, light the leaves and take a puff, drawing the thick white smoke through the untouched stem much as an explorer blazes a new path through a previously uncharted forest. For those more modern smokers who are not so traditionally inclined, there are alternatives to the break-in period, such as the "Star Wars" pipes made from carbonized graphite that was first developed for space-age nosecones. These pipes need no breaking in at all and will never burn out, even when traveling hundreds of miles an hour through the earth's stratosphere.

On more than one occasion I have heard various people advising a first-time smoker to buy a meerschaum pipe, as "sea foam" requires no break-in. I do not feel that this is practical advice. While meerschaum is noted for providing a smooth smoke right from the start, the naturally fragile nature of the material requires that it be handled with extra care, which includes not touching the bowl as it is being smoked. This, to my way of thinking, takes away a lot of the spontaneity associated with pipe smoking, especially for the newcomer in our ranks. Therefore, I heartily recommend a briar pipe for a first purchase, saving meerschaum as a well-deserved "alternative smoke."

In buying a meerschaum, the basic rule applies: buy quality. However, because meerschaum has no grain, you must console yourself by only looking for shape and if it is a carved meerschaum, being extra selective as to the quality of the carving. Because most meerschaums are produced by the

New designs of stand-up pipes are convenient to use and adapt easily to a casual lifestyle.

Two Ashton Pebble Grain (sandblast) pipes by another of England's "new wave" master pipemakers. Foreground pipe features a pinched Brindle tapered bit, an extra-step feature Ashton occasionally turns out as a subtle reminder that all their pipes are handmade.

same basic coterie of Turkish carvers, you may find the same type of pipes sold under a variety of importers' names. Among the best are those pipes previously mentioned in Chapter Two and, of course, the pipes made in the U.K., to name just a few which you will find in your tobacconist's showcases. Meerschaums are priced according to the size of the bowl and the degree and quality of carving the pipe exhibits. However, a smooth and polished meerschaum without any carving is a very attractive pipe and will color just as well as a carved version, although without all of the intricacies of the darker brown cracks and crevices where the tobacco juices and smoke has soaked through first. It is merely a matter of personal taste as to what style of meerschaum pipe you choose. Just be sure you obtain a pipe that is carved of solid block meerschaum and not the cheaper grade of meerschaum dust which will not smoke as cool or color as well (if at all). The buyer of such imitations loses on two of a meerschaum pipe's most important attributes: appearance and smokability.

Although the standard carved block meerschaum pipe has been with us since 1723, around 1980 a new type of meerschaum made its appearance and has caught on with a number of smokers, although its availability is often quite limited. It is called the Manx meerschaum, a pipe made from the African product rather than the Turkish, which is slightly harder and not as porous. These pipes have been further hardened by heating them in oil and many of them are colored to look as if they have been smoked for many years. They are also heavier than standard meerschaum pipes, but still lighter than briar. They are quite attractive and cool smoking and one of the largest producers of these pipes is Erik Nørding, who has his made on the Isle of Man, off the coast of England. They are also sold in the U.K. by Comoy's, Barling, and a few other firms.

When buying a pipe, one quickly realizes that briar and meerschaum will comprise the bulk of the selection in most tobacco shops. However, there are a few other varieties that nonetheless deserve mention. We have already discussed the clays in Chapter Two. When buying one, the main thing to do is to check and make sure it has not cracked in the shipping

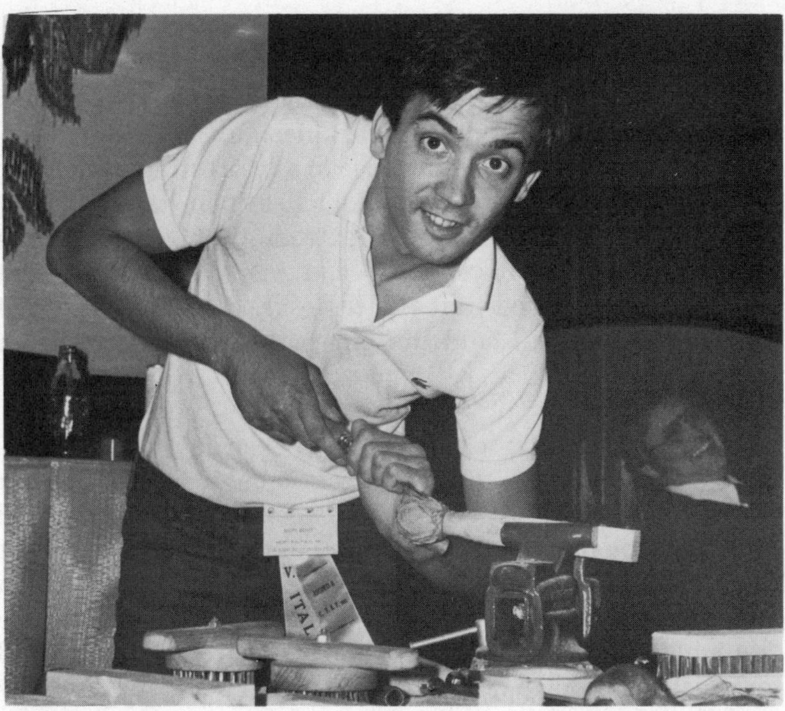

Roberto Ascorti is now the second generation to continue with his family's pipes.

The Savinelli Autograph is a handmade "first" produced on a very limited basis each year. The Autographs are graded and priced by a numerical designation, starting with #4 and #5 (which usually feature a panel sandblast), then go to the higher grades of briar found in #6, #8, 0, 00, 000, and 000E. These higher numbers refer to the quality of the briar rather than the size of the pipe. In the background is the fourth in a series of limited edition porcelain humidors issued each year by the Danish tobacco blending firm of Alfred & Christian Petersen Ltd., providing a rare smoke for a rare pipe.

process, and that the airhole is free from any obstruction. The sturdier Zenith double-walled pipes are more rigid in their construction and one need only to be concerned with buying a pipe of the right color and design.

The Tyrolean porcelain pipes are interesting to look at, but most pipe smokers today consider them to be strictly showpieces. They tend to smoke extremely hot and the bowls can often crack. However, if you insist on buying one to smoke, be advised that the little knob on the bottom of the bowl is used to hold the pipe; otherwise you'll scorch your fingers and that will end your piano concerto for the evening.

Corncobs are fun to smoke and a seven day corncob set is not a bad idea, for the same cob should not be smoked steadily, as it is highly absorbent (especially when compared to other pipe materials on today's market) and tends to get rank-tasting and soggy if not allowed to dry out between pipefuls. In addition, the life expectancy of a corncob pipe (which is short, especially when compared to briar and meerschaum) depends on how hot the bowl gets; a heavy smoking, hard puffer will go through his corncob in a relatively short period of time, while the fellow who takes his time and smokes slowly, especially with one of the wood-plugged bowls, will find that his corncob may actually last for years. I am not aware of anyone's corncob lasting indefinitely, unless they are not smoked at all. Replacing a corncob, however, is not an expensive proposition (normally 225 grams of your favorite tobacco will cost more than your corncob and may even last longer) and it is one of those pipes that you can forget in a local pub or lose on a train without having too much remorse, unless it is for sentimental value alone. If you try a corncob and decide you really want to make it one of your primary smoking instruments, I would recommend buying a great number and variety of them at one time; not only is it a convenient and extremely inexpensive way to achieve an "instant pipe collection," but, by rotating the pipes for each smoke, they will all last a lot longer. Although the bowl is highly absorbent, the shank and stem should still be cleaned with a pipe cleaner after it has cooled in order to keep the acidic tars out of your mouth.

There are also a number of what the tobacconists call "trick pipes," those that have a gimmick or two about their construction. Some of these are waistcoat pipes with fold-away stems, pipes with built-in spring-loaded tampers affixed to their bowls, pipes that smoke upside down and other such abnormalities. Most of these are smokable to various degrees, and it is up to the individual to decide whether or not such a pipe is for his collection. I personally prefer the more traditional versions.

Pipe bowls, materials and shapes are not the only thing to consider when buying a pipe. One of the most often overlooked features is the bit. Normally, we are so preoccupied with how the pipe looks that we fail to take into account how it will feel in our mouth. Both the bit shape and the bit material are interrelated. In the past, mouthpieces have been made from everything from hollow reeds to ivory and pewter. However, the two most popular substances you will find today are hard rubber (often referred to as vulcanite, an older term stemming from the last century) and plastic, which ranges from the inexpensive moulded bits found on corncobs all the way up to the hand-carved glossy Lucite. Vulcanite is more traditional and is often found on many of the high grade pipes. It has the advantage of being able to be hand cut to thin saddle-back or wide fish-tail shapes that look elegant and feel secure in the mouth. However, rubber ages rather ungracefully and will oxidize and turn green and even white in time. Fortunately, these bits can be professionally cleaned and polished to a like-new luster by your tobacconist.

On the other hand, Lucite will never tarnish and does not lose its color around the "bite marks" on the bit. Because it is harder than rubber, Lucite will take longer to bite through if you use a hard "clomp" to hold your pipe in your mouth. It will break, however, just as rubber will. Additionally, even the expensive hand cut Lucite bits must, by the very nature of the material, be more "chunky" and thicker in appearance than rubber. However, Lucite offers interesting pipe design possibilities, as evidenced by some of the inlaid Lucite bits on pipes designed by the Italian pipemakers such as Castello and Ascorti, in which the bit lip is sculpted to fit the teeth or slices of briarwood are inlaid as part of the plastic mouthpiece.

Amber is a 19th century pipe bit material that is making a comeback, especially on some of the better meerschaums as well as on prestigious high grade briars made by firms such as Ashton and Larsen. Amber is nothing more than fossilized resin which is found along the southern shores of the Baltic Sea. It comes in colors that range from an off-white to yellow to a rich, deep red. It is opaque and glass-like in structure and can break quite easily, but it still has an old world mystique about it that predates Lucite or vulcanite, although I feel the latter two materials are far more practical for pipe stems. Many of the amber bits used today are actually a powdered version of this material, moulded in a resin base. It is somewhat harder than pure amber, but lacks the clarity.

The bits of the mouthpieces come in a variety of designs, including special models made just for denture wearers. Even the airholes have variations, although I feel that as long as the hole reaches from the bowl to the end of the bit, you are on safe ground. Perhaps one of the most unique designs in today's market is the airhole found on many of the Peterson pipes, in which the hole is aimed upwards, towards the roof of the mouth. The purpose of this arrangement is to keep the smoke away from your tongue (thus avoiding tongue bite), but frankly, the roof of your mouth can be equally as sensitive. The best solution to tongue bite is discussed in the next chapter. Still, the Peterson mouthpiece does give each of their pipes a unique *bit* of individuality.

As you may have gathered, not all pipe stems are the same; basically, there are three distinct styles you will encounter, and all of them refer to the way in which the stem is affixed to the pipe's shank. The most common is the Push Stem, which simply has a tenon which is pushed with a twisting motion into the hole drilled for it in the shank. In the past, there has been a great deal written about (can you believe this?) which way to twist the bit of a Push Stem. Who cares! All the twisting motion does is help ease the tenon into the hole and prevent breakage. And if you really must know, I twist my stems back and forth (that way I satisfy everybody). The only time you should make a point to twist with a clockwise motion is when putting in or taking out a stem in which the tenon is a separate piece that has been screwed into the bit, such as is the custom on most meerschaum and two-piece bits. Otherwise, you could end up unscrewing the tenon from the bit, as the threads run counter-clockwise. But normally, all briar and corncob pipes have a one-piece stem so put them on and take them off with any sort of gentle twisting motion you like.

The second type of bit really *is* a threaded screw-on style and the threads dictate how it is put on. Just be sure the contours of the bit line up perfectly with the contours of the shank or don't buy the pipe, as anything less than a perfect match indicates careless workmanship which might be evidenced in other parts of the pipe as well.

Finally, there is the military bit which pushes into the stem, which is normally protected with a silver, gold or horn cap, adding to the pipe's overall attractiveness. Originally, military bits were designed for British horsemen, most notably those on duty in India, who suffered untold pipe casualties due to the habit of keeping their briars tucked into their uniform belts; a quick movement in the saddle and snap! another "Old Soldier" down to the repair shop. The military bit changed all that and, made it easy to quickly and simply pull the pipe apart, placing the bit and bowl into a pocket, where it was safe from harm. It could just as quickly be re-assembled for a smoke. Push bits are commonly found on Peterson pipes, some collectible Comoys and on many freeform and handmade pipes today. The main thing to guard against is a military bit that fits too loosely or that has not been shoved down firmly; these pipes become very hard to smoke when the bowl is lying on the floor and the bit is still in your mouth. Still, the military bit is one of my favorite styles and they have a nice history behind them.

Finally, when discussing how to buy a pipe, it is only fair that we acknowledge used pipes . . . or "estate pipes" as they are now being called. This is a relatively new trend in pipe buying that is centered mainly in the U.S., where it has been going on for about twenty years. I realize that this concept is totally foreign to European smokers (no pun intended), but

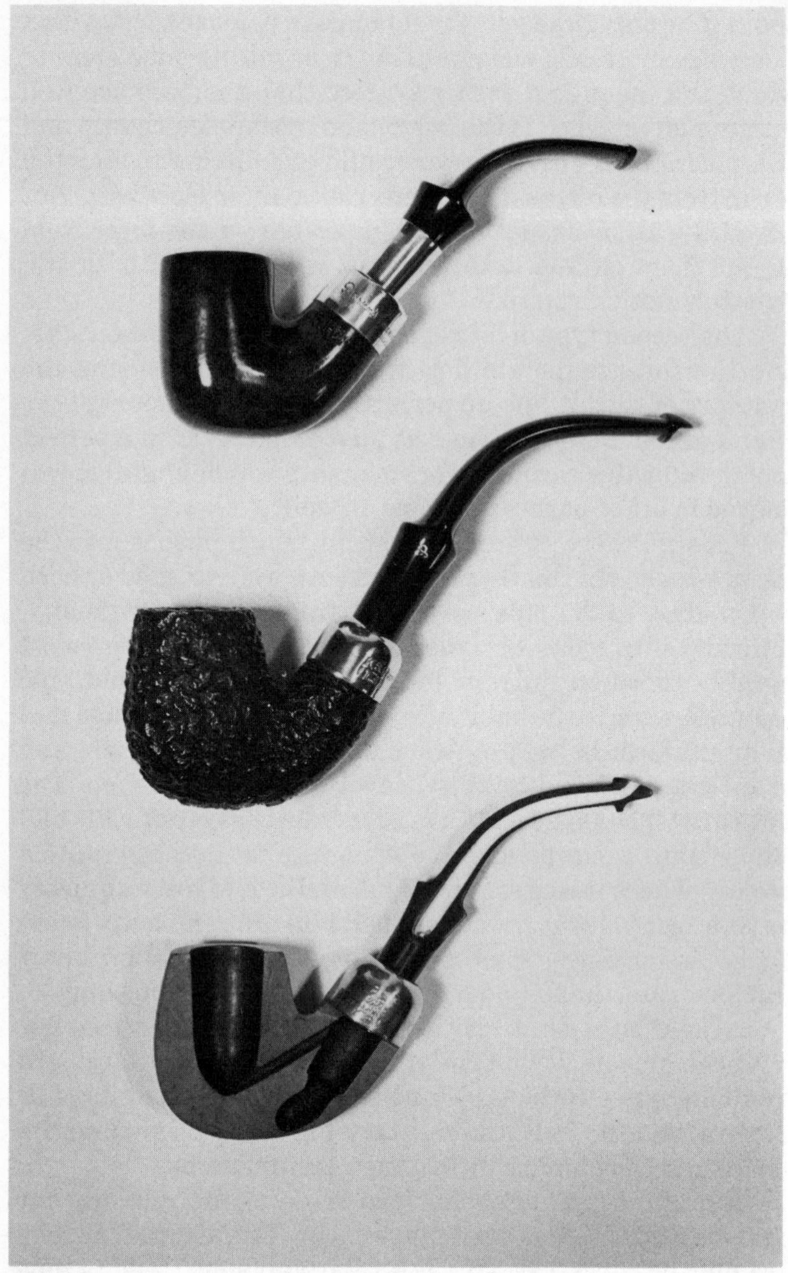

Peterson pipes are nostalgic, unique and remain popular. Top to bottom: an elegant Silver Spigot, standard sandblast and cutaway showing the Peterson system with its "reservoir" under the pipe bowl.

the American smoker's interest in vintage pipes made of old briar or carved in shapes that are no longer available has brought about a marked increase in previously-owned pipes.

Now, I admit that at first thought, there is something revolting about the concept of putting someone else's pipe in your mouth. Yet, when we eat out at our favorite restaurant, we are definitely not the first to use that particular knife and fork. They, however, have been cleaned and sterilized and that makes it all right. It is the same with an estate pipe that has been properly prepared. Of course, the obvious question we may ask is that with so many varieties and makers of pipes in the world today, why not buy a new pipe and leave the used and forgotten ones in some dusty cardboard box? It is a question I often asked until the day I saw a used GBD Prehistoric #201 with a sterling silver band around its long, slim flat shank. It was in the display case of a tobacconist who specialized in selling such things. I immediately felt a kinship with this attractive "writer's pipe." When I asked to see it, I was horrified to learn that it had already been smoked, albeit many years ago and by an owner who had long since ceased to be. Disillusioned, I gave the pipe back to the tobacconist, went home, washed my hands, and then commenced on a citywide search to find a new pipe of the same fine make and configuration. None existed and I could not get that haunting GBD out of my mind. Finally, I returned to the shop, and being assured that the tobacconist had complete hospitalization coverage should I come down with some rare 1930s disease, I bought the pipe. It has since become one of my favorite briars and I have been offered twice what I paid for it but I will not sell. Instead, I have subsequently purchased even more estate pipes and my enthusiasm for these old pieces of briar increases with each new acquisition. It is only the first one that is the hardest to buy.

Why buy a used pipe? The reasons are varied. It may be to get a shape that no longer exists or to obtain a pipe that is no longer readily available, such as the early Eight Dot Sasieni's. It is also an excellent way to buy an expensive high grade for about 30% to 75% less than you would have to pay for the equivalent pipe if it were brand new. And a used pipe is already broken in for you. However, not all used pipes are good bargains and as the estate market grows, there will undoubtedly be the seller who thinks that his 1950 bargain pipe is a rarity and will want to charge accordingly. Know your pipes; buy from a tobacconist who is experienced in used pipes and who also knows how to properly clean each piece, which should be completely reconditioned (antique pipes from the 19th century are a different matter, which we will take up in Chapter Nine). That includes reaming out the bowl, polishing the wood and mouthpiece, boiling out the bowl and shank with alcohol and sterilizing the mouthpiece. Your tobacconist can also perform this service on any boot sale treasures that you might find. Admittedly, presmoked pipes are not for everyone, but they do constitute a growing segment of today's pipe buyers, especially in the U.S.

Whether buying an old pipe or a new one, many purchasers will encounter the option of whether or not to buy a filter-system pipe. Although usually frowned upon by most pipe smokers in the U.S., these pipes are extremely popular in Great Britain and in West Germany. In fact, two of England's best selling pipes, Falcon and Dr. Plumb, are system pipes. Even some high grades, such as Dunhill, put filters in their pipes, but fortunately, from many smokers' points of view, they are usually removable. Fixed metal filters, such as those found in the London Kaywoodie and the Keyser Hygienic, base their claim to fame by variously designed (some of them quite ingeniously, I must admit) metal systems that attract and condense moisture and rancid acids before they reach your mouth. These unsavoury juices are a combination of the smoker's saliva and moisture produced as a natural by-product from the combustion of tobacco. There is no way to completely avoid them (although smoking a flavored aromatic tobacco usually compounds the problem; an English blend lessens it). Learning to deal with the matter is one of the hurdles all successful pipe smokers must overcome, and the filter is one way of attacking the problem. Unfortunately, many filters prevent the smoker from inserting a pipe cleaner into the stem to get rid of these juices. In addition, because filters tend to accumulate rancid tars in one central spot within the airhole, they can taint the taste of the smoke you are puffing and may even be slurped into the mouthpiece (and into the mouth) with a sickening and bitter gurgle. So if you must use a filter pipe, be sure you select the system carefully. And keep in mind that most of the newer high grade pipemakers, such as Ashton and Upshall, do not use any filters at all.

There are also some non-metallic, absorbent filter pipes on the market, such as the Stanwell and Duncan charcoal-filled tubes that are extremely popular in West Germany, or the unique balsa filters enclosed with most Savinelli pipes (although I personally enjoy smoking this pipe without the

A great variety of Danish pipe shapes are available today. From top to bottom: Nørding flawless silver banded straight grain, Nørding briar ribbed "Skipper," Stanwell sandblast calabash with smooth top, Karl Erik Golden Briar, Jenson four-band Royal Navy (which comes with matching tie!), and W. Ø. Larsen with combination rusticated and smooth finish.

wooden filters, which I find much more useful as a "spill" to light my tobacco). Some of the other cardboard-like "absorbent" filters can taint the otherwise pure tobacco smoke when they become saturated, although many ex-cigarette smokers feel more comfortable with them. Whether or not you use a filter, for the driest smoke possible, if your bowl starts to gurgle, insert a pipe cleaner all the way through the mouthpiece and into the heel and then withdraw it. Your pipe will instantly smoke clean and dry; you will probably have to tamp the tobacco down slightly to close up the air pocket the cleaner may have left in the heel.

No matter what type of pipe you select, I would emphatically suggest that you only buy well-known or recommended brands from a knowledgeable tobacconist. The pipe shop itself can be newly-opened in an ultra-modern mall or mouldy and vine-covered from decades of service to a local community. It doesn't matter. What is really important is the salesperson behind the counter (does he or she know what they are talking about or are they merely occupying space just to pick up a paycheck at the end of the week?). Also, is the shop well-stocked so that you have a wide choice from which to make your final selection?

In most cases, when you buy your new pipe from a tobacconist, you will get an unwritten guarantee of customer satisfaction (assuming you do not abuse the pipe or the privilege, however). In this way, your investment in pipe smoking is somewhat protected, as most pipe companies will stand behind their product and will replace a faulty pipe that burns out or has a cracked stem or does not draw well due to an improperly bored airhole. Additionally, most conscientious tobacconists will replace a pipe if it was purchased from their shop, shows no abuse, and has obviously failed in its intended purpose. Of course, a pipe that has been used as a hammer or dropped on the pavement or subjected to a number of other unpipelike abuses should not be considered under warranty. Accidents and ignorance morally void any share of responsibility on the tobacconist's part, although I have known a few who discounted a replacement pipe for regular customers. This is simply a business decision that the tobacconist must make; the customer should not expect it. But after all, the pipe shop exists solely to serve the pipe smoker, and if the owner can keep you satisfied, then he has indirectly made a long-term investment in his future.

One of the best examples I have ever encountered of a pipe company's warranty policy towards a customer occurred some years ago in the Santa Monica headquarters of the Tinder Box International. One of its Chicago stores had sold an "own brand" pipe to a customer who subsequently was smoking it while squirrel hunting in the Illinois forests one crisp autumn day. Through an unfortunate set of circumstances, the pipe smoker's .22 rifle accidentally went off, shooting the sandblasted briar right out of his mouth (thereby making it a true sand*blast!*). It was an act worthy of Buffalo Bill's Wild West Show. Fortunately, the only damage was to the pipe, which snapped from the stem and flew out of the hunter's mouth with the lead bullet imbedded in the bowl. The embarrassed fellow waited a few days to regain his composure and inasmuch as he had shot the only briar pipe that he owned, he eventually was forced to gather up enough courage to package up the wounded pipe and ship it off to the corporate offices of Tinder Box, along with a four-page handwritten note that went into a rather lengthy explanation of how the pipe came to have a bullet in it. All the customer really wanted was to have the stem repaired and to show the Tinder Box folks that the pipe was still smokable and could withstand a bullethole without even cracking. The letter and the pipe made the rounds of the TBI executives who finally decided without question to send the chap not only a new pipe, but a pound of handblended tobacco as well, as he had given TBI a bang-up testimonial on the quality of their brand label pipes in an actual field test that no one would be likely to duplicate for some time. The pipe, complete with the .22 bullet imbedded in its bowl was on display in the Tinder Box offices for many years and now resides in a private collection.

When considering whether or not to purchase a particular pipe, don't be afraid to "try it on" for size. Many tobacco shops have mirrors and protective cellophane mouthpiece covers for just this purpose. However, it is a matter of good manners and proper etiquette not to clamp down on the pipe

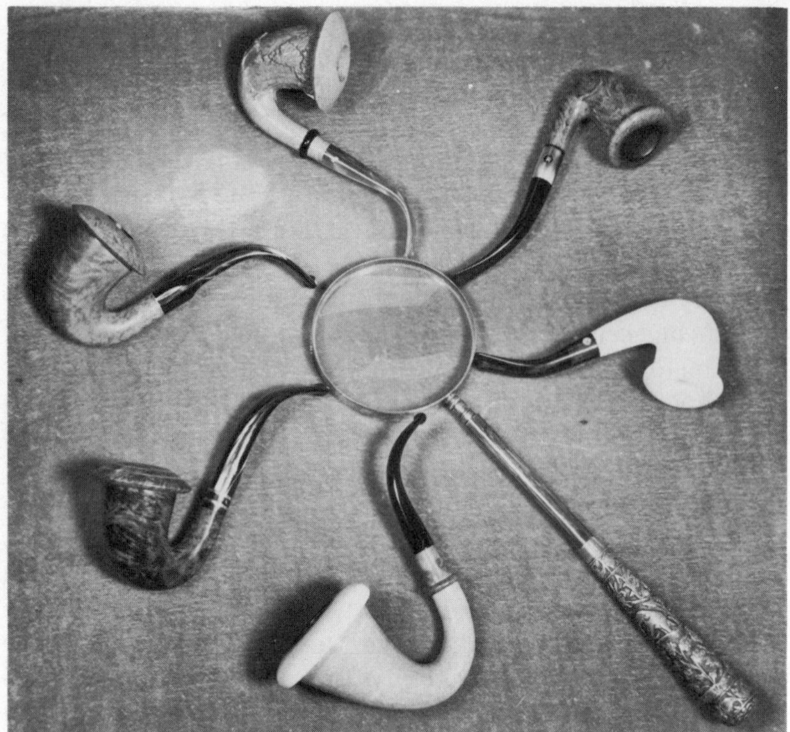

A circular covey of calabashes (starting from 6 o'clock): the original calabash gourd with meerschaum bowl, double brass-ringed briar Mistella calabash by Barontini, D'Argento briar calabash (one of the first to come out in this style) with sterling silver band and three dots on bowl rim, Ascorti New Dear, Butz-Choquin calabash Deluxe with horn ferrule, and a meerschaum calabash. With the exception of the last two pipes, all calabashes have removable bowls which may be twisted out from the body of the pipe for cleaning.

A nicely styled Manx meerschaum made for the new Barling factory.

Using news clippings and photos, Turkish carvers often immortalize world leaders they have never seen. Churchill's cigar is removable, but Truman's glasses are fixed.

Davidoff pipes are one of the newest entries in the world of international high grades for the connoisseur.

stem with your teeth until *after* you have purchased the pipe in question.

Also, don't let a tobacconist talk you into a pipe that you do not want. Most pipe shop personnel are rather low-key and will let you make the final choice, but I will never forget the time my wife and I stopped in to see a rather well-known tobacconist in New Orleans. At the time, I happened to be smoking a short, squat pipe because it was easy to carry around in my coat pocket. Normally, I smoke much larger pipes with longer stems.

"Ah ha," said the tobacconist as we entered his shop and began to look around. "I have just the pipe for you!" And he proceeded to haul out a tray full of short, squat little pipes.

"I prefer a slightly larger pipe," I said.

"Here's one you'll like," replied the obviously deaf tobacconist, taking out a pipe similar to the one I was smoking. "You seem to like a smaller bowl."

"This is just my traveling pipe," I stated. "I have forty longer stemmed, larger bowled pipes at home."

But the tobacconist insisted on trying to sell me a short squat pipe. Finally I managed to change the subject and, in essence, ended up waiting on myself. I discovered a rather old and picturesque long stemmed briar which I purchased. As is the custom in most tobacco shops, the proprietor let me fill my new pipe with one of his house blends. As I lit up for the first time, the tobacconist stepped back, looked at me analytically and said, "You know, you look much more comfortable with that pipe than the one you were smoking when you came in. Ever think of changing to a pipe with a longer stem and a bigger bowl?"

Of course, no matter how carefully you may inspect, reject and finally select the "right pipe" (for that moment, at least), there can never really be one perfect pipe that will meet all your smoking requirements for every occasion. The ultimate goal, of course, is to eventually have a variety of pipes that will be ideally suited for a variety of situations. For example, I like to vary the color and texture of my pipes to match the color and texture of my clothes or to keep in character with a particular situation. Thus, when going out for an elegant evening in which I am forced by convention to wear a suit and tie, I usually smoke an elegant pipe to match, such as a gold-banded Dunhill or a Silver Spigot Peterson. For more casual situations, such as when visiting friends or going for a walk, I'll smoke a more casual-looking pipe, like my BBB Silver Grain Bulldog or a Charatan sandblast Canadian. When sneaking away from civilization for my annual ten-day trek in the Rocky Mountains, I'll usually take along one of the better-made private brands (some of the best pipe values) or a similar medium priced quality briar like the Comoy, Stanwell or Jobey, all of which provide excellent value for the money, give me the smoking pleasure of briar, but are inexpensive and obtainable enough to be easily replaced if broken or lost. On the other side of the spectrum, if I am speaking before a group of people or am in the company of knowledgeable pipe collectors, I always enjoy sharing my treasures by smoking some of my rarer pipes, such as a 1940s era Barling, a hard-to-find Castello or one of my limited edition Christmas commemoratives (see Chapter Nine for more information on these and other collectibles). I save my larger, more valuable or more delicate pipes for at-home smoking, reserving the sanctity of my castle for such delicious smokables as meerschaums, calabashes, clays, and large, custom made briars. Finally, I have one large-bowled GBD that holds so much tobacco I only light it up when I know I can relax for at least an hour and a half of uninterrupted smoking.

Although the intricacies of pipe-buying are many, the act itself is both simple and enjoyable, and is a prelude to many memorable moments to be spent with a friend that you took great care in selecting. The main thing is to visit a well-stocked store, be at least familiar with some of the brand names you will encounter, and tell your tobacconist approximately how much you want to spend. The rest is simple: just pick out the pipes that look good and are comfortable to hold.

But the best is yet to come, for after pipe buying comes pipe smoking, an act that starts emitting those mind-soothing Alpha waves from the moment you begin filling your bowl. And discovering the secret of successful pipe smoking is just a turn-of-the-page away!

"Passing the Arcadia" by J. Bernard Partridge, 1898

Chapter Four

The Secrets of Successful Pipe Smoking

"Tobacco smoke is the one element in which . . . men can sit silent together without embarrassment, and where no man is bound to speak one word more than he has actually and veritably got to say."

– History of Frederick the Great 1858–1865, Vol. 1 –
by Thomas Carlyle

Ever since the first pipe was put between a smoker's lips, one of the great mysteries of "civilized" society has been how to smoke a pipe without having your tongue bite the mouth that feeds it. Indeed, "tongue bite," that sharp, painful burning sensation all too common with many neophyte puffers, is one of the chief reasons most people give up pipe smoking after only a few unsuccessful tries. No doubt they are left with the belief that all tobaccophiles are confirmed masochists who, in addition to smoking a pipe, also take pleasure in eating unthawed TV dinners and insist on putting heavy starch in their underwear. But tongue bite is not a malady reserved just for the 20th century pipe smoker; in 1535, French explorer Jacques Cartier, while paddling up the St. Lawrence River, discovered a tribe of Indians smoking pipes filled with chopped tobacco leaves. "They say the habit (sic) is most wholesome," he wrote, "but we found that (the) tobacco bit our tongues like pepper." It is apparent that Cartier, while obviously a noted explorer, was unable to discover the proper way to pack and smoke a pipe. Yet today, it still surprises many experienced smokers to learn that accomplished pipeologists rarely, if ever, are subject to the painful phenomena known as tongue bite, and that its avoidance is something that can easily be learned. In fact, tongue bite is not a part of normal pipe smoking at all. The sad truth is that few new pipe smokers are properly instructed on *how* to smoke a pipe, and this one glaring omission is the main reason so many potential pipe people turn away from their briars before they have even started to put a decent cake on them.

The very act of smoking a pipe is an art form derived from skills. Like most skills, it cannot be fully appreciated until you have mastered the techniques yourself. Happily, anyone can learn them and the proof of that statement is best typified by the author himself, having come from a non-smoking family. Back in the mid-1960s, when I lit up my very first briar which I randomly crammed with a fistful of nondescript tobacco, there were no veteran pipeologists standing nearby to tell me what I was or was not doing correctly. Inasmuch as practical "how-to" pipe books always have been relatively scarce, I learned from experience. One of the many pleasures I hope you will enjoy from these pages are some of those smoke shrouded pipe-puffing secrets, which I now share with you.

Tongue bite is caused by one of three things: 1) a pipe that has not been properly "broken in"; 2) incorrectly packing the pipe with tobacco; and 3) trying to smoke tobacco that is not properly humidified. All three of these topics and their solutions will be discussed in this chapter.

Additionally, many new pipe smokers are multi-pack-a-day cigarette smokers, and turn to briar either on their doctor's orders (a fairly common prescription, given to break them of the nicotine habit and generally, far more effective than nicotine gum) or out of their own desire to free themselves from an uncontrollable addiction and turn it into a controllable pleasure. It is important to realize that pipe smoking is not like cigarette smoking. Consequently, one of the most difficult things a cigarette smoker will have to do is not so much give up "the weed," but rather, to learn how to properly smoke a pipe, as all the old cigarette smoking habits must be overcome. For one thing, pipe smokers do not inhale; to do so defeats the very essence of pipe smoking, which is to "taste" the tobacco in your mouth, as if smoking a steak. Inhaling pure, untainted pipe tobacco into the lungs is like gargling with a fine California 1973 vintage Cabernet Sauvignon wine. Not only is it uncouth and ignorant, but you will never be able to fully experience the natural flavor and benefits the substance has to offer. Besides, pipe tobacco is much purer and richer than anything cigarette paper was ever wrapped around, but because the smoke is not drawn into your lungs, you do not absorb large concentrations of nicotine into your bloodstream, which is one of the reasons pipe smoking is not physically habit forming.

In addition to the health and psychological benefits of pipe smoking, the cigarette smoker should also consider the economic advantages: while it might take an average cigarette smoker about ten minutes to nervously go through a single cigarette, the average pipe smoker, using a medium-sized bowl can easily puff away for 30 to 45 minutes. Considering the fact that there are about 30 or 40 pipefuls of tobacco in every half kilo container (with a slight variance being allowed for pipe bowl size and the cut of the tobacco itself), pipe smoking represents one of the greatest values of our modern-day society, even with its shockingly high European taxes.

For the fullest measure of enjoyment, it should be remembered that a pipe is sipped, not so much like brandy but rather like a gin and tonic. In this way, the full, rich smoke is drawn into the mouth, held there briefly as the flavor is sensed, then gently exhaled in a white, scented cloud. An interesting sidelight to this is the fact that the pipe smoker cannot smell the aroma of his tobacco; only those around him have access to that olfactory pleasure. For years, I have heard others comment on the rather pungent odor of the strong English blends I smoke, but I could never really identify with their statements until the day I put my pipe in an ashtray while I went outside for a few minutes to check on the sunset. When I returned, the house was filled with a rich, heavy fragrance that was reminiscent of autumn nights, campfires, forests, and hunting lodges. It was the tobacco aroma from my own pipe, which I was smelling for the first time.

Moderation is an important key to truly enjoyable pipe

smoking; an overindulgence in anything pleasurable takes away from its benefits, often with very unpleasant side effects. A bottle of 1975 vintage Dom Perignon champagne can be a very elegant treat reserved for a special occasion, but quaff down six or seven of those costly corkages and no longer are the senses able to comprehend the qualities of that fine bubbly, but instead, they leave you with a painful, brain-throbbing reminder of your overindulgence the next morning. The same is true with pipe tobacco. Each smoker has a limit as to how many bowlfuls his or her body will tolerate. The daily temperament of each individual also affects this tolerance level, and I have found that I will smoke more bowlfuls of tobacco when busy or under pressure (no doubt subconsciously using the pipe to help me relax) than I will when my Ship of Life is floating in calmer waters.

Smoking habits can also be affected by our surroundings. For example, I rarely have the proverbial "morning pipe" unless it is a special occasion, like the first day of vacation or Christmas Day; I routinely smoke my pipes in the late afternoon or the evening. However, years ago when I worked in a corporate office where a number of my fellow executives were also pipe smokers, we would all find ourselves lighting up by mid-morning, smoking through the lunch hour and into the late afternoon. The constant aroma of someone else's pipe tobacco and the sight of others contentedly puffing away in meetings or while on the phone was too much to resist; we each had to get in there and partake of our common enjoyment. But even then, my body would tell me when to slow down, for unlike cigarette smoking, one doesn't always "need" a pipe. It should be enjoyed as a hobby, not a habit.

The art of pipe smoking begins properly enough, by filling the pipe with tobacco. Now, as uncomplicated as that may sound, it actually is the single most important step in maximizing the enjoyment from your pipe. And, if done correctly, is one of the "secret ingredients" that will not only help eliminate tongue bite, but will also enable your pipe to stay lit longer with fewer matches.

Ever since pipe smokers learned they could puff and write at the same time, there have been innumerable theories, techniques and treatises done, redone, and redundant on the correct methods of packing a pipe. Some techniques were written by people who obviously were not regular pipe smokers at all, while other methods only worked part of the time, depending on the tobacco, the mental condition of the smoker, and even, I suspect, the phases of the moon. The pipe-filling technique I am about to give you has continuously worked for me in scores of pipes and in a period that has spanned more than two decades. Moreover, it is a technique that is taught by many experienced tobacconists to first-time purchasers of pipes, realizing that a satisfied pipe smoker is also a satisfied customer.

First, check to make sure your pipe is completely clear of foreign matter. That means no left-over bits of tobacco in the airhole from the last smoke, and no gray ash or dottle in the bowl. Besides a visual check, it also helps to gently blow through the mouthpiece of the pipe to make sure there is nothing lodged inside the stem that could impede the flow of air necessary to keep the tobacco burning. I once spent a frustrating few seconds trying to light a rather large briar calabash before I realized that there was a pipe cleaner hidden within its unusually long stem. However, trying to puff under these conditions does help put the color back into your cheeks!

If your pipe is a brand new never-before-smoked briar, it is a good idea to rub a *very thin* coating of honey around the inside of the bowl with your finger, making sure you completely cover the heel and side walls, but take care to keep the sticky stuff off the exterior of your pipe. The honey on the inside of the bowl will help speed up the process of building a "cake," or thick charred coating in your pipe bowl, another one of the factors that will help eliminate tongue bite. A properly built-up cake will also keep your pipe smoking cooler and will enable you to derive the full flavor of whatever tobacco you happen to be using at the time. This cake serves as both a fireplace-type grate and an insulator for the pipe bowl. Normally, it will take about three to five bowlfuls of tobacco to begin building an adequate cake.

Personally, I happen to enjoy breaking in a new pipe. It is like meeting a friend for the first time and getting acquainted by relaxing together as we smoke. I once had a

How to Properly Light Your Pipe: A Step by Step Procedure

1) Pull out pipe cleaner that was stored in pipe from previous cleaning, and make sure that airhole is clear.

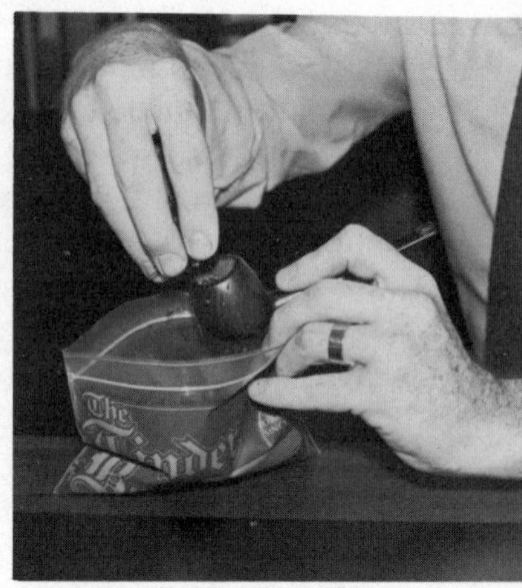

2) Trickle in tobacco until bowl is filled to overflowing.

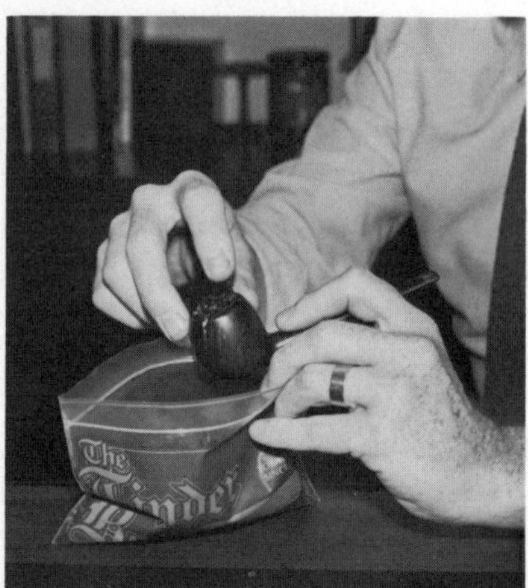

3) Tap the pipe bowl to "settle" the tobacco and tamp it down until it feels "springy." Do this three times to fill pipe bowl.

4) Light up for charring light. Be sure to let all sulfur burn off matchhead before puffing on pipe.

5) The charring light. Make sure top of all tobacco is lit, then tamp it down.

6) Light up again, this time puffing slowly and rhythmically.

7) Sit back and relax with a favorite friend!

college pal who so enjoyed smoking new pipes that he would offer to break in pipes for any of the others in our crowd, giving them a cleaned and sterilized pipe back in about a week that had a healthy cake already starting to build up within its bowl. For many pipe smokers, breaking in a new briar is a necessary evil and I often thought my school chum could have made a decent living (at least in those days) by charging money for every pipe he broke in. Although that was over twenty years ago, little did I know that someone was already working on the idea.

If anyone should get an award for tenacity in the pipe business, it is Santo Bellinghieri, who spent forty years perfecting a unique desk-top accessory that actually smokes your pipe for you! Called the Pipeking, it is a device which plugs into the wall and actually gently puffs on your pipe, consuming a bowlful of tobacco in about thirty minutes – about the same amount of time it takes a person to perform the same act. What this all means is that you can now break in your pipe with whatever tobacco you want without ever putting the stem to your lips. Then, when a proper cake is built up (usually in about 10 to 12 pipefuls, using this machine) you are ready to smoke a perfectly caked pipe for the first time with absolutely no break-in required. It is only a matter of time before some manufacturers start using the Pipeking to create truly "naturally pre-caked" briars for the growing new-smoker pipe market. Of additional importance to meerschaum smokers, I have discovered that the Pipeking can also be used to speed up the natural coloring process of these fine, white porous pipes, as about five bowlfuls of tobacco a day (allowing the fragile material to properly cool between smokes) makes every 24-hour period equal to a week. Using the special cleaning solution that comes with each unit, the Pipeking can also be used to clean older and neglected briars. Thanks to an adjustable filter system, the smoke from briar being "puffed" by the Pipeking can be regulated and contained, so that there is absolutely no aroma. Of course, the filter can be bypassed so that it seems as if a pipe smoker were actually in the room. My brother-in-law periodically comments that he likes having me visit him because he enjoys the fragrance of my pipe tobacco. Consequently, a Pipeking would seem to be the ideal gift for him, as it would help compensate for those obviously long, empty voids when I am not around.

Breaking in a pipe, whether done mechanically or "in person," is a very important process in properly preparing your briar for a lifetime of smoking enjoyment and is not something that should be rushed. I will always remember back during my earliest pipe smoking days in college when I conducted a unique experiment involving trying to get an instant cake on a pipe. I had not yet learned that there were pipes other than the cheap mass-market variety and I had grown disgusted with the harsh bitter taste of the breaking-in process I had experienced with the two pipes I already owned. Therefore, upon purchasing yet another heavily lacquered, red colored filter pipe (it wasn't so much that I was a slow learner – it was just that in those days I didn't know any better and obviously, I did not have this book to read), I packed my new briar full of a coarse Burley tobacco, fired it up with a packet of paper matches, climbed into my 1954 Austin-Healey four-banger and roared down the highway for about an hour holding my red-hot glowing pipe out the window to "properly" break it in within a record time. At about 70 miles an hour the smoke was pouring out of the mouthpiece like a steam engine! At the end of my experiment I confidently brought the pipe back into the roadster and looked at what I expected would be a nice charred, evenly smoked bowl. Instead, the pipe looked like it had been created in Dr. Frankenstein's lab; the entire exterior finish of the pipe had bubbled and cracked and the pipe itself had burnt completely through at the heel. At $3 for the pipe and ten cents for a packet of tobacco it was a relatively inexpensive lesson for me, even in those days, but it taught me something I have never forgotten: to this day I will not smoke a pipe in an Austin-Healey.

Some new pipes come with their bowls already precarbonized as an aid to cake-building, but even these should have a thin honey coating to help with those first few all-important bowls of tobacco. However, this honey-coating should only be applied to briar pipes; it is not needed in clay pipes (which are absorbent and will age of their own accord without building a cake) and should definitely *never* be applied to meerschaum or meerschaum-lined pipes, as in these porous bowls the build-up of a cake is not desirable, for it separates the tobacco from the meerschaum and will impede the coloring process (as discussed in Chapter Two), thereby defeating the unique benefits of meerschaum as a pipe smoking material. Likewise, honey should not be used in the porous corncob unless you plan on eating it after smoking it.

Of course, a briar pipe that has been "broken in" will already have this cake, which should never be allowed to get any thicker than a 5p piece (about 1.5 mm), otherwise there is a danger of it becoming so thickly encrusted it will expand when hot, to the point where the cake could conceivably crack your pipe bowl. Moreover, thick cakes mean your pipe will hold less tobacco. Tools used to keep the cake trimmed down to the proper thickness are discussed in Chapter Seven.

With your pipe empty and clean, it is now time to add that most precious of ingredients, the tobacco. In Chapter Five, we will be discussing the various types of *Nicotiana Tabacum* available to today's pipe smoker, but for now, suffice to say pipe tobacco generally comes in one of two forms: caked (pressed tightly together) or loose (much more common and encountered when buying various house blends from tobacconists, or when buying most pre-packaged tobacco in foil pouches). Either way, before filling your pipe, the tobacco must be carefully broken up and separated so that no matts or solid clumps will be present to impede the mixture of air and fire that is responsible for keeping the tobacco burning evenly. Even tobacco that is finely cut, such as Virginia, or the last vestiges of a long leaf English blend that have been sitting on the bottom of your humidor will occasionally have a tendency to "lock leaves," and should be gently separated with the fingers before it enters the hallowed region of your pipe bowl.

The pipe-filling procedures must actually be repeated three times in order to properly pack a single bowlful of tobacco. First, take a pinch of tobacco in your fingers and trickle it into your pipe until the bowl is loosely filled and completely full, almost to overflowing. Then, using your finger or a pipe tamper (whichever is handier), gently press the tobacco down into the bowl, not hard, but until it feels slightly springy. Normally, this will compress the tobacco so that it fills the bottom one-third of the pipe bowl. Repeat this tobacco-filling process a second time, pressing down slightly harder, which should now bring the tobacco to about one-third from the top of the bowl. Finally, gravity-feed tobacco into your pipe bowl for the third time, filling it to overflowing and press down on the load firmly, so that the tobacco is now even with the top of the pipe bowl. Be sure to retain that "springy" feeling in your tobacco. Otherwise, you may be pressing down too hard and by compressing the tobacco too tightly you may make it difficult or even impossible to keep your pipe lit. When this happens, it is best to empty everything out of the bowl and start over. It is also important that you only pack a pipe with fresh, humidified tobacco, as dry tobacco will crunch down and produce a hot and quick burning smoke, which immediately translates into tongue bite. When filling your pipe, it's a good practice to occcasionally draw some air through the mouthpiece, to make sure you are not packing your tobacco too tightly and to insure that the airhole has not become plugged with a tiny chuck of tobacco. The correct tobacco-filling procedure takes a little practice, but after a few times you will automatically develop this all-important skill and will be able to actually "feel" when you have a properly filled pipe full of tobacco.

We are now ready to light up, thereby inaugurating our potential pleasure with a baptism by fire. For this all-important act, use *only* wooden matches or a butane lighter. Paper matches are impregnated with chemicals that will taint the tobacco and its taste, as will lighter fluid. When using wooden matches, pause a second after striking the match, so that the sulfur will burn off and you will not get a bitter mouthful of sulfur smoke mixed in with your tobacco smoke. (A butane flame actually burns hotter than a wooden match, and care must be taken to avoid charring the rim of your pipe bowl during the lighting process.)

Pipe lighting is a two-part procedure. The first step is called the *false* or *charring* light. Its purpose is to create a completely charred "lid" covering the top portion of your bowlful of tobacco, thereby making a "fire platform" which will permit your carefully packed pipe to smoke evenly all the way down to the bottom or heel of the bowl. To begin the charring light, move the flame from your lighter or match slowly over the entire area of the tobacco, taking care not to scorch the edges of the pipe bowl – it may discolor soon enough of its own accord after a number of repeated smokes. As you light the tobacco, draw in on your pipe with long, smooth puffs, thereby sucking the flame down into the tobacco. When the entire top surface of the tobacco has been completely and evenly lit, take the pipe from your mouth and gently press down on the ashes with a pipe tamper (these ashes usually rise above the rim of the bowl during the charring light), pushing them down upon the unburned tobacco underneath.

Now you are ready for your second light. Once again, move the flame over the entire area of the tobacco as you puff slowly and rhythmically. That's all there is to it. Besides giving you a better smoke, getting these step-by-step pipe lighting techniques down pat can give you a decided advantage in an argument. For example, as soon as you feel you are starting to lose in a verbal match to your opponent, give him the last say for the moment, and noticeably pause from the encounter to fill, light, and tamp your pipe (furthering the popular conjecture that all pipe smokers are deep, philosophical thinkers). Then, as the first wave of gray haze lifts from your briar and your antagonist is starting to feel a bit uneasy because of the lull, look him squarely in the eye, slowly take the pipe from your mouth and utter the profound bombardment of words you have by now had ample time to conjure up.

Your pipe will stay lit longer if you periodically keep the ashes tamped down upon the remaining tobacco and if you gently blow a whisper of air into the stem occasionally; your breath will act like a miniature bellows to keep the tobacco burning. That is why pipe smokers who talk with their pipes in their mouths require fewer matches to keep their briars lit; the breath from their speech helps keep the glow alive. Thus we can say that these pipe smokers are *stimulating* conversationalists in the truest sense of the word.

As you smoke your pipe, moisture will invariably accumulate in the bottom of the bowl and within the stem. Sometimes this is evidenced by an annoying gurgling sound. This liquid is caused by the burning of your tobacco, for one of the by-products of combustion is moisture and it is important to realize that some tobaccos burn "wetter" than others (more about this in Chapter Five). In addition, some individuals smoke wetter than others and it is not uncommon for some saliva from your mouth to invariably mix in with these tart tobacco liquids. All too often, you will suddenly get a sharp acidic taste as these juices are drawn into the smoke. This moisture must be removed from the pipe before enjoyable puffing can continue. Thus, it will occasionally be necessary during the course of your smoke to run a pipe cleaner through the mouthpiece of the stem and into the heel of the bowl in order to absorb the juices, removing them by withdrawing the pipe cleaner. Normally, one or two cleaners will do the job. But be sure to pass the cleaner through the mouthpiece; *do not* attempt to separate the stem from the bowl while the pipe is still hot from smoking, or you could crack the shank of the pipe.

The etiquette of using a pipe cleaner in mixed company is a problem that I have never seen dealt with in print before, for it is a somewhat unpleasant procedure: the pipe cleaner comes out looking rather dark and smelling quite rank. Therefore, if dining or seated with a group of people, I will excuse myself and venture off to some unobserved part of the house or restaurant to perform this brief pipe cleaning act in private. If in a car, business meeting or similar enclosed situation where I cannot get away, I will simply put my pipe down and let it rest until it can be cleaned discreetly. However, when in my own den or in the company of fellow pipe smokers, I use pipe cleaners wantonly and with little regard for their preservation whenever the situation warrants it. They are an extremely inexpensive means for insuring the continuation of "clean" smoke. One of the worst situations a pipe smoker can imagine is being stranded on a desert island with ten pounds of choice tobacco, a case full of quality high-grade briars – and no pipe cleaners! However, a word of caution: used pipe cleaners are rather smelly and are best disposed of in the fireplace or hidden deep within the darkest confines of a garbage bag outside the house.

It is important to remember that any pipe will go out if left unattended. In fact, no matter how well you've packed it, no matter how thoroughly you've lit it, all pipes require additional lightings before the entire bowlful is consumed. That is part of the joy and relaxation of pipe smoking . . . the frequent lightings and re-lightings and watching the billowing clouds of smoke as they slowly rise playfully and stumble over each other until, exhausted, they finally disperse across the room. An average pipeful of tobacco usually lasts from thirty to forty-five minutes (depending upon the size of the pipe bowl and the forcefulness of the puffing), and during that time I have used as little as three and as many as twelve matches just to keep my briar alive and well. Of course, many pipe smokers pride themselves on only using one match to keep an entire bowl burning right on down to the heel and ever since 1723 there have been pipe smoking contests to determine who can keep a bowlful of pre-measured tobacco (usually 3.3 grams of Burley cube) going the longest, using only two wooden matches. These pipe smoking contests are billed as "the slowest race in the world." It should be noted that the world's first pipe smoking contest was held in the 18th century in the Oxford Theatre in London. The winner received 12 shillings for first prize, but

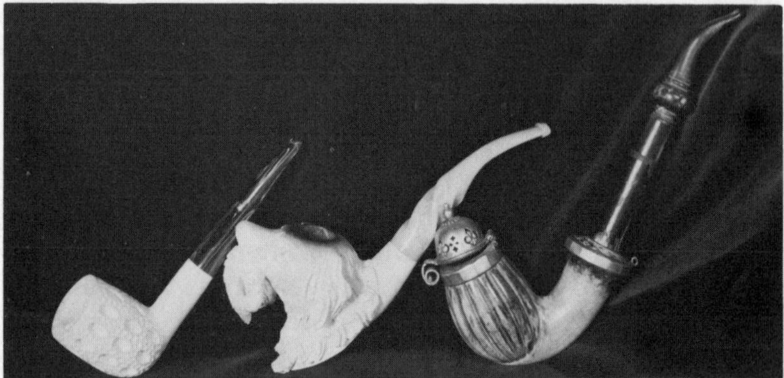

The gradual coloring processes of a meerschaum, beginning with a brand new pipe (L.), starting to color after a number of bowlfuls (M.) and after years of steady smoking (R.).

there is no record of his actual time. Today, pipe smoking contests are especially popular on the Continent, where World Cup championships are held annually in various countries and hosted by local pipe clubs. Unlike many pipe smoking contests in the U.S. and Great Britain, where cube cut Burley is often mandated, these annual European contests usually use a commercially blended tobacco of the hosting country or a sponsoring company. Thus, some rather spectacular times are possible. Yet using only Burley, the best U.S. time is two hours, six minutes and 39 seconds, established in 1975 by William Vargo of Swartz Creek, Michigan.

By way of comparison, the European world record was set in 1981 when Swiss Pipe Club founder Pierre-G. Müller kept his pipe going for three hours, 20 minutes and 47 seconds. Our friend Müller went on to win the contest again for the next two years, as well as claiming numerous regional events, and today his Geneva office is a pipe-trophy collector's paradise. Conversely, the *fastest* pipe smoker in the world, again using only one match, was a garage mechanic in New York City, who accidentally mixed gasoline – instead of Irish whiskey – in with his favorite blend. His time for consuming a single bowlful of tobacco was 1.3 seconds. And the world's record for using the *most* matches on a single

The pipe smoking contest has been called the "world's slowest race." They are not exactly spectator events, but are lots of fun for the pipe smokers.

bowl of pipe tobacco goes to a Cape Cod puffer who, on December 4, 1927, went through 239 matches just to keep his pipe lit in the wake of a fierce North-eastern gale. Now, *that* is a determined pipe smoker.

Normally, however, when we smoke our pipes we are neither in a world championship pipe smoking contest nor in a wind tunnel. We are probably in the sanctity of our homes or at least, somewhere within the realms of civilized society. Thus, in the course of smoking a bowlful of tobacco, you will undoubtedly have to re-light your pipe many times. Unlike cigarettes and cigars, which smoke stronger each time they are relit, it is one of the phenomena of pipes that the taste and quality of the pipe tobacco will not be materially affected by continual relighting after it has gone out, although finishing the same bowlful two or three days later will normally take the hair off your arms – or put it back on, as the case may be. The most dramatic case of re-lighting a long dead pipe occurred back in 1947, when Admiral Richard E. Byrd revisited the Antarctic hut he had left 12 years before. Inside, he found his old pipe filled with tobacco. He immediately picked it up, lit it, and commented, "A good smoke!"

No matter how many matches you use, no matter how often you tamp, and however long it takes to consume the contents of your bowl, the primary objective to strive for, especially with a new pipe, is to smoke *all* of the tobacco, right down to the heel, for that is the only way to build up a perfect cake, thereby insuring many memorable smokes for you and your briar in the years ahead. All too often, one encounters an otherwise well-loved pipe that has a perfect cake built up around the upper walls of the bowl, but not on the bottom or the lower sides. What a waste of tobacco . . . what a waste of briar . . . what a waste of time! It is the telltale sign of the "incomplete smoker," an unfortunate soul who has failed to procure the very last vestiges of pleasure from his pipe, and in so doing, has cheated both himself and his briar from giving both the longest and the best smoke possible.

Here are a few more smoking hints: when a pipe gets to hot to handle or to hold against your cheek without burning your skin, you have been smoking it too hard or too fast. The best thing to do is to put it down in an ashtray for a few minutes and let it cool off before relighting and puffing again. I once put a hot pipe down for about fifteen minutes and then picked it up and was able to start puffing smoke again without even relighting, so I *know* it had been burning hot! Additionally, by leaving a layer of ash in your pipe instead of fluffing it out every time you tamp the tobacco down, your pipe will actually burn a little cooler. However, I never worry about this too much unless I am smoking out of doors, where miniature eddies of breezes can cause your tobacco to burn slightly hotter than when smoking indoors.

Smoking in the wind can create its own set of problems by causing your pipe to burn hot and can actually ruin a new pipe or a briar that hasn't been properly caked. One of the reasons briar is the most desirable wood for a pipe is that it is porous (can breathe) yet is hard, which means it can be charred without burning. However, it still is wood and too hot a temperature within the bowl can cause a burn-out. That doesn't mean you send your pipe to a psychiatrist and then take it to Jamaica for three weeks of rest. It simply means that the side of the bowl actually starts to burn instead of charring. The end result is a blackened hole in your pipe. Burn-out is caused by one of two reasons: puffing too hard and fast on a brand new pipe (broken in pipes with a healthy cake lining in the bowl are protected from this malady) or by inadvertently having a new briar pipe that has a hidden flaw or soft spot in the bowl. This soft spot will usually burn before it chars. On a brand new pipe, most responsible tobacconists will replace a burned-out flaw with another pipe as long as you originally purchased the first briar from them and did not abuse it. If the tobacconist won't replace a faulty pipe, the factory certainly should. Pipe firms are usually a reputable lot and are truly embarrassed by any flaw found in their product, even when it is Mother Nature, and not their workers, who is the culprit.

Burn-out can also be caused by smoking a pipe in a high wind or an open top convertible. Some companies, such as Peterson and Dunhill, make pipes with metal ventilated lids which fit over the bowl to help "break up" the wind, yet which provide enough ventilation to keep the pipe burning. It is a design idea that harkens back to the old Tyrolean pipes discussed in Chapter One. Of course, there is nothing wrong with smoking a pipe in a car with an open sun roof or a "T" roof, as the wind never hits the pipe directly and the pipe smoke is immediately aerated from the car interior. In fact, as far as transportation is concerned, today's modern Trans-Am styling is the best thing that's happened to the travelling pipe smoker since the buckboard was replaced by the enclosed coupe.

The most spectacular case of a pipe burn-out I ever witnessed occurred in 1981 at the annual Tinder Box National Pipe Smoking Contest. Joliet, Illinois tobacconist Dick Davis was so intent upon winning that when his brand new briar burned through the bowl due to a soft spot in the wood, Davis just kept on puffing, even after a bright red glow appeared on the *outside* of the pipe! Eventually the bowl caught fire, burned all the way around the stem and fell off onto the table. Undaunted, Davis kept on puffing away on the wooden stem until he was officially declared "out" by the judges. Still, he may go down in history as one of the first men to literally smoke a *pipe* and not the tobacco.

Of course, you should be serious about your pipe smoking just as long as you do not take your pipe smoking too seriously. While it is both necessary and commendable to have the proper smoking techniques firmed up and practiced in mind and actions, pipe smoking is nonetheless a pleasurable pastime, not a regulated vocation. The pipe should provide enjoyment, not frustration. After all, pipe smoking is among the gentlest and most relaxing of all human activities, and these are the legacies to which every pipe smoker falls heir, whether he smokes an inexpensive corncob or a priceless freehand straight grain.

For the owner of a newly purchased fine-grained briar, there is nothing more captivating than to gaze at the polished sheen on the bowl as the pipe is smoked. This gloss is put there by wax, which of course heats and melts deeper into the pores of the wood as the pipe is smoked. I have a hard time grasping this polished bowl with my bare mitts for the first few times I am breaking in a new pipe and prefer to hold

Inclement weather never stopped a pipe smoker. These four pipes were made for puffing in a blustery breeze (L to R front row): Kaywoodie Airway with built-in swing-away screen; Dunhill Shell fitted with rose gold windscreen; (L to R back row): Orlik briar lid Hurricane pipe; BBB fitted with a separately-purchased clip-on metal screen.

Two weeks worth of smoking ready for cleaning, with all the necessary accoutrements close at hand.

the pipe by its stem while smoking it rather than risk dulling the finish that the maker has so proudly buffed to a high luster. But eventually I succumb and hold the pipe the way it is normally held. Of course, the shine on the briar turns dull almost at once, but a newer finish starts to take hold, a finish that will eventually transform into the rich, time-worn patina of a well smoked, aged briar that has stood sentinel with your thoughts throughout many a year. Of course, the wax polish can be resurrected at any time, simply by adding carnuba wax to the pipe and buffing with a soft cloth or a chamois. But it is the older-looking antiqued luster that makes most briars look the richest. This finish can even be accentuated by rubbing the warm pipe against the sides of your nose, around the nostrils, and along your forehead – places where a large concentration of natural body oils appear. These oils can then be rubbed with the fingers into the pipe as you smoke it, imparting a deep tone to the wood. In this way, you and your briar actually start to become as one.

Whatever style of pipe you smoke, all good things must come to an end and so it is with our bowlful of tobacco. Eventually, sometimes with much reluctance, other times suddenly with nary a struggle, the glowing bits of tobacco will fade, the embers will die, a final curl of gray smoke will drift up and away, severing itself for all time from the very pipe that contained its life, and our repast with Lady Tabacum will be over for a while. Only the fading warmth of the bowl in our hand will be left as a brief reminder of our latest encounter with one of life's simplest yet greatest of pleasures.

But then, this only sets the stage for a whole new ritual, that of caring for your pipe once its service is temporarily ended, much as a sportsman cares for his prized hunting dog after a rewarding day in the fields and marshes.

To be sure, there are some smokers who disdain the "chore" (their word, not mine) of cleaning one's pipe, almost as if it were a penance to pay for having had the enjoyment of so gracious a smoke. Yet pipe cleaning can be as rewarding as filling a cherished briar in anticipation of a smoke, for cleaning prepares the pipe for a future cordial meeting between tobacco and flame once again. Samuel Clemens (aka Mark Twain), one of America's most prominent pipe smokers, seemed to sum up the pipe cleaning rites most eloquently when he wrote, "There is a real sense of pleasure in setting before one's own fire with racks piled about, each briar, clay or meerschaum catching the flickering light in its own way. And there is that feeling of achievement at seeing the racks, some moments later, filled with clean, sweet pipes, each ready and waiting to be filled with a favorite blend."

Indeed, Clemens knew how to enjoy his pipes, whether he was smoking them or not. In fact, it is rumoured that he once turned down a lucrative speaking engagement because it fell on the night he regularly set aside for pipe cleaning.

As necessary as the pipe cleaning process may be, you should not be in too great a hurry to get started. First, you must let your pipe cool down completely. Otherwise, you run the risk of cracking the shank when you try to remove the stem from it, due to the pipe's expansion and contraction caused by the heat from your tobacco. After smoking your pipe, the first thing to do is to fluff out the ashes and dottle (those burned-up and gooey blackened bits in the heel of the pipe) or gently tap the pipe in the palm of your hand so that the muck falls out. Never rap the pipe against your heel or a hard object, as more pipes are broken this way than by any other means. It looks great in the movies but doesn't work in real life, especially with a pipe that you purchased with your own hard-earned money and which is not a studio prop. Once the pipe is emptied, I usually push a pipe cleaner through the stem so that the end is resting inside the bowl. Put the pipe away, bowl lower than the mouthpiece, until you are ready to clean it. Never smoke your pipe before it has been cleaned or it will eventually start to taste bitterly sour and will have to be cleaned with a liquid pipe solvent or by using the Pipeking device with its cleaning solvent, as discussed in Chapter Seven. Badly neglected pipes should be taken to a tobacconist who specializes in pipe rejuvenation, where they will literally boil out the bowl with alcohol to bring it back to its original smoking quality.

Most pipe smokers own more than one pipe and are thus able to smoke a clean, fresh pipe while the last one smoked is still "resting." In any case, it is always advisable to let a recently smoked and cleaned pipe air out and dry for at least a day before taking it up again. The ideal number of pipes for a smoker to own is seven, the theory being that a specific pipe is to be smoked each day of the week, thereby insuring that the pipe for each day will be clean and dry. In fact, as we shall see in Chapter Nine, there are some very rare matched briar "seven day sets" that are created by master pipemakers and specially packaged in velvet lined wooden cases just for this reason, although due to the high costs of premium briar with matching grain and the resultant scarcity of such sets, they are often purchased by investors and collectors as well as by discerning smokers. Still, there is nothing to stop any smoker from assembling his own "working man's" seven day set made up of any pipes that catch his fancy and pocketbook. Moreover, the commendable goal of always having a fresh pipe to smoke is little enough excuse to go out and buy yourself another new pipe should the mood suddenly strike you.

Personally, I have always thought the seven day set theory was a bit unrealistic, for it assumes that pipes are cleaned the day – or at the very worst, no more than six days – after they are smoked. In actual practice, I rarely clean my pipes the day after I've smoked them. In fact, it is often a full week or more before I can find the time to settle down and thoroughly clean my pipes with all the loving attention that they deserve. However, as a temporary measure I may fluff out the ashes and run a pipe cleaner through the stem and into the bowl. The fact that I have so little free time is the very rationale I have successfully used to amass a collection of over 900 pipes, thereby insuring that I can go through at least 12 full seasons of the year before forcing myself to throw another log on the fire on a rainy Saturday afternoon, surround myself with all of my pipe cleaning accoutrements, and, with perhaps my last remaining clean pipe clenched firmly in my teeth, thoroughly immerse myself in the enjoyable task that lies ahead (and in fact all around me) . . . bringing my beloved pipes back to life. For me, pipe cleaning is therapeutic.

The best example of the pipe-for-every-day philosophy that I have discovered is an Associated Press story in 1939, which reported that Robert Thompson, secretary of the Lake Placid Chamber of Commerce (the Adirondack town that years later would help make winter Olympic history) smoked a different pipe every day of the year. His collection of 380 pipes meant that not only was he covered for Leap Year, but could even squeeze by for two more weeks without smoking the same pipe twice.

Like any endeavor of such magnitude, there are certain specialized tools one must have in order to perform the pipe cleaning task properly. Fortunately, none of these items are expensive. First and foremost are pipe cleaners, those elongated fuzzy-coated lengths of wire that are indispensable to the pipe smoker before, after and during his bout with briar or meerschaum. Frankly, it is a toss-up as to whether a pipe smoker will use up more matches or pipe cleaners in a year's time, but the fact is that pipe cleaners are the smoker's ultimate throw-away. You use it once and into the fireplace it goes (the only sure way to get rid of the foul-smelling things, leaving nothing behind but a tell-tale wire strand in the cold gray ashes the next morning).

Pipe cleaners should be used with every kind of pipe except with clays. The clay material is fragile and a cleaner rammed down its stem can crack it. Yet, it is a little known fact that a clay pipe can be cleaned simply by putting it in the fireplace while a hearty blaze is roaring. After the ashes have cooled, remove your pipe and you will find it as white as the day you bought it. I discovered this quite by accident, when my favored "Christmas pipe," a white clay churchwarden that had become nice and mellow with age, suffered a terrible fall one day. Being clay, it did the only thing expected of it and broke. Dismayed at losing such a faithful companion that had spent so many late nights with me reflecting upon the eventual fate of the world, I tossed it into the fireplace. The next morning while cleaning out the ashes, I made the discovery I now share with you. The clay bowl was as white and clean as snow. But to prove Cicero was right and that there really is nothing new under the sun, years later I read about this very same cleaning process for clays in a book entitled, *Tobacco: Its History and Associations*, which was written in 1859!

But most pipe smokers favor the briar and meerschaum, which are cleaned with pipe cleaners. Pipe cleaners come in three basic styles; the thin and untapered absorbent ones, the thick-to-thin tapered absorbent version, and the coarse bristle "Reem 'n Clean" style, not as absorbent as the others and best suited for reaming out coagulated goo and gunk from a badly neglected or hard-smoked pipe. Personally, I use all three; the Reem 'n Cleans are used to scrape out the shank, where most of the gook occurs, the untapered absorbents are used for pipes with very thin air holes in their stems and the tapered, (my favorites) are used for cleaning the airholes and shanks in larger-bored pipes, swabbing out the bowl of all loose ash, and cramming into the pipe, thick end pointing into the bowl after a smoke to let any remaining residue in the wood absorb into its fluffy little body overnight. The thicker ends of these tapered cleaners, especially when doubled up and used as a swab, also aid tremendously in absorbing moisture from pipe bowls and the reservoir cavities of pipes such as the Peterson. Because I go through so many cleaners, I never buy just one package at a time; I buy my pipe cleaners in multiples of ten packages at once. There is no price break, but that gives me 4,500 pipe cleaners and it is a tremendous feeling of security when lighting up, I can tell you.

In addition to pipe cleaners, you should also have a pipe tool (some of which are illustrated in Chapter Seven) that has a thin, sturdy wire pick to break up bits of caked tobacco or dottle from the heel of the pipe bowl, and a flat miniature shovel-like device for scooping out the residue. Sometimes these inexpensive little devices are referred to as a "smoker's friend." An absorbent paper towel is also handy for wiping off the tobacco-juice from the tenon of the stem that goes into the shank of your pipe. A soft cloth, such as chamois, flannel or even a clean piece of a discarded T-shirt is useful for polishing the stem and bowl just before the pipe is ready to be put away in the rack. This cloth may also be used to buff the polish on silver or metal fittings that are found on some pipes. There are also specially treated pipe-polishing cloths and stem-polishers that are both sold and used by many tobacconists. So much for the basic tools; now, on to the task of actually cleaning the freshly-smoked briar.

After the pipe has cooled and the bowl has been emptied, gently twist out the stem from the bowl by holding the bowl in your left hand and carefully twisting out the stem and mouthpiece with your right hand. Obviously, left-handed smokers need only to reverse this procedure. The reason for a twisting rather than a pulling motion is to avoid placing undue strain on the relatively delicate shank, which can all too easily become cracked even on the best of pipes. Of course, if you have a pipe with a metal screw-in bit, your method of stem separation will already have been preordained.

With your pipe now separated into the bowl and stem sections, take your pipe cleaners and pass them through the air holes of each. It normally takes about three to five pipe cleaners to remove all the stains from the stem. The bowl, where all the combustion has occurred, is usually quite dirty and will require from five to seven cleaners, including one that has been doubled over to serve as a swab for wiping out the interior of the bowl. Pipes using the Peterson system, as discussed in Chapter Three, in which a "tobacco-juice reservoir" has been added to the bottom of the bowl, should have this extra accumulation sopped up with an absorbent paper napkin and then cleaned with a folded-over pipe cleaner. Be careful when twisting out the bits from such pipes, as the liquid from these reservoirs can spill out, imparting an acrid odor and stain to everything it touches.

When you have finished cleaning your briar (i.e., all the cleaners come out from the air hole the same color as when they went in), you may want to pass a cleaner lightly moistened with a commercial pipe cleaning solvent (available in all tobacco shops and referred to as "pipe sweeteners") through the pipe, although I find this sometimes imparts a slight artificial flavor to the next few puffs I will take on the pipe, interfering with the natural taste of the tobacco. Some adventurous individuals even use a pipe cleaner soaked in brandy or rum as a freshening agent, pushing the alcohol-laced wire fluff through the stem and into the bowl (being careful not to get any of the patina-erasing liquid on the outside of the pipe). While I have tried this and admit it is great fun on occasions, especially when sucking on the pipe cleaners to remove all excess liquid before passing them into the pipe, it is an abominable waste of a good beverage when commercial pipe cleaning liquids do the job so much better and for far less money.

I give each of my pipes the extra "pipe sweetener" treatment about twice a year, as the alcohol-based solvent does help to dissolve the accumulation of tars that can build up in any pipe, no matter how thoroughly it has been cleaned. If you do use these mixtures, do not let them drip onto the bowl of your pipe as they may injure the finish of the wood and discolor it. Pipes in which an unusually large amount of moisture has accumulated should be left separated from the stem after a thorough cleaning and allowed to air out for a day or two. The final procedure in pipe cleaning is to reassemble the pipe, with an absorbent cleaner left inserted into the air hole and passed into the heel. This technique helps draw out any moisture that may still lurk in the briar of the pipe's interior. The question of how long to leave the pipe cleaner there is quite another matter.

Sometimes the smallest of objects can create the largest of controversies. Like the neutron, the snail-darter and the pipe cleaner. For years pipe smokers have been admonished by "experts" to leave a pipe cleaner in the stem of the pipe after thoroughly cleaning it. I myself have fallen victim to this hoax until one day I accidentally discovered THE TRUTH. It was during the construction of a larger den onto my house. Because the older, smaller den was where I conducted most of my pipe smoking activities, and with the arrival of the contractors and their sledgehammers, my older, smaller den had ceased to exist while we all decided just how many walls the new den was to have. In between arguments, I packed up the majority of my cherished briars and stored them in the garage, saving just enough pipes to get me through the construction period. A short lifetime later, when the job was completed and we at last discovered why the toilet flushed every time we turned on the living room light, I brought the rest of my briars out of storage. Some had been dutifully put away with the traditional pipe cleaner thrust into their shanks (theoretically to absorb whatever moisture lay within the wood, as every pipe smoker knows), while others were more hurriedly cleaned and packed without the traditional pipe cleaner. I soon discovered that there was absolutely no difference in the smoking quality of my briars to differentiate which ones had been stored with pipe cleaners and which ones had not. In fact, some of the briars which had not been stored with pipe cleaners actually smoked drier than before! I reasoned that this was because the air had been allowed to circulate through the pipe stem, unheeded by a thick inhibiting pipe cleaner. Moreover, when removing those cleaners left in my pipes, they all came out clean, leading me to conclude that a properly cleaned pipe will remain that way and a dry pipe cleaner left in the stem and bowl will only impede the drying-out process.

However, if your briar pipes have been neglected for a long period of time, or if the bit tastes bitter and has oxidized to a grayish white, normal pipe cleaning procedures may not be enough and you may have to take your briars to an experienced tobacconist to have them rejuvenated. He will boil out the shank with alcohol, ream the cake to a proper size, clean and polish the bit (even bending or straightening it to a new shape in hot sand if you wish) and polish the bowl with a special carnuba wax. However, the exterior of a well cared-for older pipe can usually be brought back to life by carefully cleaning the delicate bit with #400 wet sandpaper, polishing the bit and stem with special pipe cleaning compounds or cloths sold by tobacconists, and then buffing the entire pipe with carnuba wax and a soft chamois or flannel cloth.

The technique for smoking and cleaning a meerschaum pipe is much the same as for briar, with a few notable exceptions:

1) The bare hands should never be allowed to come in direct contact with the meerschaum bowl, as oils and acids from your skin can affect the waxes in the meerschaum and cause the bowl to color unevenly, leaving blemishes over an otherwise smooth area. Some say it is permissible to handle a cold meerschaum pipe, but I never overindulge in this practice out of respect for the fine coloring potential of the

material. When smoking a meerschaum, hold the pipe by its stem, or wear a special cloth glove, such as those sold by various importers. There are those who scoff at this practice, but a simple glance at their mottled and sparsely-colored pipes tells the entire story. Some 19th century meerschaums even came with special leather coverings, to protect the pipe bowl from the smoker's hands as it was puffed.

2) Even after a meerschaum pipe has cooled, it is best not to risk blemishing the bowl with residue from your hands that may linger and show up during the next smoke. Thus, when holding the bowl for cleaning, always use a cloth or wear a glove.

3) Be sure to gently scrape away any semblance of cake that starts to form inside the meerschaum bowl. Because of their porous nature, meerschaums need no breaking in and a cake will only act as a physical wall that will impede the natural coloring process of the pipe as it is smoked.

4) Most meerschaums have stems that screw into the shank and may require some force to turn the threads. Be very careful when handling and cleaning these pipes, as they are more fragile than briar.

5) Do not use liquid pipe sweetener on meerschaum pipes, as it will actually soak into the pipebowl. Instead, use plenty of pipe cleaners, including the wire bristle "Reem 'n Clean" type. Due to their absorbency, meerschaum pipes can be smoked day after day without tasting sour, as long as they are thoroughly cleaned between smokes.

6) To help your meerschaum age and turn color quicker (as described in Chapter Two), try blowing a little smoke on it as you puff. The microscopic particles of smoke will be absorbed into the surface, while they also work their way to the outside from the bowl from the burning tobacco itself. My wife calls this "cheating," but with all the pipes I've got, I may not be around long enough to see my few meerschaums turn a rich chocolate brown. Why not help nature along a little? Years ago, meerschaum pipes were artificially aged on occasion by coating them with a mixture of dyes and linseed oil and then applying heat to the pipe. However, I prefer the natural smoking method, as it gives these pipes a deep mellow color that has yet to be artificially duplicated.

More popular in Europe than in America, the smoking of clay pipes is worthy of mention. Although I find it historically and meditatively interesting to smoke a clay pipe on certain occasions, they are somewhat impractical in that they must always be held in the hand. To try and clench one in your teeth will invariably break the pipe, either in your mouth or on the floor. In time, however, if smoked long enough, clays will turn off-white or a yellowish brown and sometimes may even go to "black and oily," like the famed clay of Sherlock Holmes, although it will take many years of steady smoking to get it that way and a lot depends on the composition of the clay itself. Additionally, clay pipes can "season" with use and can actually provide a relatively mellow smoke, which can be quite relaxing when one is in the proper frame of mind. It sometimes helps to be wearing a tricorn or at least to be drinking a flagon of ale.

With your pipe cleaned and polished, the final step is to store it with the bowl lower than the stem, so that any remaining moisture that surfaces can drain away from the mouthpiece and towards the thicker portion of the pipe cleaner in the heel. However, some smokers prefer to store their pipes with the stem downward, as was often the fashion in the 19th century (many Victorian-era pipe stands reflect this practice). The theory is that all of the remaining juices will flow away from the bowl so as not to taint the next smoke. Unfortunately, the law of gravity being what it is, these juices invariably end up in the tip of the mouthpiece, a fact I have unwillingly demonstrated to amused friends whenever taking a pipe from one of the two antique pipe racks I use. From my experience at least, I find it far more agreeable to burn up any rancidity in my pipe bowl rather than have it burn me on the mouthpiece. In either case, to properly dry out, a pipe should be surrounded by fresh air, not locked up in an air-tight container or in a drawer. For this purpose, many of the current array of pipe stands are best and they are discussed more fully in Chapter Seven. But even more important than what your pipe goes into, is what goes into your pipe. And the many types and smoking qualities of tobacco are what we will be discussing in the next chapter.

Drawn & Engraved by F.W. Fairholt

TOBACCO PLANTS.

1. Nicotiana Tabacum. 2. N. Rustica. 3. N. Persica

PUBLISHED BY CHAPMAN & HALL PICCADILLY 1859

Chapter Five

SEARCHING FOR THE PERFECT TOBACCO

"May I die if I should abuse that kindly weed that has given me so much pleasure."

– William Makepeace Thackeray

One of the world's great cliches used to be, "Put that in your pipe and smoke it!" Ah, how unchallenging life would be if that were all there was to it. There is far more to pipe smoking than merely grabbing the first colorful tobacco tin you happen to come across; even when sufficiently equipped with a proper pipe and the knowledge of how to smoke it, correctly packing your carefully chosen briar with the wrong tobacco can completely negate any smoking pleasure you might otherwise be entitled to receive. It is often a misunderstood fact, but pipe tobacco is like a cologne: it may smell good in the bottle but it takes on a different aroma depending on the body chemistry of the person who is using it. And so it is with tobacco. Each smoker has a different chemical balance with his body that determines what tastes good and what is distasteful. Moreover, personal habits often dictate what type of tobacco we wish to smoke, as some tobaccos burn hotter when smoked outdoors, or taste better when smoked after a meal, or emit an aroma that may be more acceptable to co-workers. Thus, choosing a tobacco is as individualistic as choosing a pipe, for no single tobacco can ever be "perfect" for every pipe smoker.

Four hundred years ago most pipe smokers had to be

content with what they could readily obtain in the way of pipe tobacco and in some of the more primitive areas, dried tobacco leaves or cornsilk was the optimum choice. However, living in today's Golden Age of Pipe Smoking, we have a decided advantage over our ancestors, as a casual glance in any moderately stocked tobacco shop will reveal numerous tins and pouches from a multitude of suppliers, each containing a different mixture, not to mention the tobacconist's own lineup of private house blends that have been carefully selected to appeal to a wide variety of tastes. And therein lies the problem.

Choosing a tobacco, especially for the newer pipe smoker who is unfamiliar with many of the brands (and I know of no one who has smoked them *all*) is much like ordering a meal in a restaurant that has a 24-page menu. The selections are so vast and most of it sounds so good, but if we have not eaten there before, or do not know someone who has, our freedom of choice is totally useless. And for the first-time pipe smoker, the menu might just as well be written in a foreign language.

Unfortunately, this situation is compounded by many of the tobacco manufacturers themselves, or more properly, their advertising policies, for few of the brands actually tell you what that particular blend smokes like. If one were to believe the promotional copy in brochures and on tins, then virtually every tobacco in the world "smokes sweet and cool, slow-burning and delicious." This is the cruelest blow a copywriter could throw at the very pipe smoker he is trying to attract, for by virtue of using the same adjectives for different blends, we are erroneously led to believe that everything smokes the same. It doesn't. Therefore, it would be helpful if all the tobacco manufacturers got together and devised some form of international (dare I say "universal" . . . ?) grading system for each tobacco, to be printed on the containers for all to see and judge them by. All we want are the aged and cured facts. For instance: Tobacco Taste – strong, medium, mild. Aroma – sweet, nutty, forest-like. Burning Rate – slow, medium, fast. There could also be a numerical rating system so that the strength of all tobaccos could be public knowledge, with No. 1 being supremely airy and light, No. 5 being a medium blend and No. 10 used for an extra heavy and thick taste, with all the other numbers in between used for designating the various measurements leading up to these three primary categories.

But strength is not the total tobacco story, for there is also taste, and like various foods at different mealtimes, the taste of a particular blend may fluctuate and change as it is smoked at different times of the day. I have always felt that it was impractical to expect a pipe smoker to be inseparably wedded to the same tobacco day after day, week after week. Variety is what keeps the taste buds tingling and it is the thrill of popping off the lids of new tins every now and then that keeps the spirit of adventure alive and fresh around the old pipe rack. Admittedly, there is a sense of protective security in finding one stable, likeable pipe mixture and sticking with it through thick and thin, like an old loyal friend, and every pipe smoker should have at least one of these blends to fall back on when no more surprises can be tolerated at the end of a hectic day. However, just as we smoke a different pipe each day to match our different moods, why not vary our tobacco also, in an effort to better satisfy our fluctuating cravings and to match our pipe smoking with the biorhythms of life. For example, a very mild tobacco might be ideally suited for the "morning pipe" while a mixture of medium strength would go well in the mid-afternoon, as an aid to settling lunch and calming one's outlook on the rest of the day. In the evening, a slightly headier brew would help us relax as only a well-packed briar can do. Of course, these are only generalities and many a pipe smoker may prefer to stick with his "morning pipe" all day long, or perhaps limit his smoking to a single bowlful of the evening blend, no matter what time of the day it is smoked. Personally, I enjoy medium English tobacco in the evening and even have a hard time adjusting to the heavy, thick clouds of Latakia and Perique when I walk into a tobacco shop early in the day. On the other hand, I like to eat cold pizza while reading the Sunday morning paper. It is all a matter of personal taste, which brings us back to the topic of tobacco selection. It is not something to be taken for granted if we are to get the utmost satisfaction from our pipe, no matter what time of the day it is smoked.

In his classic Victorian volume of tobacciana entitled *Whifflets*, published in 1897, A. M. Jenkinson stated, "... there is nothing among men that will quicker bring even a righteous man into scorn and contempt than the use of a poor mixture by which he spoils other people's pleasure and degrades his own palate ... Indeed, appreciation of good tobacco is a test of true gentlemanly instincts ... a man who smokes bad tobacco when good tobacco is abundant ... has his sense of taste and smell deficient or blunted ... it follows that if his judgement on tobacco be wrong, it is very likely to go astray on other important things."

As a prelude to selecting the perfect tobacco, it helps to know a little bit about the plant itself, where it comes from, and how it gets from the ground and into our pipes. Aside from giving you an even greater knowledge and appreciation of the pipe smoking art, you can also use this information to utterly amaze your friends with a sixty-second dissertation on the finer points of tobacciana the next time they watch you light up.

To begin with, there are about fifty different varieties of tobacco, the most common of which is Nicotiana, originating in the Western Hemisphere, although the plant is now grown worldwide. Besides the United States, tobacco flourishes in Canada, Italy, Greece, France, Germany, Sweden, New Zealand, Yugoslavia, Hungary, China, Russia, Japan and Puerto Rico. After all, it *is* a weed, although rarely has a weed been cultivated through the centuries with such reverence.

Only three of the many tobacco plant varieties have any real interest to the pipe smoker. The most popular, of course, is the historic *Nicotiana Tabacum*, a native plant of South and Central America and the very plant that our hero John Rolfe shanghaied from Trinidad to Virginia in 1612. Second in popularity, especially for those smokers preferring the English blends, is *Nicotiana Rustica*, a native of Mexico which is now grown in Europe, Africa and Asia and which is responsible for producing the rich-tasting Turkish, Latakia and Sumatra tobaccos that we often enjoy after a particularly heavy meal. Last in the tobacco trilogy is *Nicotiana Persica*, the smallest of the tobacco family and named because it was originally grown only in Persia. In the United States, where the bulk of the world's pipe tobacco is grown, the top producing states are North Carolina, Virginia, Kentucky, South Carolina, Georgia and Tennessee.

It seems somewhat ironic that in order for North American pipe smokers to obtain some of the highest quality European blends, the tobacco must first be grown in the United States, shipped overseas for processing and packaging, and then shipped back to America again.

True to the very nature of the flavor it will ultimately produce, the very best tobacco is grown in the very best of soils. The southern states of North America have some of the most fertile soils and climatically ideal environments for growing the tobacco plant and the average yield is over 500 kilos of tobacco per acre. Furthermore, a single plant can produce a hundred grams of tobacco and if you want another useless fact, approximately two kilos of processed tobacco will produce 500 grams of ash. Now put *that* in your pipe and smoke it!

In the United States, the pipe tobacco saga begins when the seeds are first planted in protected seed beds from December to May, when the very heartiest of the young shoots are then transplanted to a larger tobacco field in May and June. It usually takes from 6 to 10 weeks for the young plants to grow strong enough for the transplanting process. Scientific fertilization and in some cases, crop rotation, is needed to produce a healthy harvest. The plants are then carefully nurtured and pampered like the valuable commodity that they are. At the proper cycle in the plant's growth, it is "topped," whereby the top stems are trimmed off so that more of the plant's strength goes into the leaves. The "suckers," or new shoots that spring out of the stems as a result of the "topping" process are also trimmed away so that none of the growing strength is deprived from the main body of the tobacco leaves. The tobacco plant is very sensitive to both moisture and heat, conditions which can cause dark spots and even holes in the leaf. As the healthy leaves ripen, they begin turning yellowish green in color, sometimes with yellow spots, and they become rougher and thicker in texture. The crop is harvested as early in autumn as possible, as the tobacco leaves are highly susceptible to frost.

The plants are trimmed close to the ground and laid gently on the warm earth so that the leaves are not damaged as they cure in the sun to a point where they are "wilted," yet still flexible. Another method of harvesting the tobacco plant is to only take off the mature leaves, leaving the stalk in the ground to nurture the remaining leaves of the plant. In this way, a single plant will produce more mature leaves, but the process takes longer. (The old methods of hand weighing and stripping the tobacco with sharp knives, whereby the stalk is removed from the leaves and a worker "feels" whether or not the tobacco is dry enough have largely been replaced with modern machinery and in more sophisticated concerns, with complete automation.)

Just as the curing (drying) process of briar is so crucial to the final smoking qualities of the pipe, so is the curing and fermentation process critical to the ultimate flavor that the tobacco leaf will finally have in the bowl of your pipe. This all-important phase is the next step the tobacco leaf must take.

All tobacco is cured by one of three methods: 1) air-cured, in which no artificial heat is applied, 2) fire-cured, in which the tobacco is dried by the heat of open or mechanically controlled fires in drying sheds, and 3) flue-cured, wherein metal flues or conducting pipes are used to transmit heat of 90 to 170 degrees Fahrenheit throughout the tobacco sheds without subjecting the delicate leaves to smoke. Normally, only air-curing and flue-curing are used for pipe tobacco.

After the curing process, the tobacco leaves are graded according to color and texture. Then they are aged (sometimes referred to as fermenting) whereupon the leaves are stacked and stored for anywhere from six months to three years, depending upon the tobacco and the blend it is to be used for. This fermenting cycle is a very crucial process, for it will help determine the final flavor and aroma the tobacco will have.

The numerous varieties of aged and cured tobaccos are then sold at auction to the various pipe blend manufacturers, whose bidders carefully inspect each basket of leaves before making an offer. The selection of your favorite pipe tobacco is therefore a very personal business, even before you put your first match to the bowl, for someone else has already decided how that particular mixture is going to taste; it is up to you to determine whether or not their decision was the right one for you.

The tobaccos are then shipped to various blending companies, primarily in the U.S., England or Denmark. For much of the U.S. market (and to meet a recent and growing trend in England), aromatic tobaccos are sprayed with chemical additives, such as diethylene glycol and mixtures of sugar, glucose, molasses and various food flavorings. Up until 1986, these tobacco additives were not allowed in Great Britain, which is why pipe smokers traditionally refer to U.K. tobaccos as English blends, as they are composed mainly of unadulterated tobaccos, give a purer taste and have a slightly more pungent aroma. However, both English and aromatic tobaccos can run the gamut of being mild or strong; it is the taste of the smoke and the way the tobacco burns in your pipe that will ultimately please your personal palate.

After a brief storage period of about a week, the tobacco is then put through machines that clean the leaves and remove the woody stems, although a few high quality manufacturers still prefer to have this operation done by hand. For some tobaccos, such as Latakia, the stem, or portions of it, actually comprise an important part of the final flavor, and therefore are not discarded.

At this point, if the tobacco is to be an aromatic or semi-aromatic blend, casings are added. Casing is simply another word for flavorings, and they are responsible for the person sitting next to you saying, "My, your pipe tobacco smells just like chocolate!" In addition to chocolate, honey, rum, cherry, apple, peach, banana, coffee, liquor and a host of other flavorings can be added to the aromatic leaves at this point in their manufacture. In fact, were it not for the noticeable lack of steak, salad and potato flavors, one could almost make a complete meal out of tobacco casings alone.

Next comes the blending process, one of the most critical operations in the final preparation of any pipe tobacco. It is much like preparing a gourmet meal; it is the various ingredients, their proportions and even how they are served (packaged) that creates the ultimate flavor and spirit of the tobacco, which directly translates into the enjoyment a pipe smoker will receive from it. Because each tobacco has its own burning rate, color, flavor and other characteristics, which also include the way it is cut, the object is (or should be) to produce a resultant product in which each of the elements compliment each other – and the pipe smoker as well. It is not surprising, then, to learn that each pipe tobacco company has its own individual formula and methods of blending their various tobaccos and many are often jealously guarded secrets within the industry.

Finally, the tobacco is packaged and shipped to your local tobacco store, where you eventually arrive with pipe and pouch in hand, glance over the multi-hued array of packets, tins, and glass humidors and scratch your head, wondering whether or not you should spend some of those weighty pound coins in your pocket just to find out what a certain brand may taste like. As I mentioned before, the lack of a factual taste-guide on the tobacco container (giving specifics rather than generalities) is a great disservice to the pipe smoker, especially the newer ones just entering our fraternity.

Of course, if one has plenty of money and lots of time, it would be one of life's great adventures to obtain a packet or pouch or tin of every tobacco available and smoke a quarter bowlful of each (contrary to popular belief, you only need four or five puffs of a tobacco to know whether you're going to like it or not; it does, however, take a full pipe to convince

The three types of pipe tobacco (L. to R.): Ribbon (English blend), Cube (aromatic Burley blend), and Flake.

most smokers if that tobacco will be with them for any length of time), taking copious notes, throwing the foulest-tasting of the batch at the dog and keeping the pleasanter blends with you until at last, by process of elimination, one would have discovered *the* ultimate tobacco for his or her own personal taste. (Remember, tobacco, like clothes, colors or food, strikes each person differently, depending upon his chemical and psychological makeup. That is why I hate to recommend tobaccos, movies or electricians to anyone.)

However, a far more practical solution in the never-ending quest for The Perfect Tobacco is your local tobacconist, the dedicated professional who works in his own smokeshop daily and who has thus devoted a part of his life to becoming intimately familiar with most of the pipe tobaccos today – or at least with those he carries in his store. He is probably the most knowledgeable pipe smoker you will meet on a retail basis. Although he may have his prejudices, the true tobacconist will listen to what you have to say, try to determine what you are seeking in the way of taste (many smokers don't know what they want until they find it), and then guide you onto three or four blends which may fit into your particular category. These tobaccos can be commercially-prepared pre-packaged brands or privately packaged

Some of the more popular packaged pipe tobaccos from America include these aromatic Cavendish, Virginia and Burley blends.

"house blends." Thus, it is not uncommon to discover that Sherlock's Homesbrew is exactly the same tobacco as Cowboy's Corral in another tobacco shop a thousand miles away. It is still the same quality, however; just a different name in a different town. It is also possible to have a tobacconist mix two or more of his standard blends to create a special taste exclusively for you. Many tobacconists keep file cards on their customers for just this purpose and Alfred Dunhill began his firm's now famous My Mixture tobaccos in this way.

But before we start mixing and matching various blends or begin searching for the perfect ready-made mixture that has the advantage of being able to be purchased anywhere in the pipe smoking world, we should first familiarize ourselves with the various terms that are commonly used to describe our most noble weed.

First, it is important to realize that all pipe tobacco can be divided into two categories, *English* and *Aromatic*. English blends have been with us the longest, as they are pure, unadulterated mixtures of specific types of tobacco plants, usually Latakia and other Oriental varieties, each imparting its own distinctive taste to the final product. English tobaccos generally taste and smell stronger than aromatic blends. However, they are, as a rule, the favorite choice of many pipe smoking connoisseurs as well as people

Hans Petersen of Danish tobacco blenders A. & C. Petersen inspects shipment of Virginia from hogshead container.

who like to drink their whiskey straight. Aromatics, on the other hand, are a relatively new addition to the pipe smoking world, and in America at least, aromatics are far more popular with pipe smokers on a ratio of three to one. An aromatic tobacco is one which has had some form of flavoring agent added to it to give it an enhanced taste and extremely fragrant aroma, something which endears aromatic smokers to practically everyone around them. In fact, I suspect that it is the purchases of aromatic tobaccos by non-smokers for their pipe smoking friends on their birthdays, Christmas and other smokable occasions that has given this new product such a large lead over the tried-and-true English blends. Aromatics are usually blended with a Burley or Cavendish base and are normally much milder than English tobaccos but they sometimes have the annoying habit of smoking "wet." That is, as the heat from the pipe tobacco permeates the bowl, some of the aromatic additives will coagulate and turn into moisture, which ends up in the heel of the bowl along with the natural moisture caused by burning tobacco as well as with the saliva from the smoker's mouth. Thus, a natural situation can be turned into a dramatically annoying and frequent "gurgle." Not all aromatics are guilty of this phenomena, but many of them are, and it is up to the smoker to choose between a rich, perhaps stronger but drier smoke or a sweeter one requiring the use of more pipe cleaners. There is no universal answer, as both types of tobacco sell well throughout the world and rather than prejudice the pipe smoker, I would merely suggest that three different varieties of both English and Aromatic tobacco be tried and then the one that offers the least resistance should be the path to take for further tobacco exploration.

However, here is a handy hint: if you finally decide that the best tobacco for you is one that, unfortunately, smokes wet, then you might consider smoking that tobacco in a clay or meerschaum pipe, both of which are more absorbent than a briar. But do not smoke an unusually wet tobacco in the porous corncob, which would simply be asking that historic pipe to commit suicide well before its time.

Throughout my pipe smoking career, I rarely found a

single source that told me exactly what each of the most popular blending tobaccos were, so that I might have a better understanding of what a specific mixture contained in taste and personality. I finally ended up compiling a list of my own, which I would now like to share with you. Hopefully, it will tell you more than you already knew, while I continue my research (yes, I really *am* trying to eventually smoke all of the tobaccos in the world!). Although most of these tobaccos come from the U.S., rising costs have now forced many blenders to buy "offshore" crops from other countries.

Virginia – Its name is somewhat of a misnomer, for although it was first grown by English colonists in Jamestown, today it is far more prominent in the tobacco fields of North and South Carolina, as well as Florida and Georgia. Virginia tobacco is most commonly a bright yellow color and no doubt for that reason is called "Bright" tobacco by growers, although a dark Virginia does exist. Bright Virginia, when smoked, has a pleasantly sweet, woodsy taste, which makes it popular in many blended pipe tobaccos, although too much Virginia in any mixture will tend to burn "hot." Used in moderation, however, it lends a superb flavor to practically any blend.

Burley – First grown in America in 1864, Burley primarily comes from Tennessee, Kentucky and Ohio. The leaves are a light yellowish green to yellow-brown in color and it is an extremely light tasting tobacco. In fact, I once smoked a bowlful of Burley just to see what it was like and had to keep watching the smoke coming from my pipe to make sure the tobacco was still lit. Burley has an almost transparent flavor when used by itself, and this fact, combined with its unique ability to absorb the flavorings that are often added to aromatic tobaccos, makes Burley an excellent host and binding agent for these popular mixtures. Consequently, Burley is one of our largest tobacco crops today.

Latakia – A distinctively Oriental tobacco, which is only grown in northern Syria and consequently, is very expensive. Latakia is dark brown and almost black in color and is one of the few tobacco plants in which the stem and leaf ribs (being the sweetest-tasting portions of the weed) are used, along with the leaves themselves. Latakia produces a rich, heavy taste, almost like smoking a Porterhouse steak, and is usually found in most quality English smoking mixtures. When blending Latakia, a little can go a long way, but for the connoisseur, too little is never enough.

Perique – A very rare and slow burning strong-tasting tobacco with an air of mystery about it, due to the fact that Perique is only grown in a small, triangular section of the U.S. in St. James Parish, in the bayou country of Louisiana. The plant is a blackish brown in color with a distinctive taste and aroma. Perique is just the opposite of Burley, and achieves its strong taste from being pressed and then fermented in its own juices. It is one tobacco that should never be smoked by itself; smoking straight Perique is the equivalent of having a lobotomy. However, when used by skilled blenders, Perique can produce an even-burning, distinctively-tasting mixture that would be like no other if this mysterious variety of tobacco did not exist.

Maryland – Unlike Virginia, most of Maryland tobacco is grown in the state for which it is named. It is a rich brown in color and is occasionally used to increase the burning characteristics of other tobaccos, such as Burley.

Turkish – Not a single strain, but rather a broad classification of at least a dozen tobaccos that are actually grown in Greece. It is a quality leaf that burns well and evenly and has a wide range of slightly aromatic tastes. Turkish tobacco is rarely used in pipe tobaccos, although it is found in some of the more exotic blends.

Cavendish – A generic term for tobacco that has been flavored with sugar, maple or rum and then heated and pressed in recurring cycles to give it a darker color. This process produces a heavy-sweet and mild taste when added to other tobaccos. Cavendish is extremely popular in the United States.

In addition to the different types of tobacco used in pipe blends, there are also different cuts, which is the way the leaf is trimmed, and determines the final shape of the blended tobacco that you will be putting in your pipe bowl. The type of cut can also affect the burning rate of your tobacco and therefore, how it will taste. A coarsely cut tobacco will burn slow and is a good choice for the fast and heavy puffer as well as for the smoker looking for a milder taste (blend notwithstanding). A finely cut tobacco or one composed of thin strands of leaf will burn faster and somewhat hotter, although this is ideal for the slow, meticulous smoker, as he does not have to puff as much in order to keep his pipe lit. The trick in finding the perfect blend or blends for your individual tastes is to *experiment*; do not be afraid to venture out into the unearthing of new brands, new tins, new mixtures. For me, the adventure of searching for the "perfect" tobacco has never ceased, although I have my favorites (at this current writing, there are about fifteen of them).

The basic cuts we encounter today are shag, cube (occasionally called "chop" cut) and ribbon (sometimes referred to as "long cut"). English blends traditionally are long cut because they are blended with Virginia as a base, and Virginia is a long cut tobacco. These finer, string-like strips are easy to keep lit and burn fast, making them ideal for slow, methodical smokers. On the other hand, Burley is almost always a cube cut, which makes it burn slower because of this thickness. In Victorian times, shag was a very coarse-cut tobacco and was the favored smoke of Sherlock Holmes. Today, however, shag has come to mean (paradoxically) a finely cut tobacco which is often found in Cavendish tobaccos.

Another form of tobacco which is still occasionally encountered, although not as popular as it once was is Plug or Cake Tobacco. Plug tobacco has been soaked in honey, which acts as both a bonding agent as well as a sweetener, then moulded by packing or forcing the gooey tobacco into holes (or "plugs") that have been drilled into hickory logs. Popular in many rural areas of the U.S. over a hundred years ago, plug tobacco could be conveniently carried in pocket or pouch and a measured amount could then be trimmed off with a pocket knife or more preferably a Bowie for smoking or chewing, as the situation warranted. Cake tobacco was very popular in Europe during the 19th century, but is less so today, due to the added effort it takes to prepare it for smoking; cake tobacco appears like clumps or pressed-together wedges and must be broken up by hand before it can be packed into the pipe bowl.

English mixtures come in a wide variety of tastes, which can run from very mild to extremely heavy.

Blending is the final step in the pipe tobacco process. Actually, the fine art of mixing and blending the various types of tobacco in order to create the "perfect blend" did not get started until 1877. Prior to that time, one type of tobacco in a package or cut from a plug was all you got. Some early 1860s-era packages of pipe tobacco in my collection bear this out, and the coarse paper is often rubber stamped with verbiage such as Clark & Snover's Stripped Smoking and Chewing Tobacco, Queen of the Valley Chewing Tobacco (which presumably could also be used for smoking) from the J. W. Loomish Company, and A. H. Mickle & Sons Grape Tobacco, the package of which sports a line drawing of an attractive young Victorian lady holding a bunch of grapes over her head, leaving one to wonder if only the stems and leaves were to be smoked.

Later, with blended tobaccos, the packaging became more ornate and the tobacco manufacturers proved that they were not without their sense of humor, as evidenced by a 100-year-old package from Wheeling, West Virginia, in which the smoking product was christened Elephant Butts and featured an appropriate illustration of that jungle animal's anatomy. The English tobacco company John Solomon, Ltd. still sells an aromatic, blended-in-America brand dubbed "Barking Dog . . . because it never bites!" In the 1920s and 30s tobacco packages became bolder in the use of color and picturesque packages bearing the names of Union Jack and Plow Boy are still found in U.S. antique shops and boot sales and can be acquired for about the same price as modern brands, although the older varieties should be strictly preserved for their collectibility and not their smoking qualities.

Today, there are countless blends and brands of pipe tobacco and given the law of averages, it is not surprising when we find that many of them are similar in taste, while others are so unique as to be totally unduplicated. A good case in point is Dunhill's recent introduction of soft pouch tobaccos of Rubbed Flake, Mild Aromatic and Mild Blend, light-tasting aromatics that, hopefully do not spell the end of the tin, but each with a distinctively modern flavor that bridges the taste gap of many smokers. On the other hand, truly dedicated followers of the rich English blends can often make a painless switch between Dunhill's Nightcap, Royal Yacht, John Cotton No. 2 and Rattray's Red Rapparee, while many smokers of Escudo, McConnell's Oriental, or Balkan Sobranie will smoke those mixtures and nothing else, even to the point of taking large amounts of these blends with them on extended trips, for fear of running out. In the U.S. this is an exercise in pipe smoking paranoia, for these two aromatics and the one English are among three of America's most popular tobaccos and are readily available in most cities. Smaller towns and foreign countries, of course, are another story. When travelling to Europe I often take my own tobacco, because ironically, English tobaccos are cheaper in America due to our more lenient tax laws. But I still end up buying brands in the U.K. that I cannot get in the U.S., not only to smoke, but to also acquire the tin. Additionally, I will often take apart the leafy contents of an unfamiliar brand when I get home and examine it under a microscope, just to determine what makes up the contents of its inner workings.

For many pipe smokers, myself included, there is no such thing as brand loyalty when it comes to selecting a pipe tobacco. For me, the closest I have come to a repeat performance with any one single mixture is occasionally buying half pound bags of a wonderful medium English concoction sold by the Century City Tobacco Shoppe in West Los Angeles, California, called, appropriately enough, Hacker's Sporting Blend. The proprietor of the shop insists he named it after me, but all I know is that he has an awful lot of golfers and computer hobbyists buying the same brand.

It is unfortunate that most tobacco manufacturers do not print the exact contents of their mixtures on their packages, so unless the curious pipe smoker actually buys, opens and smokes a particular blend, he will have no idea of what it tastes like. It has been suggested that this is all a plan on the part of tobacco makers to get the pipe smoker to buy his product but I do not believe it. A good tobacco will sell itself once its merits are discovered. This "mystery of taste" situation is rather annoying (and sometimes expensive, especially in the case of imported blends) for which there seems to be no immediate cure. "A mild, fragrant aroma" printed on a pipe tobacco package tells us poor pipe smokers absolutely nothing about what is inside the tin. In preparation for this book, I spent a great deal of effort in assembling all of the major blends and smoking a pipeful of each, in the hope of including a "Tobacco Rating List" of what each one tasted like. Unfortunately, when sharing my "findings" with a number of pipe smoking friends, I soon discovered the impracticality of all this, as what tasted "mild" to me was listed as "strong" by someone else. A lot depends upon the type of pipe one is smoking, its overall condition (has it been cleaned, does it have a heavy or light cake built up within it, how has the briar been cured, etc.,) as well as the taste preference of the individual smoking the pipe. Therefore, the experiment failed, but I did end up with one heck of a lot of pipe tobacco!

Normally, all pipe blends start out with either Burley, Cavendish or Maryland tobacco as a foundation, then other tobaccos and flavors are added to create the end result desired by the manufacturer. Virginia, Latakia, Perique and Turkish tobaccos tend to make heavier blends. Burley and Cavendish mixtures create a light taste. Also, certain countries, such as Holland and Germany, tend to produce tobaccos which are uniquely characteristic of their soil and climate, creating a "national taste" that serves as an undercurrent to the blend itself. Still, even with all these facts, there is no easy "first-time" solution to finding the right tobaccos for your taste. The best bet is to initially tell your tobacconist what you want, trying his recommendation and then going from there to either stronger or lighter, more aromatic or more English blends. In this manner, sometimes the tobacconist with a large assortment of house (private) blends can save the smoker a lot of time and trouble, as he is able to mix a number of different types together for you to create a blend that is all your own. That can be good or bad, because if you travel a lot, you may not be able to pick up the identical mixture in another town. Of course, this is much more prevalent in America, where there are various "chain" tobacco stores in which one tobacconist may be able to duplicate your blend from another store, as each member of the chain usually (but not always) carries the same handblended tobaccos. Unlike a factory-blended tobacco however, when buying your own mixture from a single-store tobacconist, it is wise, in my opinion, to purchase an adequate supply before leaving on any extended journey. And there is nothing wrong with phoning your favorite pipe shop from out of town and asking them to send you your own tobacco blend by overnight delivery. Pipe smokers in some of the remotest regions of the world have been doing this for years and once, while planning a trip to Africa, I arranged to have an adequate supply of my personal tobacco shipped on ahead so that it would be there when I arrived.

Much of the increase in pipe smoking in recent years has been a direct result of various medical reports that are usually published on an annual basis, citing the fact that both pipe smokers and nonsmokers have substantially the same reduced risks of contracting cancer, especially when compared with cigarette smokers, whose lung cancer potential is five times greater than a pipe smoker's. Additionally, unlike health warnings on cigarette packages, which have been mandated in the U.S. since 1966, there are no such warnings required for pipe tobaccos.

As a result, many new pipe smokers come fresh from the nicotine-laden ranks of being heavy cigarette smokers. Consequently, although a light to medium tobacco is normally my recommendation for the new pipe smoker, the first-time owner of a briar who is used to going through multiple packs of cigarettes per day may find more satisfaction from some of the heavier blends, such as MacBaren's Three Nuns or St. Bruno. The hardest thing cigarette smokers have to learn, however, is not to inhale, so that you still get the feeling of a nicotine "hit," but are no longer drawing the smoke into your lungs.

Whether you are a new smoker or an experienced pipeologist, when deciding which tobacco to buy, it is important to remember that the burning rate of pipe tobacco depends upon four things: 1) how dry it is, 2) how rapidly the smoker puffs, 3) the way the tobacco is cut, and 4) how it has been packed into the bowl. Each of these factors is examined within the pages of this book, as understanding them can help you enjoy every bowlful to its fullest and can prevent that burning sensation on the tongue that many novice pipe smokers experience.

A commonly asked question among new pipe smokers is, "How much tobacco should I buy?" That, of course, depends on how much tobacco you smoke and whether you are satisfied with your present mixture. In the 1700s, it was common for the average man to smoke two pounds of tobacco a year. Of course, pipe bowls were smaller then, roughly one-half to two-thirds the size of a medium briar today. Nowadays, tobacconists normally consider 500 grams to be a month's supply for the medium to heavy pipe smoker. However, I often smoke only one or two bowlfuls a day, increasing my tobacco usage in the autumn and winter months and unconsciously cutting back during the spring and summer, which seems to have a correlation with the activities of the squirrels in my backyard. (Some day I shall write a treatise on that observation.) Consequently, I find that 500 grams usually lasts me for a good four to six months. But then, I often experiment with new brands and in addition to my main supply, there are always four or five opened tins scattered about the den or hidden under the living room chair, where the cat has been playing with them. Therefore, the answer to the question of how much tobacco to buy is simply that the heavier smoker should buy in a larger quantity while the lighter or occasional pipe smoker might be satisfied in purchasing smaller packets; normally, hand-blended tobacco is sold by the half kilo and it is not unheard of to ask for 10 grams of tobacco just to try it. The pre-packaged tins and foil-sealed containers of tobacco usually come in 1½ ounce (42.5 gram) packaging, a not altogether unwieldy amount.

However, no matter how much tobacco you buy at one time, in order to be smokable, it must be kept properly humidified. In the purest sense of the term, this means kept at a constant temperature of 18 degrees Centigrade and at a humidity level of 70 percent. Now, unless you live in a self-enclosed, scientifically controlled environment, it is realistically impossible to maintain that degree of perfection. In fact, the only place I have ever seen it done is in the storage warehouses of the major tobacco companies. Many smoke-shops pride themselves on their "walk-in humidors," which create a semi-controlled atmosphere for their bulk tobaccos, where they are kept fresh until placed on the counter in smaller glass humidors. But aside from these two types of environments on the industry and consumer levels, loose tobacco will quickly dry out. Of course, individual packages of pipe tobacco are sold in pressure-sealed tins (which make a reassuring "whoosh" when opened for the first time, telling you before you even stick a finger into it that the tobacco was packed fresh and still is) or in air-tight foil pouches. But once the seal is broken on either of these containers, or as soon as your tobacco is loosely packed in your favorite pouch, it will quickly dry out if not kept artificially moist. The best way to do this is to keep one of those small individual moisturizers in with your tobacco. I keep one in my pouch and another in my humidor, just to play it safe; dry tobacco burns hot no matter how it is cut.

Speaking of humidors, they are one of the most important accessories a pipe smoker can have, especially if he goes through more than one bowlful a day. A humidor is simply an air-tight container with some form of moisturizer used for storing your tobacco. Humidors are normally made of some non-contaminating material, like porcelain or wood and the moisturizer can be anything from a piece of sponge affixed to the lid to highly porous clay. The wetness of the humidor's moisturizer should be checked once a week, especially if the container is constantly being opened and closed numerous times each day. Not only are humidors indispensable for keeping your tobacco as fresh as the day you purchased it but it can also be used for breathing new life into a dried-out blend and making it smokable again. But be careful not to get your tobacco too wet, or it will be hard to keep lit and will smoke with a juicy bitterness.

An age-old method for keeping pipe tobacco moist has been the ruin of many a pouchful of weed and should be publicly dispelled once and for all: it is the practice of placing a slice of apple or pear or other moisture-bearing fruit in with your favourite blend. Not only will this interfere with the natural taste of your pipe tobacco, but the slice of fruit will immediately start its natural "rotting process" which, if left in the pouch or humidor long enough, will quickly cover your tobacco with a nice white fluffy mold, thereby ruining your ration of *Nicotiana Tabacum* beyond resurrection. The slightest trace of mould will also render your pouch or humidor completely useless unless it can be totally sterilized. This was one of the many self-taught lessons I learned in college, when I first started smoking a pipe. Not being able to afford a proper humidor, I kept my ration of Old Hayseed in a plastic jar with a screw-top lid. Noticing that it would quickly dry out, I asked a few "knowledgeable" pipe smokers what to do and promptly got the standard instructions about the apple slice. It just took one week for the mold to form and I always regret not having the foresight to use my make-shift humidor for a "show-and-tell" session in my biology class. In spite of the fact that my entire life's supply of tobacco had been ruined, I tossed it out, but kept the humidor, washed it, and refilled it with another dollar's worth of the weed. But those little spores were still at work, invisible to the naked eye. This time it took them three weeks to finally surprise me with a whole new family of white fluff. I was tempted to keep the stuff for a pet (I had no companionship in those early years) but finally chucked the whole mess out in the trash and made do with weekly purchases of Half & Half, which came in sealable pouches. The moral of this story is: keep all moist organic material out of your tobacco. If you cannot find or afford a moisturizer from your local tobacconist, use a piece of damp, rolled up tissue, which usually lasts for about a day. For more information about humidors, see Chapter Seven.

Another questionable means of not only keeping your tobacco moist but also of flavoring it, is an old habit usually passed on to an unsuspecting nimrod by an old smoker, who advocates sprinkling a few drops of rum or brandy onto your tobacco. Frankly, I view this practice as either a poor waste of good liquor, or a good waste of poor liquor. In both cases, it is not necessary, as most aromatic tobaccos today are "flavored" enough and in varying degrees of strength to meet any taste requirement. Keep your rum and brandy in their respective glasses, not in your humidor. (I *know* you're going to try it; everybody does. Just remember, you are what you smoke!)

For the first time pipe smoker as well as the curious expert, there is a great deal of smoking enlightenment to be had by buying one of the variety packs of tobacco put out by firms such as Dunhill, or by having a tobacconist make one up from his various blends. In this way, for very little expenditure, you can experiment with a broad range of from six to ten different blends, just as you would at a wine tasting party.

Tobacco is a paradoxical substance, for it can act as both a stimulant and a relaxant, depending upon the individual smoker. Some business people in competitive industries such as publishing, finance and entertainment use the pipe as a method for sharpening their wits while after hours these same individuals use the combination of pipe and tobacco as a means for "coming down" after an adrenaline accelerated day, preferring to smoke their pipe in the solace of the evening, when the phones are silent and never-ending deadlines can be temporarily forgotten. Whether the tobacco is strong, medium or mild does not really seem to matter in the ultimate analysis of things for in this particular case, it is simply a matter of how the tobacco treats us, rather than how we treat it. Yet throughout our pipe smoking existence, whether it lasts for only a few years or until the Final Puff, there will always be the real or the subliminal quest for perfection, the chance of finding Utopia in a foil-lined packaged or sealed tin, much the way J. M. Barrie did when he wrote his classic volume *My Lady Nicotine*, in which he extolled the virtues of his favorite mixture, the Arcadia:

> ". . . I seldom recommend the Arcadia to men whom I do not know intimately, lest in the after-years I should find them unworthy of it. But just as Aladdin doubtless rubbed his lamp at times for show, there were occasions when I was ostentatiously liberal. If, after trying Arcadia, the lucky smoker to whom I presented it did not start or seize my hand, or otherwise show that something exquisite had come into his life, I at once forgot his name and his existence."

May we all ride upwards on that white, rolling cloud of elation with our very next bowlful!

Chapter Six

Pipe Smoking for Women

"The question, Shall women smoke?
has already been answered.
They do."

– A. E. Hamilton,
from *This Smoking World* (1927)

Ever since its introduction into the civilized world, pipe smoking has held a magnetic fascination for women, not only as observers, but also as participants. As early as the 17th century, when the new-found fad of public pipe smoking was just beginning an unbridled climb towards its immense popularity, ladies attending the theater were often offered a small clay pipe as a between-the-acts refresher. In 17th century Japan, women of respectability were frequently accompanied by servants who carried their mistresses' pipe and smoking tools. And during the reign of France's Louis XIV, a group of ladies of the court, growing bored by the polite and mundane conversation they were forced to engage in with guests, would often excuse themselves from the gathering and, borrowing clay pipes from the officers of the Swiss guard, would quietly slip away to their rooms to smoke. During colonial times in America women often smoked pipes quite openly and one of the most recurring stories one comes across in researching the annals of tobacco history is the accounting of a Quaker girl named Sarah Fell, a stepdaughter of George Fox, who would purchase clay pipes and tobacco for her sister Susannah. Among the early Quaker women, pipe smoking in the Colonies was quite common, although evidence seems to indicate that it was more readily tolerated in the rural areas of the country. In fact, pre-revolutionary women usually found it more convenient to smoke their clays in their homes rather than on the streets of the larger towns and cities.

The wife of the seventh President of the United States, Andrew Jackson, was one of the first documented cases of prejudice against women pipe smokers. When Jackson was elected to the presidency in 1829, his wife was forbidden to take her corncob pipe with her to the White House. But she was not the only First Lady to feel the sting of discrimination: Mrs. Zachary Taylor, wife of the 12th U.S. President, was able to get her pipes to Washington, but she had to smoke them clandestinely, behind closed doors.

Pipe smoking for women in America has never been easy, a fate not so readily shared by their European counterparts, although throughout history, women pipe smokers have never been what one would refer to as "socially conspicuous." Still, ever since the 1600s it has always existed, in one form or another, and with varying degrees of acceptance that was usually dependent upon the geographic location of the pipe smoker herself. For example, today, in some areas of Europe, Africa and the United States, a woman pipe smoker is often encountered without too much culture shock. The reason is simply because for one reason or another, women pipe smokers are more readily acceptable by the mores of these widely divergent areas. A long social history of acceptance may be the reason for the European woman's tolerance, tribal custom may be the influence in Africa, while in the U.S., California has traditionally been the launching pad for some of America's newest trends; avant-garde models and actresses are often encountered smoking slimline briars on Rodeo Drive in Beverly Hills, because this particular area is usually uninhibited towards new ideas. And while women pipe smokers are certainly not a new phenomena, they are not yet as commonplace as they could or should be. There are many reasons for this, the most important of which is social prejudice.

From its inception, pipe smoking has largely been looked upon as a predominantly male pastime. No doubt this concept had its origins with some of the very first pipe smokers, who were priests, chiefs, and other male officials of a tribe. This exclusive early use of the pipe by men was further reinforced when male sailors and explorers brought the first tobacco leaves back from their travels.

Like men, at first women began to take up pipe smoking out of curiosity and many enjoyed it enough to continue the practice, but evidently not in sufficient numbers to make it a regular part of social custom for any great length of time. For while society has often *permitted* women to smoke a pipe, rarely have they been *encouraged* to do so.

Thus, English writer Thomas Brown was slightly ahead of his time when he wrote to a lady in 1700 regarding her pipe smoking endeavors:

> ". . . Though the ill-natured World *censures* you for Smoaking, yet I would advise you, Madam, not to part with so innocent a Diversion." Browne went on to describe some of the virtues of pipe smoking for women, saying, "It is healthful . . . is a great help to Christian Meditations . . . It is a pretty plaything . . ." and finally,

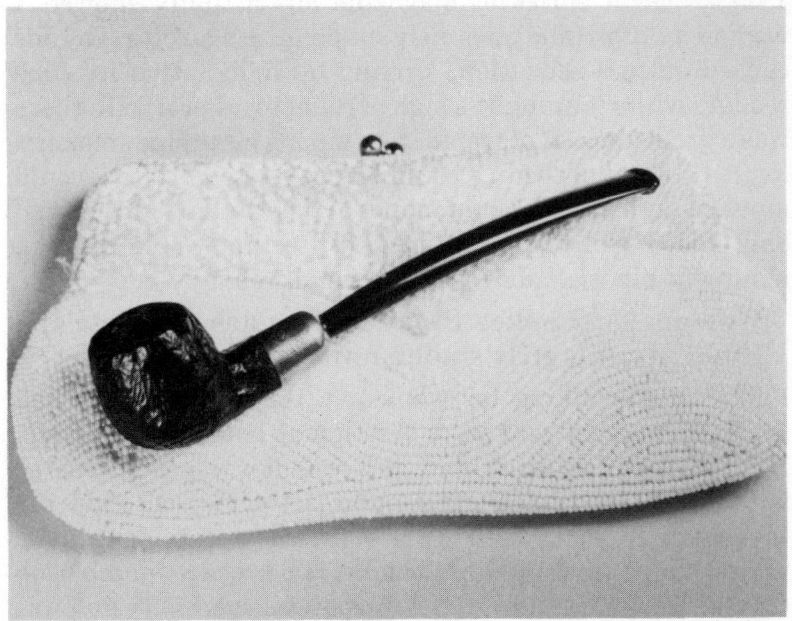

This silver mounted Dunhill shell Ladies' Pipe dates from the 1920s.

"It is fashionable, at least, 'tis in a fair way of becoming so."

The real turnaround for women smokers, in Europe at least, came over a century later, in 1885, when the Princess of Wales openly offered cigarettes to her guests at a luncheon. This was during the time of Queen Victoria's reign, when the use of tobacco in any form was royally frowned upon. In America, the "smoking revolution" took a little longer in coming and can most probably be linked with the passage of the 19th Amendment in 1920, which finally gave women the right to vote. With this "official" recognition of their democratic equality came a new feeling of freedom for women, which they subsequently expressed with the adoption of shorter hairdo's and a radical change of clothing fashions that shocked a rather conservative, male-dominated society. As part of the women's liberation movement of the 1920s, cigarettes were now being openly lit for the "fairer sex" at parties, in restaurants and even on the streets! Although it was common knowledge that women were smoking, this activity was not publicly recognized until 1927, when a series of magazine ads actually showed a woman *holding* (and obviously *smoking*) a cigarette. The ads caused quite a sensation, stirring up indignation in some readers while it brought a sigh of relief to others. Still, there was a great amount of trepidation among male pipe smokers, for if this unholy thing could happen to cigarettes, could pipes be far behind? A newspaper article of that same period only added fuel to the anticpated fire that would burn in feminists' pipes all across the nation. It read:

Woman, 93, Smokes Pipe 81 years despite Mate's Kick; says all girls smoke now, so she is in style!

Public pipe smoking for women in the 20th century had become a fact and when the prestigious London pipe firm of Dunhill began making diminutive ladies' pipes encrusted with diamonds, rubies and sapphires, the fad was suddenly in vogue. In fact, their 1923 Christmas catalogue even touted a pipe smoking handbag kit and brocade match book covers! Ten years later, GBD introduced their City de Luxe Debutante series of slim pipes for women; the tobacconist's display featured six of the pipes with pouches in various colors and a copyline which read: "For My Lady's Leisure Moments". Yet, many restaurants of the time prohibited women smokers of any kind.

Then, an interesting phenomena began taking form. Society, for reasons best known to psychologists, starting interpreting the cigarette as a feminine method of smoking and gradually accepted women in this capacity. But pipe smoking was regarded as strictly a male-oriented endeavor and the briar became a symbol of one of man's last untouchable bastions. This notion has always seemed to be a bit ironic, for pipe smoking, like jogging, cooking and reading, is one of life's pleasurable activities that can be done by both men and women with equal skill and enjoyment.

Unfortunately, the social stigma connected with women pipe smokers still exists today; to say otherwise would be to ignore the facts. This prejudice is not as widespread as it once was, no doubt owing to the latest women's lib movement of the 70s and the generally more relaxed attitude of society in general, but the bias exists, no matter how slight or weakened it might be. However, following the example set by the Princess of Wales a century ago, the best way to deal with a prejudice is simply to ignore it.

One of history's more prominent women pipe smokers, Baronne Dudevant, did just that. Her full name was Amandine Aurore Lucie Dupin, but she was better known as George Sand, a male pseudonym the Baronne was forced to adopt in order to sell her novels, which became immensely successful. "Madame" Sand smoked pipes that ranged in design from painted oriental to carved cherrywood and perhaps it was the fact that she was looked upon as being unconventional that she was able to smoke her pipes in public. Yet Gertrude Stein was also a celebrated intellectual who made no secret of the fact that she smoked a pipe.

It is difficult to estimate how many women pipe smokers there actually are in the world, but in the United States alone the number is generally believed to be around 10% of the total pipe smoking population. That would make them definitely a sizable force to be reckoned with and one that, by all indications, is on the rise.

However, women pipe smokers are an "invisible market." We do not see them because the majority of them are what the tobacco industry refers to as "closet pipe smokers," a term that I find somewhat inaccurate. No one ever smokes a pipe in their closet unless they have an unusually severe moth problem and the term itself seems to imply that there is something to be ashamed of. There is not.

Nonetheless, it is a fact that most women pipe smokers do not smoke outside of their own homes, although this may be gradually changing as women in business encounter more of the stress and anxiety that on-the-job pipe smoking helps to relieve. Additionally, there is the health factor to consider, as women who are habitual cigarette smokers look towards the pipe as one of the few workable solutions that can help free them from a nicotine addiction that may have

In the 1600s, pipes were often offered to ladies as a form of refreshment.

harmful side effects throughout the childbearing years and beyond.

The question of whether or not pipe smoking can be harmful to women can be answered in the same way as it can be answered for men: moderation and practice of the proper pipe smoking techniques without overindulgence are the secrets to long-term pipe smoking enjoyment without incurring any negative side effects. I recall a yellowed newspaper clipping about the plight of an 81-year-old woman named Rossale Spuler of Chillicothe, Ohio, who "has had a good clay pipe going in the corner of her mouth longer than she cares to remember." The article was focusing on her plight of not being able to find a local source for clay pipes anymore, and she was down to her last one!

One might think that women, longevity and clay pipes might seem to go together, for the oldest woman pipe smoker I have found was Jane Garbut, who died at age 110; this was back in 1856, when women – and men, for that matter – did not live as long as they do today. It was recorded that Ms. Garbut smoked a clay pipe daily and that she had retained all of her faculties up to her dying day.

A fairly common thread that I have discovered among the pipe smoking women I know or have interviewed is that they all possess a definite knowledge of who they are or have a strong desire to express their individuality. For women,

Savinelli's Davina is a currently-made ladies' pipe that is stylish and elegant.

This photo from the 1950s was an attempt to popularize women's pipes.

smoking a pipe should be done simply because the person wants to smoke a pipe and for no other reason. It should not be done just to prove a point. In addition, if a woman does not feel comfortable smoking a briar in public, she should not do so, for it would defeat the very essence of pipe smoking, which is to relax and enjoy those pleasurable moments the pipe can offer. Of course, it is human nature that the more women see other women publicly smoking a pipe, the less inhibited they will be to try pipe smoking for themselves.

A surprising number of women pipe smokers start out simply by taking an exploratory puff of their husband's or boyfriend's pipe and decide that they like it enough to buy a pipe of their own. Personally, if your spouse *has* to smoke I can think of no better way than with a pipe and it seems that a couple in love with pipes as well as with each other could have a lot of fun buying gifts for themselves at Christmas. I strongly suspect that it will only be a matter of time before some enterprising pipemaking company comes out with a "His 'N Hers Pipe Smoking Set" of matched briars or meerschaums. Do you think that they will give credit to this book?

Most new women pipe smokers today are in their 20s and 30s, although there certainly is no age limit that dictates when a woman should start smoking a pipe. Anytime you feel like it is the right time. However, extra care should be taken in selecting a woman's pipe, especially if it is her first one. Some pipes designed for women smokers are "trendy" and take on different styles in different years. The problem with many of these pipes is that they were designed by men who only seem to pay a cursory glance at this very viable and growing market without considering it from a practical, long range viewpoint. For example, a few years ago a line of women's pipes was introduced that appeared very elegant and colorful. Unfortunately, the bowls were so small they could only hold enough tobacco for a short fifteen minutes smoke and because of their diminutive scale, they smoked "hot." Moreover, the wood was varnished, which made it impossible for any smoker, no matter what their sex, to truly enjoy the tobacco. In short, this product turned out to be a "gimmick" pipe and consequently, it did a disservice to women pipe smokers everywhere.

A woman's pipe should be of a practical size for enjoyable smoking.

Keri Hulme is a pipe-smoking New Zealand authoress whose first novel, *The Bone People*, won the prestigious Booker Prize in 1985.
Credit: Michael Short

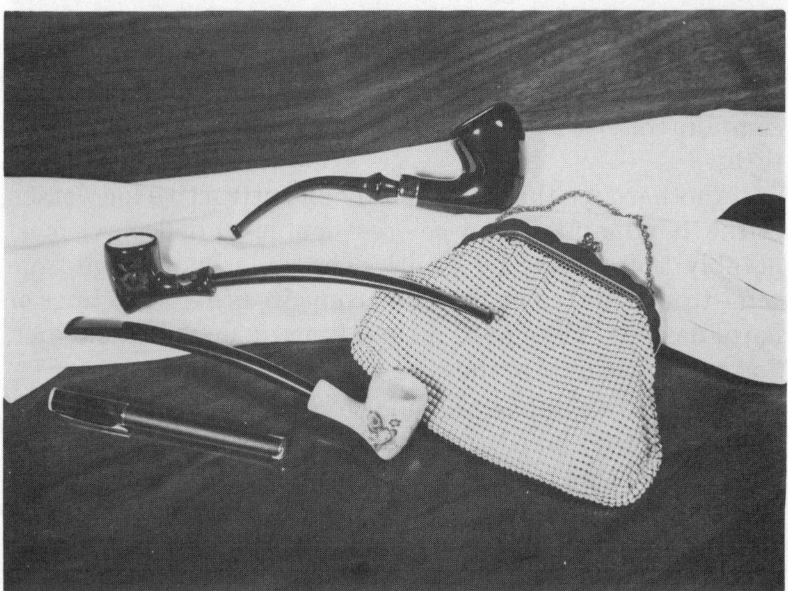

Zenith makes a variety of elegant ladies' pipes.

There is no reason why a woman's pipe cannot be feminine looking and still be practical, with a naturally oiled or stained briar bowl, such as the Savinelli Lady's Pipe, which comes with its own carrying purse. A number of other pipemakers have already made some rather innovative advances in design, such as special paneled or oval bowl designs, multicolored Lucite stems, colored bands of synthetic material or precious metals inset in the shank and even semi-precious stones that are bonded onto the stem. Cosmetics aside, the main thing a woman should look for in a pipe is a properly-finished bowl (see Chapter Two) that is of sufficient size. Many women smoke standard sized pipes, but women pipe smokers should exercise the same care that a man does when selecting a pipe: buy one with a shape and of a size that will compliment your own facial features and bone structure. An Apple or Churchwarden and even the straight-stemmed, high-bowl shape of the Crosby design offer practicality as well as a graceful look that can be obtained in a variety of wood hues ranging from natural blond to black sandblast.

In addition to briar, meerschaum is another pipe material that I would highly recommend for women. Not only does the pipe provide an excellent smoke, but the meerschaum itself is an attractive material and these pipes can often be found carved in graceful, delicate shapes that can compliment both a woman's wardrobe and her facial features.

Another pipe that I personally find attractive for women is the handpainted and colored double-walled clay, most notably those made by Zenith. The styles can range from semi-traditional to modern and come in either solid hues or floral designs. They need no breaking in, do not smoke hot, and can be cleaned in the sink with hot water.

The choice of tobacco should be given the same amount of thought as the choice of a pipe. Do not make the mistake of buying the same tobacco your husband or boyfriend smokes just because you like the way it smells. Remember, a pipe smoker does not smell, she only tastes. Therefore, for the first-time smoker, I would recommend a light blend such as a Cavendish or a very light English, depending upon your preference. Try a few bowlfuls of each, including the aromatics, letting your pipe and tastebuds rest for a day or two before switching mixtures. Keep in mind there is no law that states you have to smoke the same brand of tobacco day after day; as I mentioned in Chapter Five, I invariably change my tobacco blends with each new pound I purchase. As an aside, most of the long term pipe smoking women I have spoken with seem to favor the very light to medium English blends rather than the aromatics, which they tend to find too "gooey."

Like pipes, women should also select their smoking accessories with the same attention to style and practicality. In view of so many tobacco pouches and traveling pipe cases now on the market, coupled with the growing number of women pipe smokers, it may only be a matter of time before one of the larger manufacturers begins making a special woman's designer line, with tobacco pouches made of suede or patent leather and pipe cases covered in real or synthetic fur. Additionally, pipe tampers are easily adaptable to the feminine hand and we already have the slim designer lighters. All that is left is for the pipe and tobacco industries to recognize the woman pipe smoker as a real and viable customer.

For a woman, lighting her pipe in the privacy of her home is no major media event, but lighting up in public could be a traumatic experience if she is not prepared for it. Debbie Raymond, heiress to Paul Raymond's entertainment empire, has no trouble adjusting to pipe smoking. "I have found it a very pleasant change from smoking cigarettes and my pipe is going to become a familiar sight in all the clubs!" she says. Likewise, three-time U.S. pipe smoking champion Jean Bain states from experience, "You can do supposedly masculine things in a very feminine way."

Her statement is based on fact. And at a cocktail party, I once watched with interest as a very sophisticated lady casually lit her pipe during a conversation with two men and did it with such cool matter-of-factness that neither of the men openly seemed to notice and never changed or altered the course of their conversation. Likewise, one of ex-U.S. Ambassador Millicent Fenwick's aides has stated that,

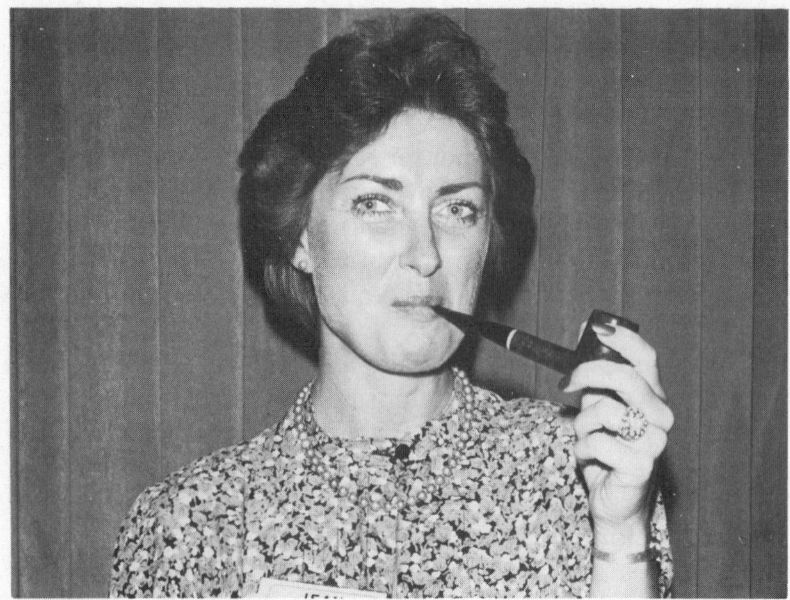

Jean Bain began smoking a pipe in 1970 and is a 3-time Women's Champion of a national pipe smoking contest in the U.S.A.

Dancer, award-winning singer and noted magazine editor Debbie Raymond finds her pipe has become a symbol of freedom as well as relaxation.

". . . she smokes a very small, plain pipe and she does it in such a way you are hardly aware of it."

Generally speaking, women are very conscientious pipe smokers. They pack their tobacco with care, they light up correctly, and they puff slowly and rhythmically. In short, they seem to savor their pipes to the fullest. Perhaps the best example of this I ever saw was during a national U.S. pipe smoking contest I was judging in 1982. Occasionally, some of the entrants in these contests are women, most of whom participate simply for the novelty of the event. However, this time the overall champion was a woman who beat every other man and woman in the huge smoke-filled auditorium with a time of one hour, 23 minutes and 55 seconds. Her winning was especially notable because it marked the first time she had ever smoked a pipe! She simply asked her husband about the correct pipe smoking procedures, took careful mental notes, and went on to outsmoke everyone else in the room, much to the delight of her nine-year-old daughter who was watching from the sidelines.

In recent times there are relatively few ads showing a woman smoking a pipe, but I think that perhaps the time is coming. If so, it may have the same effect as the first female cigarette ad back in 1927, which acknowledged a trend that was already well under way, thereby giving it added momentum. Meanwhile, it is interesting to note that new international rules are now being added especially for women contestants in European pipe smoking events. In the U.S., the number of women tobacconists is on the rise and in Hollywood, a great many actresses have taken up the pipe, although few will admit to it publicly. Still, who can forget the stunning beauty of Silvana Suarez (Miss Argentina and Miss World of 1979) who was photographed by an Australian newspaper just as she was lighting her silver banded briar? Indeed, the pipe doth have charm and provides equal pleasure for all. Consequently, it really does not matter whether advertisers wish to publicly recognize the woman pipe smoker or not. The fact is, she exists and the pipe smoking world is all the better for it. Whether she chooses to puff her pipe at home, at the office or at parties, the woman pipe smoker is a symbol for the universal awareness of the pipe and its continued growth in our society today.

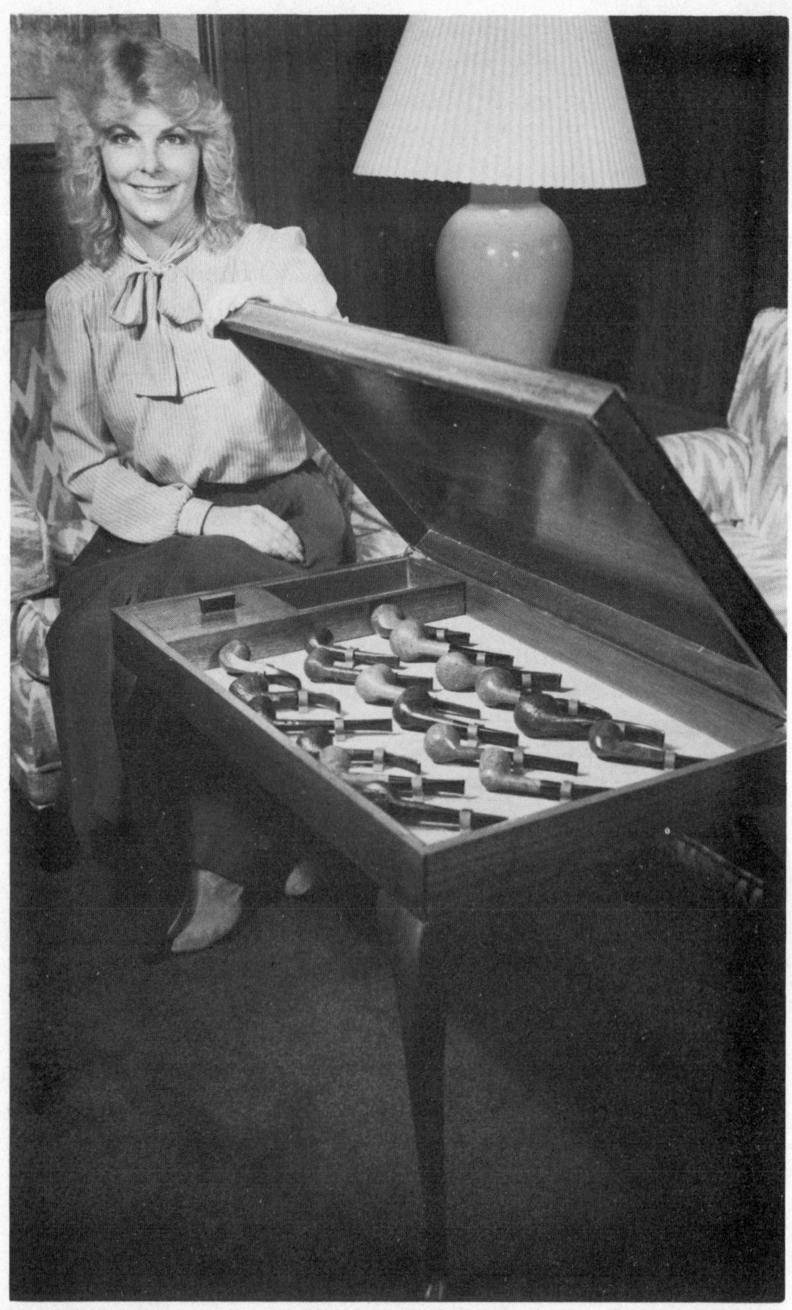

The ultimate smoking table, by Dunhill: eighteen White Dots encased in mahogany, leather and velvet. The table has separate compartments for tobacco and accessories.

Chapter Seven

Pipe Smoking Accessories

Come! don't refuse sweet Nicotina's aid . . .

– motto taken from an old tobacco jar

One of the true pleasures of having a pipe smoker for a close acquaintance is that there is never a dearth of ideas as to what to give her or him for birthdays, Christmas, or on any of a number of other gift-bestowing occasions. Likewise, one of the many pleasures of *being* a pipe smoker is that there is always some extra accoutrement you will need, so as to provide you with an excuse to send for the latest smokeshop catalogue or to stop in and visit your favorite tobacconist. Having a bevy of pipes and a goodly supply of tobacco simply is not enough. There are pipe lighters, cleaners, reamers, tampers, tobacco pouches, humidors, pipe stands and numerous other accessories with which to pamper yourself and your pipe. In this chapter, we will discuss and show a fraction of the many treasures that can actually aid us in the pleasures of pipe smoking.

There is no particular order of importance, but I suppose we should first start with the tobacco tamper, something no self-respecting pipe smoker is ever without, unless he enjoys going through life with a blackened and burnt index finger.

Pipe tampers are also known as "tobacco stoppers" and, next to matches and pipe cleaners, are the most frequently used pipe smoking accessory. They used to be made of wood, bone, ivory and metal and in fact, still are. They can be as inexpensive as a wide-headed nail or as costly as a silver-entwined and carved ivory rod. Your local tobacconist or mail order catalogues such as those put out yearly by firms such as Comoy's, Dunhill, and many department stores are the best places to find a variety to choose from. The main criteria is to select a pipe tamper that will clear the rim of your pipe bowl. As basic as this may sound, there was a company a few years back that marketed a fascinating assortment of Olde English brass pipe tampers in a variety of designs. Sales dropped rapidly when smokers got them home and found that they were too wide to fit into their pipes!

The main problem I have always had with pipe tampers is that the more expensive they are, the quicker I will lose them. It seems to be a preordained rule I must follow. I once made the entire staff of a janitorial cleaning crew immensely wealthy (and myself proportionally poorer) by accidentally losing no less than five ivory-and-gold tampers in my office within a month's time. I have since switched to the very inexpensive "horse shoe nail" variety that I often am given free just for walking into a pipe store; naturally, I have yet to lose a single one of those uninspired metallic creations.

Pipe cleaners are another indispensable aid to the smoker, but these have been dealt with more than adequately (considering their low cost and disposability) in Chapter Four. Suffice to say that prior to the invention of the pipe cleaner, smokers were forced to use bits of string, small wire brushes made especially for the purpose, and (as many 19th century catalogues advertised) chicken feathers, which sold for 7/6 per gross in bundles of 12. Thank heavens we live in the 20th century.

Although pipe cleaners are traditionally used to pass into the body of the pipe occasionally during a smoke in order to soak up the juices formed by the tobacco combustion and the smoker's own saliva, there is a relatively new item on the market that soaks up these unsavory liquids even as the pipe is being smoked. They are the invention of Erik Nørding, one of Denmark's most respected and talented pipemakers. Called EricsKeystones, they are tiny pebbles of specially dried moraine-clay, a type of which is only found in Denmark (near where Nørding lives, I suspect). Three or four of these light tan-colored pebbles are dropped into the pipe before it is filled with tobacco. Then, as the pipe is smoked, the clay effectively absorbs all moisture, preventing that annoying gurgling sound we hate to hear from our pipes in mixed company. After the smoke has ended, the pellets are emptied out with the dottle (they are only good for one pipeful), and the pipe smoker will notice that the pebbles have now turned a dark brown color, as EricsKeystones have absorbed not only the juices, but some tars and nicotine as well. I have found that because they create a slight air space in the heel of the pipe, it is far easier to smoke all of the tobacco in the bowl and occasionally the stones themselves will be scorched, although they have absolutely no effect upon the taste of the tobacco. For the smoker who feels he must have a filter in a system-less pipe and doesn't want to buy a new briar, Erics-Keystones could be a practical alternative. In addition, they greatly increase smoking pleasure for the pipe puffer who has a habit of over-salivating, as well as for the aromatic smoker, as these tobaccos often have a tendency to burn "moist." Nørding does not sell direct, but your local

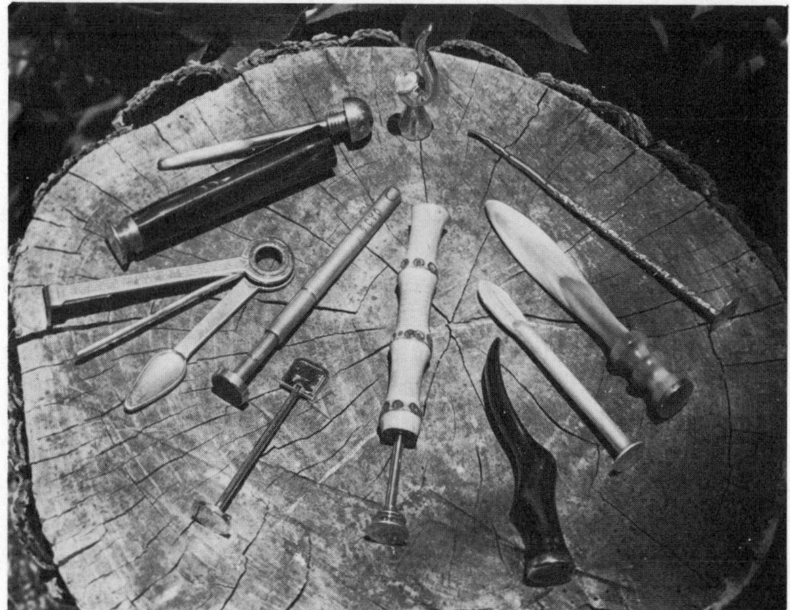

Pipe tampers come in a variety of styles and price ranges.

smokeshop should be able to get some of EricsKeystones for you. However, do not use them when first breaking in a new pipe, as their presence will prevent your pipe from caking at the heel.

The proper storage of that most necessary of ingredients, tobacco, should not be overlooked by the serious pipe smoker, for unless the blend is properly humidified, your pipe will be totally unable to give you all the potential enjoyment it is capable of, and which you so rightly deserve. While most smokers buy a 25 g to 50 g pouch of their favorite tobacco at a time, it is always convenient (and usually more economical) to purchase larger amounts of 225 grams or more to keep at home or in the office, so that you will not run out in the wee hours of the evening or during a holiday and are not forced to leap on a bus or unleash the Jaguar during a rainstorm just because you have no tobacco. Thus, practically every pipe smoker in the known world owns at least one tobacco humidor (which are usually referred to as tobacco jars in Europe). But convenience is only part of the reason we keep our favorite blends secured away in a humidor. They are also necessary for keeping our tobacco moist.

Most humidors being sold today are made of wood, porcelain or glass, but they all should have some sort of humidifying agent in a recessed compartment of a tightly-fitting lid. This humidifier is usually a sponge or a piece of water-absorbent clay. Care must be taken not to let the moisturizing agent come in direct contact with your pipe tobacco or mould may set in, ruining your supply of smokables. The moisture content of both tobacco and wetting agent should be checked about once a week. That's what you should do; I normally wait until my tobacco is tinder-dry before plucking out the sponge, uttering a gasp of horror and racing to the sink with it as if it were some dying thing I happened to find prostrate in the Sahara. In a day's time, however, all is well again. My tobacco is moist and my smoke does not burn hot any more. The lesson here is that dry tobacco *can* be re-humidified. Just be sure that your sponge is moist, not dripping wet when you put it back into the humidor lid.

Another reason for storing tobacco in a sealed porcelain or glass humidor is to prevent it from absorbing other odors

Tobacco humidors have changed over the years. On the left is a Tedd Cash replica of a 1790 Hudson's Bay tobacco box with a glass "burning lens" that predates the match. On the right is an old unopened humidor-can of pipe tobacco while the middle humidor is a modern porcelain replica with a sponge humidifier in the brass lid.

Elegant matching humidor, ashtray and pipe rest sets are available from numerous firms such as Davidoff or Dunhill, as evidenced by their silver smoker's set pictured here.

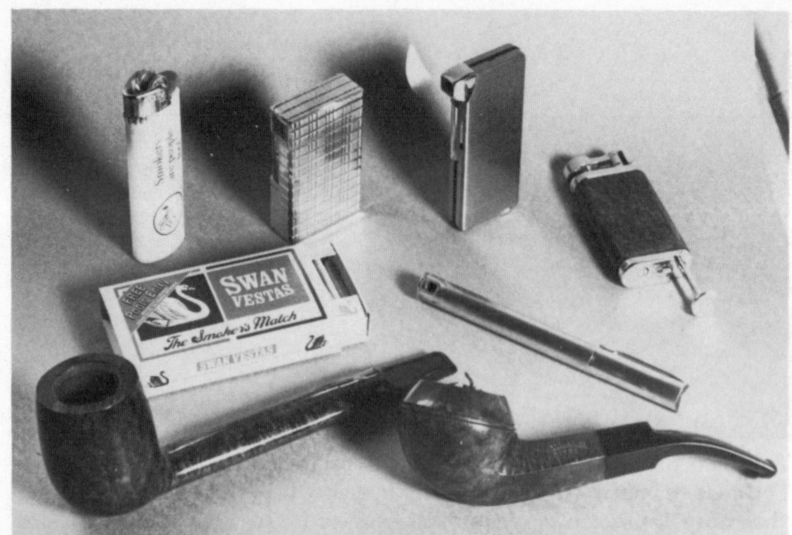

Six ways to light a pipe: Savinelli Old Boy with built-in detachable tamper, Colibri 90 degree Electric Quartz, gold Dupont, disposable gas (butane) and Colibri clip lighter. Of course, there are always the reliable wooden matches. The pipes? A Parker Tanglewood Canadian and a Hardcastle Extra Bulldog.

Your tobacco shop markets numerous pipe stands in wood, plastic and pewter that are designed to hold a variety of pipe styles.

which may permeate the air from time to time, such as the garlic stew that's been simmering on the stove all week. Tobacco is highly susceptible to the air around it.

Storing certain tobaccos in a humidor also helps to age them, just as storing leftovers from a delicious meal makes them taste all the better the next day, after the flavors have blended. An interesting phenomenon with some tinned tobaccos is that, upon opening them, they may taste slightly different from when they have been exposed to the air a while, much like letting a bottle of red wine "breathe".

Humidors can come in all varieties of styles, designs and colors to match your mood and decor. They can be covered with leather, made of porcelain, carved of wood, and even cast of silver. One of the most elaborate humidors, understandably enough, was Sir Walter Raleigh's tobacco box, which according to Mr. Ralph Thoresby of Leeds, was cylindrical in shape and measured 13 inches high by 7 inches in diameter (32 cm × 17 cm). It was covered with leather and had a "collar" with holes in it for holding his clay pipes. The container itself could hold about a pound of tobacco – clearly a month's supply for the average smoker today, but in Sir Walter's time, with those diminutive clay bowls, filling the box must have been a bi-annual event. But no matter in what century it is found, the tobacco humidor has always been a friendly addition to a room and its presence makes any dwelling a home, because you know a pipe smoker lives there.

However, it is a fact of life that pipes are not always smoked in the confines of the home and like any true friend, we find great pleasure in taking our briar, meerschaum, or corncob along with us as a stabilizing force as we meet and slay the various dragons of our daily forages into the worka-

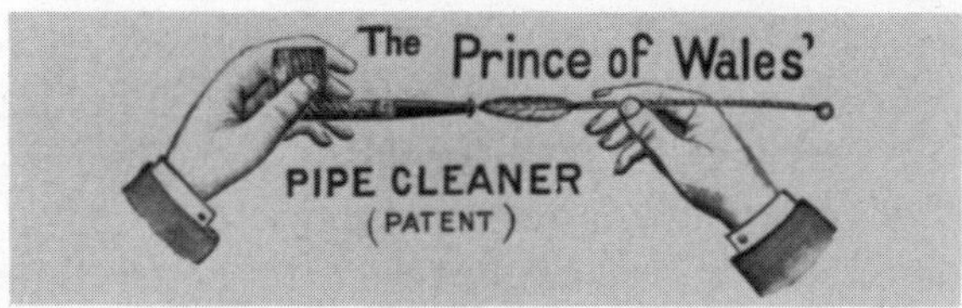

Around the early 1900s, BBB sold this rather handy adaptation of the standard feather pipe cleaner.

day world. For this reason, and as a means of keeping our pipe well-fed and taken care of while "in the field," the tobacco pouch is indispensable. In the early part of the 1600s when pipe smoking was becoming extremely fashionable in England, no well-appointed gentleman would think of venturing out without his clay pipe, tobacco-box, tongs (for plucking up a hot coal), priming iron, tinderbox, and touchwood. The tobacco was normally kept in a metal, ivory or hardened leather tobacco-box, usually elaborately engraved or decorated and featuring a storage area for one or more clay pipes. In another part of the world, the Chinese used elaborately decorated silk bags for carrying their tobacco. Later, a slung-over-the-arm style tobacco bag was used by gentlemen of the Old and New Worlds smoking their pipes while out in public and still later came the tobacco pouch, a handy, fold-over device that easily fits into the pocket and by virtue of its practicality, is still with us today.

There are many different styles of tobacco pouches, but some of the best are made of leather and are lined with a rubberized or synthetic material to keep the moist tobacco from damaging the animal skin, which can impart an unpleasant taste to the tobacco itself. Pouches are also being made from rubber or synthetic material, but nearly all of them are usually sealed with a zipper or by folding the material over itself. With the exception of the inexpensive plastic zip-lock bags that the tobacconist puts your tobacco in when you buy it, I have rarely found a pouch that is 100% airtight. One of the best tobacco pouches I ever had was made out of Australian kangaroo hide and given to me by my wife years ago, before we were married. Even though it was a simple fold-over style, that pouch would keep my tobacco moist for a week or longer. Later, well after the wedding and I, under her influence, finally succeeded in making a moderate success of myself, I purchased a rather expensive black leather pouch with a zipper and a separate compartment for my pipe and lighter. What luxury! But for some reason, that pouch never could hold moisture and my tobacco would seem to go bone dry the minute it entered the pouch. I once even considered entering the pouch in the Guinness Book of World Records as being the driest spot on earth. It literally seemed to suck my tobacco dry the very day I filled it. I have recently discovered that some of the newer brands do not exhibit this phenomena and I always believed that I had really purchased an experimental dehumidifier made from camelskin.

Unfortunately, very few of the tobacco pouches I have encountered today are completely airtight, and therefore, only a one or two day's supply of your favorite blend should be carried (usually that is all that will fit into the pouch anyway) in order to keep it fresh. I also like to keep a water-soaked metal moisturizer (sold by most tobacconists) in the pouch, which is then "sealed" either by a zipper or by folding over a flap. Naturally, environment plays an important factor as to how long your pouch will keep your tobacco moist and a lot depends on whether you are trudging across the moors in a thunderstorm or hiking across the Sahara in the summer with your pipe and pouch. Some pouches also have a self-contained compartment for storage of your pipe, but I find this a rather bulky arrangement. I much prefer to use these compartments for carrying my pipe tamper, matches and a few pipe cleaners instead, a much more practical arrangement, as that way nothing gets lost or forgotten (if you've ever tried to tamp your pipe down with your finger while driving a car you know what I mean).

Interestingly, just as clay pipes are once again becoming popular, there is a growing resurgence in the small, pocket-sized iron, brass and German silver tobacco boxes of the late 1700s and early 1800s of the American fur trade era, when such devices were carried by Kit Carson, Jim Bridger and John C. Fremont, all of whom were devout pipe smokers. Today, these well made "modern antiques" are fashioned by a fellow named Tedd Cash. Some of the current re-issues even have a magnifying lens in the cover, putting this design before 1826, the date when the sulfur match was finally perfected by an English chemist in Stockton-on-Tees.

Prior to the invention and public acceptance of the match, pipes were lit with burning embers, smouldering pieces of charred cloth (called "tinder"), flaming cedar wicks, candles, or anything else that happened to be aflame at the time. Indeed, pipe smoking was not a "strike anywhere"

With a little imagination, some scraps of wood and a rubber clip, homemade stands can be built to display pipes of unusual configurations, like this 18th century Wedgwood pipe of blue Jasperware.

What could possibly be the "Ultimate Pipe Cleaning Kit" is made by Porsche. Seven precision tools are French fitted in a magnetically-locked wood case. Silver combination tool is by DuPont. Pipe on left is a Willmer Belfair; on the right is Butz-Choquin Flamme flame grain.

Many pipe companies produce elegant assortments of leather tobacco pouches and pipe cases for the travelling pipe smoker on the go.

The U.S.-made PipeKing will not only break in your new pipe by smoking it for you, but can also rejuvenate bitter briars and will help color meerschaums as well. The filters prevent smoke from being emitted into the room. In Europe, an electric converter is needed for this device.

proposition in those early years. The sulfuric match changed all that, although they were very expensive and difficult to obtain at first. However, the economies of manufacture soon made wooden matches readily accessible and today they are still the favored method for igniting the connoisseur's pipe. From 1830 until 1914 matches were carried in Vesta Boxes, a pocket-sized metal container (shaped much like the cigarette lighter of today), usually with a hinged metal lid and a serrated edge on which to strike the match. The vesta box was replaced by the alcohol-burning flint-and-wick lighter, much to the chagrin of all knowledgeable pipe smokers (see Chapter Four, in case you missed it), which thankfully gave way to the more proper butane lighter in the 1960s, an approved form of pipe lighting that is still very much with us. In the butane lighter department, there are a number of companies now offering versions that shoot the flames straight out at a 90 degree angle from the lighter, making it easier to "dip" the flame into the bowl without scorching it or singeing the hair on your fingers, or for the ladies, without bubbling your nail polish. So popular has the butane lighter become that now special pipe-lighting models are introduced with regularity each year, so the best bet is to ask your tobacconist to show you the latest models designed exclusively for pipe smokers. Be sure to ask about the warranty and repair policy, as some lighters are better than others and have a lower rate of return.

Pipe racks are, in my mind at least, a rather uninspired necessity for the pipe smoker. They are needed to properly store your briars out of harm's way, with the bowls down so that any moisture within the wood is drained away from the mouthpiece. A pipe rack also enables the smoker to proudly inspect each of his pipes prior to picking the "best" one for that particular moment, as they stand at attention like so many briar soldiers, waiting to pass in review for you before your ultimate selection for the evening's smoking campaign, one in which the pipe and smoker always emerge the victors. However, many of today's pipe rack designs are rather plain and do not always display the briar as attractively as possible. The best pipe rack I have seen in recent times was a model that featured an enclosed dust-free case and a mirrored back, so that both sides of the pipe could be viewed. Unfortunately this product is no longer being made. In my collection I have two rather attractive pipe racks from the 1890s, but they both hold the pipes with the bowls up, exactly the opposite of where they should be.

It is the Europeans who often store their pipes with the bowls upwards, so that all the moisture is drawn into the stems. In America, the unquestioned practice is to store our pipes with the bowl downward, so that everything is directed away from the mouthpiece. Both positions seem to suggest that the pipe will be dripping wet with saliva when placed in the rack, when in fact, nothing could be further from the actual condition of your pipe if you have smoked and cleaned it properly. As discussed in Chapter Four, your pipe should be thoroughly cool, cleaned and therefore dry by the time you place it back in the rack. At worst, you will have inserted a pipe cleaner into the airhole to help sop up whatever moisture there is. A pipe rack should hold your briars in a position where air can circulate around them, thus helping to dry them out completely. The best advice I can give you for a pipe rack is to get one that you find reasonably attractive and that will hold more pipes than you presently own, so that you will have an excuse to buy more!

As both an alternative and a complement to the pipe rack, pipe rests are handy little objects to have around the house and office and make for great gift suggestions on the proper occasions, as they come in a variety of designs that can depict any subject matter, from a favorite hobby to a favorite sport. They are made of wood, pewter and ceramics and their primary function, aside from displaying one or two pipes in an attractive manner, is to keep your pipe from getting knocked off the table accidentally. They are also useful as a resting place for your pipe between puffs when you are busy doing other things with your hands.

I prefer to store my more fragile pipes, such as clays and meerschaums, in the boxes in which they originally came, rather than leave them lying about, waiting to get broken by some wayward child or cat. The only exception I make to this rule is my well-smoked clay churchwarden, which I prop up next to some antique tobacco tins that I have displayed for the envy of others. I also have a smaller but equally favorite clay stuck in a beaded buckskin Gage d'Amour, an 1840s era tobacco pouch that was designed to hang around a trapper's neck or in his lodge. I have mine, which is well tainted with campfire soot from various autumn outings, hanging from a peg in my den; the clay pipe completes the ensemble and is easy to get when I feel like a frontier smoke.

In these days of specialization, it is comforting to know that there are ashtrays made just for pipe smokers. These usually have a pipe-shaped recess for resting your briar upright and often sport a cork knob in the center of the recepticle. This soft cork knob is theoretically used for knocking the upside-down bowl or your pipe against it, to empty the pipe of ashes. (Even Emily Post, writing on the Etiquette of Smoking in *Good Housekeeping* magazine of September, 1940, admonished pipe smokers not to knock their pipes against a fragile ashtray.) However, maybe I am doing it wrong, but I keep on knocking the ashtray all over the table or at best, creating such a racket on the table that people often stop in the middle of their conversation just to watch me hammering and pounding away, like some sort of deranged carpenter. I like these ashtrays, don't get me wrong, because their presence in my home clearly indicates to even the most casual observer that I am a pipe smoker. It's a badge of office, like a college diploma, fraternal ring or regimental tie. But frankly, I find it far more practical to merely pat the après-smoked pipe bowl in the soft palm of my hand and let the ashes drop gently into the ashtray and all over that little cork thing. I suppose it is really just a matter of experience, but after more than two decades, I am still not qualified to enter the pipe pounding Olympics, whereas by now I've gotten my palm-tapping down pat.

A pipe reamer is not something a pipe smoker needs right away, but eventually it will come in handy for trimming down an overly-thick cake. Simply using a pocketknife to do this chore may result in a cake with an uneven thickness and the point of the knife could accidentally (and often does) run into the side of the briar, causing a nick and a potential burnout spot. Most reamers are adjustable or come in sets of various sizes to fit different diameter bowls. By a slow and careful twisting of the sharp cutting blades within the bowl, a pipe reamer can trim away a thick cake in minutes. I also use my reamer for carefully scraping off some of the carbon buildup in my meerschaums so that the coloring process can continue, but care must be used as overexuberance can inadvertently cause some of the soft meerschaum to be trimmed away as well.

Practically all pipe smokers, within the past century at least – no matter how obscure or how famous they might have been or still may be – have owned at least some of the basic pipe smoking accessories that we have discussed in this chapter. If the truth be known, few of us care about the obscure pipe smokers, but in the next chapter we shall meet some of the more famous ones and we might find out we even have something in common with all of them.

In the United States, patriotism has played a major role in the identity of many tobacco brands. In this advertisement from the 1890s, America's symbolic Uncle Sam is shown proudly puffing on a briar filled with Union Leader tobacco. Today, the same advertisement could be used to promote an individual's freedom to smoke a pipe.

Chapter Eight

Famous Pipe Smokers in History, Literature & Entertainment

"I do not believe that intelligence and creative thinking are injured by smoking."

– Emile Zola

It stands to reason that such a notable creation as the pipe should itself attract an ageless gathering of notable personages around it. After all, should not society spotlight the pipe, just as it focuses its public eye on some of history's most admired and influential celebrities? It's no surprise then, to learn that the pipe, which personifies all that is respected, intellectual and honorable among mankind, has created an entire new sub-species of Homo Sapiens, the *Pipe Smokerus Venerabilis.* It is a fact that, up until the ill-fated Watergate scandal, no criminal had ever been known to smoke a pipe. And in a recent police case study of the Westside of Los Angeles, which has had its share of crime, there has never been an arrest made of a single pipe smoking individual. Moreover, Britain, which has a relatively low crime rate, has a comparatively high rate of pipe smokers. It is plainly evident, then, that pipe smoking only attracts the very best that civilization has to offer. We are not talking about income or net worth or the size of an individual's dwelling or the cost of his car; what we are referring to here is *character*, the one common link that all pipe smokers, from the Dark Ages and puffing through the millenniums to perpetuity, have in common with each other. We are all a noble lot, and history has chosen to record the names of some of the more notable in our pipe smoking realm.

Take the earliest of our clan, for example. The written word and the art of pipe smoking have been inseparably linked ever since the clay was introduced to England. That literary chap Sir Francis Bacon was among the first to take up pipe smoking in polite society and one of the great mysteries of olden days is why his contemporary and fellow drinking companion Shakespeare never joined him in a bowlful of the "scandalous weed" when he was all too willing to share a flagon of ale at the famed Mermaid Tavern. Perhaps it was because Will the poet was esteemed by King James, and fully realizing that where there was smoke there was ire, decided not to risk arousing the wrath of his anti-tobacco king. Lord Byron and Lord Tennyson not only shared the gift of being able to create some of the world's most lasting poetry in their times and beyond, but are further linked together by the fact that they had a common love of pipe smoking, and no one will ever know how many clays were responsible for inspiring some of England's most immortal sonnets. It was Tennyson who exhibited the unique quirk of never wishing to smoke the same pipe twice. He kept a box full of clays at his feet while he worked, and after finishing the first and only bowlful of a new pipe, he would break it in two and toss it into a second empty box which he kept just for that purpose. Later poets and essayists such as Ralph Waldo Emerson and Carl Sandburg would share Tennyson's earlier inspiration for the pipe, but not his penchant for creating the first premeditated "smoking break." Early in the 19th century, famed English essayist, Charles (Elia) Lamb was once asked how he came to be such an ardent pipe smoker. "I toiled after it, Sir," was his reply, "as some men toil after virtue!"

That same type of philosophy might have been expressed a bit differently by the home-spun upbringing of Davy Crockett, the frontier hero from Tennessee who remained a faithful corncob pipe smoker before he went to Congress and well after, taking his favorite pipe with him to the Alamo. But as far as a dedicated pipe smoker who was also a prominent public figure, perhaps one of the greatest visible

Professor Albert Einstein was a lifelong pipe smoker and preferred briars with deep bents.

literary champions of the pipe was the celebrated author and humorist Samuel Langhorne Clemens, who no doubt gave himself an inner chuckle with his riverboat-days inspired pen name of Mark Twain, but who took his pipe smoking seriously, as we have already noted in Chapter Four. Clemens knew how to enjoy his pipes. He and his wife Olivia used to hold dinner parties at their picturesque home in Hartford, Connecticut, where the celebrated author would entertain his guests with his wit and wisdom under a white haze of tobacco smoke as it rose up from his shaggy head and drifted towards the high ceiling of the billiard room, which was decorated with a motif of pool cues and pipes. Like some of the characters in his stories, the author "Mark Twain" smoked corncobs, but was more partial to calabashes and Peterson pipes and is known to have kept at least two of the Irish briars by his bedside. Once, during a speech about his youth, he recalled, ". . . Afterward I learned the delight of a pipe, and I suppose there was no youngster of my age who could more deftly cut a plug of tobacco as to make it available for pipe smoking."

Other pipe smoking authors include Herman Melville, Rudyard Kipling, Somerset Maugham, and Sinclair Lewis. However, one of the most enthusiastically exuberant writers in praise of the pipe was Scotland's J. M. Barrie, the celebrated author of *Peter Pan* but who also wrote an equally lasting work entitled, *My Lady Nicotine*, in 1890. The book has since become a hard-to-find classic among pipe smokers and one of the Great Mysteries of Life among those who have read this volume is the true identity of the Arcadia Mixture that Barrie held in such high esteem. So let it be known for now and all time that the Arcadia was none other than the no-longer produced Craven A Mixture, once sold by Carreras Ltd. in London. In fact, at the request of the tobacconist, and owing to Barrie's immense popularity at the time, the celebrated author wrote:

> Dear Sirs: In answer to your letter, it is the Craven Mixture – and no other – that I call the Arcadia in "My Lady Nicotine."

The letter was dated January 19, 1897, and for years it

Award-winning motion picture actor Jack Lemmon, who is equally skilled at both comedy and drama, is also a dedicated pipe smoker who favors the high grades.

Noted Hollywood television producer Aaron Spelling is rarely seen without his pipe. Although he lives in a $12 million mansion that boasts over 56,000 square feet of living space, a bowling alley, screening room, four garages and a separate guard house, he prefers to smoke a small pipe with an unpretentious Group 2 or 3 bowl.

Former U.S. President Gerald R. Ford is a lifelong pipe smoker. He prefers ". . . a small, easy to carry pipe," and his favorite tobaccos are Field & Stream and Walnut, both traditional American blends, appropriately enough.

Britain's ex-Prime Minister Harold Wilson (now Lord Wilson) did much to popularize the pipe in his homeland. It is very possible that the pipe he is smoking in this photo was given to him by President Ford, who purchased it as a gift for the Prime Minister at Curtis Draper's pipe shop in Washington, D.C.

was reprinted with pride on every tin of Craven, with the letter "A" being added afterwards, for Arcadia. Barrie never received a shilling for the endorsement he so freely gave, even though it invariably helped sell enough tobacco to enable the shop owner to retire from the tobacco business three years later.

If Craven A (disguised as the Arcadia Mixture) was one of the most celebrated Victorian English pipe tobaccos, then by far one of the most celebrated Victorian English pipe smokers is so legendary a figure there are some who doubt that he even existed. It is none other than the world's first consulting detective, Sherlock Holmes. In the course of 60 different Arthur Conan Doyle stories, Holmes smokes a pipe in 54 of the adventures, while his more sedate colleague and chronicler Dr. Watson is only reported to be smoking a pipe in seven of the tales. Yet, for all of his pipe and tobacco expertise, Holmes persists with some of the vilest smoking habits ever recorded upon the printed page. For example, he saves all of the "plugs and dottles" (those tar-stained remnants left in the moist heel of the pipe) from the previous day's smoke, dries them out and resmokes them! Holmes also keeps his tobacco in the toe of a Persian slipper that hangs by the fireplace in what must be one of the driest spots in all of London. And he stores his pipes with the bits lower than the bowl, thereby letting everything drain into the mouthpiece.

It is not too presumptuous to assume that Holmes' pipe smoking habits may have been partially patterned after those of Sir Arthur Conan Doyle's, a pipe smoker himself, who added perhaps a bit more drama to foster reader interest. Yet, Holmes followed the philosophy of smoking a different tobacco at various times of the day (as we discussed in Chapter Five), to match his changing moods. For example, in "The Engineer's Thumb," he is reported "Smoking his before-breakfast pipe." In "Charles Augustus Milverton" he is "smoking his morning pipe," his "evening pipe" is smoked in "Wisteria Lodge," and his morning pipe is puffed again in "The Three Garidebs," at which time he goes back for a second bowlful. Given Holmes' penchant for experimentation with various types of tobaccos, it is logical to assume that, at various times, he changed his pipe tobacco so that a different one was consumed at different times of the day. However, we all have our favorites and Holmes had a preference for Shag tobacco, while Watson smokes Ship's, a not altogether mild rough-cut and coarse blend. Together they must have made a pungent pair, permeating the sitting room of 221B Baker Street with the heady aroma of their pipes forever in literary history.

So powerful is the pipe smoking characteristic of Sherlock Holmes that it has touched virtually every actor who ever played the role of that detective in front of an audience. One of the first was William Gillette, a famed Turn of the Century Thespian who portrayed Holmes from 1901 to 1937 and who indirectly caused the affected use of the calabash in a good-humored retaliation for a spoof of his own highly successful Sherlockian stage play (Holmes never smoked a calabash in any of the Conan Doyle stories, preferring instead, the briar, clay and cherrywood pipes). Peter Cushing is a well known British pipe smoking actor who appeared as a natural in his Sherlock Holmes role in the 1967 version of "The Hound of the Baskervilles." Yet, up until recently, the most famous of all theatrical personifications of Sherlock Holmes was Basil Rathbone, an accomplished actor who only took up pipe smoking to better portray his roles. But now that title may have to be surrendered to British actor Jeremy Brett for his uncanny assimilation of the Holmes pipe smoking character.

Of course, one of the most famous actor-singer-pipe smokers was Bing Crosby, who adopted the pipe as a part of his personality so completely, that today the "Crosby" pipe is a term which immediately conjures up a mental picture of the thin-stemmed, high-bowled briar that was a favorite of "Der Bingle."

Clark Gable was a pipe smoker; years later, actor Lee Van Cleef puffed on his meerschaum as he played a bounty hunter opposite Clint Eastwood in one of the many "spaghetti westerns" of the 1960s. And muscular actor Arnold Schwarzenegger continues to find strength whenever he picks up one of his many briars to smoke.

Actor William Conrad, who was the voice of Marshall Matt Dillon on the old 'Gunsmoke' radio series and who today is an accomplished stage and screen actor, is also an

Mark Twain found that his pipes helped him see the more enjoyable side of life. Here he is shown relaxing with a favored calabash.

General Douglas MacArthur, in a rare photo taken without his sunglasses but still with pipe, was originally introduced to the corncob by General "Black Jack" Pershing.

J. R. R. Tolkien always enjoyed a good briar, although he knew that pipes were not Hobbit-forming!

Well-known disc jockey, "Top of the Pops" personality and BBC1 music host Dave Lee Travis maintains perfect harmony with his pipe. No wonder he was awarded Pipeman of the Year in 1982.

Scottish-born Malcolm Jamieson is a popular actor on numerous British and American television programs. To the public he is perhaps best known as Claude Dupont in the BBC series "Howard's Way"; to his friends he is also recognized as an enthusiastic pipe smoker who favors meerschaums.

enthusiastic pipe collector and smoker. He owns over one thousand pipes, of which 400 are Charatans, many of them rare freehands, of sizes and shapes that would make each of them a centerpiece in any collection. His pipes are so well smoked that one calabash looks like an antique, even though Bill insists that he bought it new. Because of his special fondness for Charatans, Bill was one of the first "outsiders" to visit the old London Charatan factory back in the late 1960s and he still has fond memories of the trip; when the Charatan company found out that an actor of his stature was such a devoted fan of their pipes, the firm presented him with yet another briar for his collection. He owns and smokes a number of antiques, but prefers the high grades and when he opens a drawer to search for some tobacco, a gold-banded Nørding is casually lying in among the bags of Burley. Like many pipe smokers, Bill Conrad has spent years looking for the "perfect" tobacco. "Dunhill must have three thousand and one custom blends," he says, "of which 3,000 must have been mine, looking for the right mixture!" Today he smokes Amphora Red.

Ted Shackelford, the talented television actor who first started hearts throbbing on "Knot's Landing" and who since has branched out into motion pictures, uses his pipes to help him relax while on the set and refers to his high grade briars as "props." "They are great devices," he says, giving an admiring glance to the Dunhill double sandblast he is smoking. "You can hide behind them, use them to accent your character, or simply sit in a chair and be contemplative with them." Ted has a deep appreciation of quality briar and takes special pride in selecting the pipes that he smokes, picking each one out with the same care as he exercises when reading a screenplay. Weaned from cigarette smoking, pipes have now become an enjoyable part of this popular actor's life.

The late Edward G. Robinson not only smoked pipes but even had a pipe tobacco named for him, complete with his photograph on the package. James Whitmore, famed for his one-man shows depicting such historical figures as Theodore Roosevelt and Harry Truman, is a dedicated pipe smoker. Musician David Rose, who composes many of the popular American television themes, puffs a pipe and enjoys collecting unusual shapes. British actor Edward Fox is a pipe smoker who was first seen by American television audiences when he portrayed the pipe smoking Duke of Windsor. Actor James Sikking, whose talents were brought to the public's attention in the highly-acclaimed television series, "Hill Street Blues," is a pipe smoker, as were Egyptian president Anwar Sadat, psychologist Carl Jung, and even Paul McCartney's father.

In the field of science Albert Schweitzer, Jonas Salk and Albert Einstein are only a few of the many who are part of the pipe smoker's fraternity. An interesting story about Einstein was once related by the late Bennett Cerf (a pipe smoker himself), in his book *Try and Stop Me* (Simon & Schuster, 1944). It seems the world-renowned scientist ran out of pipe tobacco during a seminar he was giving one afternoon. One of the students suggested that the professor crumble up some cigarettes and fill his pipe with them.

"Gentlemen," said Einstein as he lit up, "I think we have made a great discovery!"

However, in the end, the experiment proved to be a failure, as anyone who has tried it can testify.

In art, as in literature, the pipe smokers are many and Norman Rockwell is one of the first to come to mind as portraying himself as the image of America in a now-famous self-portrait, complete with briar jutting forcefully out of his mouth. On the other end of the scale, Vincent Van Gogh was a pipe smoker who included pipes in many of his paintings such as "Still Life with Straw Hat" (1885), "Chair and Pipe" (1888) and "Still Life With Onions." Van Gogh appears with his pipe in his mouth in two of his most memorable self-portraits, painted before and after the "ear incident," proving that he might sacrifice his ear, but never his pipe!

The military has never been without its pipe smokers, the most famous of which was General Douglas MacArthur and his well-known corncob. But what most people do not know is that the media-wise general was first introduced to the corncob by General John "Black Jack" Pershing, a Missouri-born lad who had a natural penchant for corncob country. Dwight Eisenhower was another pipe smoking general and serves double distinction in joining the long ranks of America's pipe smoking presidents, which encompass John Adams, Andrew Jackson, Herbert Hoover and Gerald Ford.

Other well-known pipe smokers include Jules Maigret author Georges Simenon, British novelist J. B. Priestley, and ex-Prime Minister Lord Wilson (who was proclaimed Pipeman of the Decade in 1976). As might be expected, many of England's royal family have maintained the pipe smoking tradition, including King George V and the Prince of Wales (Duke of Windsor). In the old Charatan factory, a document existed from King Edward VIII, in which His Majesty commanded that the "enclosed pipe be repaired while the messenger waits". That was probably one of the fastest and most thorough pipe repairs in history!

Of course, it takes famous people to make famous quotes, and when those quotes concern pipe smoking, they are worth repeating here:

Kenneth Grahame, the celebrated author of *The Wind in the Willows*, wrote in 1898 of a morning pipe, that it is "smoked on a clearer palate, and comes to unjaded senses like the kiss of one's first love." That it reminds us of a leisure time and relaxed ways of "Sunday, holidays and the like – the whole joy and peace of which are summed up in that one beautiful pipe after breakfast, smoked in a careless majesty . . . Then only can we be said to really smoke. And so this particular pipe of the day always carries with it festal reminiscences: memories of holidays past, hopes for holidays to come; a suggestion of sunny lawns and flannels . . ."

19th century English biologist and writer Professor Thomas Henry Huxley, in speaking to a debate on "Smoking" among the members of the British Association, stated, ". . . There is no more harm in a pipe than there is in a cup of tea. You may poison yourself by drinking too much green tea and kill yourself by eating too many beef-steaks. For my own part, I consider that tobacco, in moderation, is a sweetener and equalizer of the temper."

Finally, there are some people who might not have been noteworthy at all, were it not for the pipe. Take the case of Jim Purol. As of this writing, he holds the world's record for smoking the most pipes simultaneously, having managed to

Although England's Arthur Wontner made many films, the five Sherlock Holmes movies he did in the 1930s earned him the title of "*the* Sherlock Holmes of British film", a role in which his pipe shared equal billing.

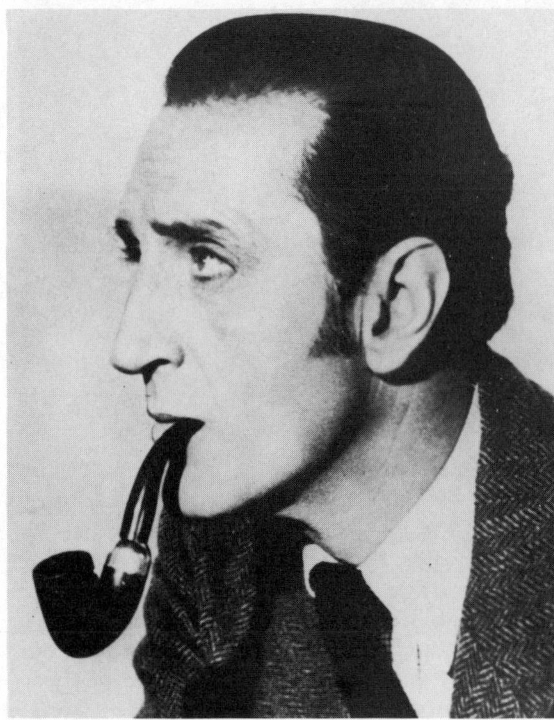

Basil Rathbone was the ultimate screen personification of Sherlock Holmes, and became a pipe smoker just for the part. He is shown here smoking a Peterson, which he used in many of the movies.

William Conrad has been a lifelong pipe smoker and owns one of the finest Charatan collections in the country, as evidenced by the straight grain Charatan freehand he is smoking. A Nørding rests in the ashtray on his desk.

Britain's former champion boxer, Henry Cooper, enjoys his pipes, including the specially made one he is smoking that is carved like a boxing glove. It was awarded to him as 1984 Pipeman of the Year, a title he can add to all the rest, including Former British, Commonwealth, and European Heavyweight Champion, winner of three Lonsdale Belts, and being awarded the OBE and the KSG.

Television star Ted Shackelford gave up cigarettes for pipes and has not regretted it. Not only does he enjoy smoking his Dunhill and Upshall high grades, but the briars have added to his public image.

British actor Edward Fox is a pipe smoker who made a notable impression with American television viewers when he portrayed the pipe smoking Duke of Windsor.

cram 38 briars into his mouth at one time. One wonders at how he was able to keep them all lit and he probably had to hire the entire Liverpool football team to do the tamping.

Then there is the late Lord Shinwell, Britain's first (and no doubt only) individual ever to become Pipeman of the Century. He lived to see his 100th birthday in October 1984, after having smoked a pipe every day since 1898, when he took his first puff at the age of fourteen.

Thomas Nast's famous sketches of Santa Claus always portrayed the jolly old elf with a pipe, which has changed from clay to briar over the years, proving St. Nick can adapt to the times, just as long as he doesn't have to give up his pipe. This drawing was for a 1881 edition of *Harper's Weekly*.

Not the most famous, but certainly the most prolific pipe smoker in history was a fellow from Holland named Mynheer van Klaes, who consumed approximately four tons of tobacco during his rather successful lifetime. Upon his death, his will stipulated that all the smokers of the countryside should come to his funeral and smoke their pipes throughout the ceremony. Then, according to his wishes, as his coffin was lowered into the ground, all mourners scattered the ashes of their pipes into the grave. As each one filed out of the cemetery, they were presented with ten pounds of tobacco and two new pipes bearing van Klaes' name and family crest.

And they say you can't take it with you!

Chapter Nine

The Collectible Pipe

A pipe to make the royal Friedrich jealous,
Or the great Teufelscrockh with envy gripe!
A man should hold some rank above his fellows
To justify his smoking such a pipe!

– On Receipt of a Rare Pipe
W.H.B. (19th Century)

Being a collector of more than one type of inanimate object, I have often pondered late into the night, accompanied by only a smoking briar to serve as friend, hand-warmer and night light, just what makes such a thing valuable? Why is a gold coin worth more today than yesterday? What makes grandpa's old jalopy sit in the garage rusting because nobody can be paid to haul it away while three states over, someone is frantically advertising in all the rare car magazines trying to find just such a vehicle? And why are some limited edition "collectibles" nothing more than calculated rip-offs of the public while others soar in value immediately after their first offering?

Welcome to the world of collectibles, a multifaceted society founded on facts, guided by rationale, and ruled by emotion. It has existed ever since man first began to know the meaning of the word "possess" and has come to encompass everything from stamps to steamboats. Needless to say, this aura of accumulation has not escaped pipes and pipe smokers, although many people are not yet aware that they collect anything other than an awful lot of good smokes from their briars. Others are not only cognizant of the fact that they own some of the world's rarest pieces of briar and meerschaum, but take extra care to see that their smokable treasures are securely locked away from mortal view and scorching match. Fortunately, there is room for all variances of the collecting philosophy in this rather far-ranging assemblage of individuals, who may or may not actually smoke the pipes they so enthusiastically acquire and covet.

Though not openly publicized until recent years, pipe collecting is far from being a new phenomenon. During the reign of King Louis XVIII, the Duc de Richelieu's pipe collection was reported to be worth over 100,000 francs. President Andrew Jackson was a pipe collector and so was King Farouk. Pipe collecting has also attracted numerous entertainment celebrities such as Bing Crosby, Edward G. Robinson, William Conrad, Jack Lemmon and others throughout the world, many of whom I cannot mention due to requests of anonymity, which I must honor. However, I feel safe in stating that one of the most prolific pipe collectors of all time was a man by the name of William Bragge (a dubious name for any collector) who passed away in 1884 and left his widow with an estate of over 7,000 pipes.

Because of the intrinsic role they continue to play in both history and art, it is a shame that until recently, pipes have been somewhat ignored by the mass media, pushed into the background by more inanimate tokens of man's collecting folly, such as baseball cards, beer cans and matchbook covers (the *paper* kind, which as everyone knows, are of absolutely no use to the civilized world). However, in the U.S. at least, a series of events took place that started to change all that and began gradually to bring pipes from the backstage shadows into the full spotlight of public view. The first incident took place in 1976 when, because of my involvement as publicity consul for the 200-store Tinder Box chain, I selected a number of antique pipes from their corporate collection, assembled them in exhibit format, and began displaying them around the nation in various tobacco stores. Through a concentrated public relations effort, these pipes began appearing on television news shows and in newspapers all across the United States. Suddenly, pipes made from meerschaum, seashells, amber and pewter were media stars, albeit their exposure was purposely confined to the local areas in which they were being displayed. But at least the public was finally being exposed to antique pipes as works of art that had a very real value as collectibles.

A few years later, a number of combination “pipe shows and swap meets” began popping up in various cities around the U.S. These shows created an atmosphere where pipe collectors could buy, trade, sell and display their smokable treasures. More importantly, they showed the public that pipe collectors existed and convinced individual pipe enthusiasts that there were others just like them. Nothing like that had ever happened to the American pipe smoker before. Unlike the antique pipe display that I had created a few years earlier, these pipe shows concentrated mainly on 20th century briars, many of which were still being smoked by their owners, or were at least “smokable”. Names such as Dunhill, Charatan and Barling began commanding more money than some of the lesser-grade pipes, even though the pipes were “used”, or estate pipes as they were now being called. Because of their exposure to some of the older premium briars and a gradual sophistication in taste, American demand was growing for many of the older English brands that were no longer available or were in short supply. Comoy Blue Ribands, Dunhill ODAs and Charatan freehands began commanding premium prices. Today, 20th century pipe collecting has become one of the “hottest” hobbies in America, although our European brethren often have a hard time understanding this phenomenon.

In Europe, it is clearly the antique pipes that are collected and the 20th century ones that are smoked, with a very distinct differentiation made between the two. Most European pipe smokers are just that, and do not think of their briars as a collection. By contrast, many Americans take great pride in displaying and smoking the same pipe and there are some who will purchase an extremely rare newly-made straight grain, for example, and put it away in a safe, never to see the light of a match. The same is true for many of the limited edition year pipes and commemoratives, although I take great pleasure in smoking my Dunhill Sherlock Holmes commemorative, believing that all pipes are made to both covet and to smoke! Interestingly, antique

The young lady holds two extremely rare antiques. On the left is a walnut burl Ulm pipe made during the first half of the nineteenth century. It is fitted with an elaborate silver cap that has two tiny deer on either side. The stem is made of horn and carved ivory. The pipe on the right is carved meerschaum with an amber cap and solid gold fittings around the rim of the bowl. The stem is of yellow amber.

Two exquisitely carved meerschaum pipe bowls from the 19th century – even the teeth have been carved inside the Viking's mouth.

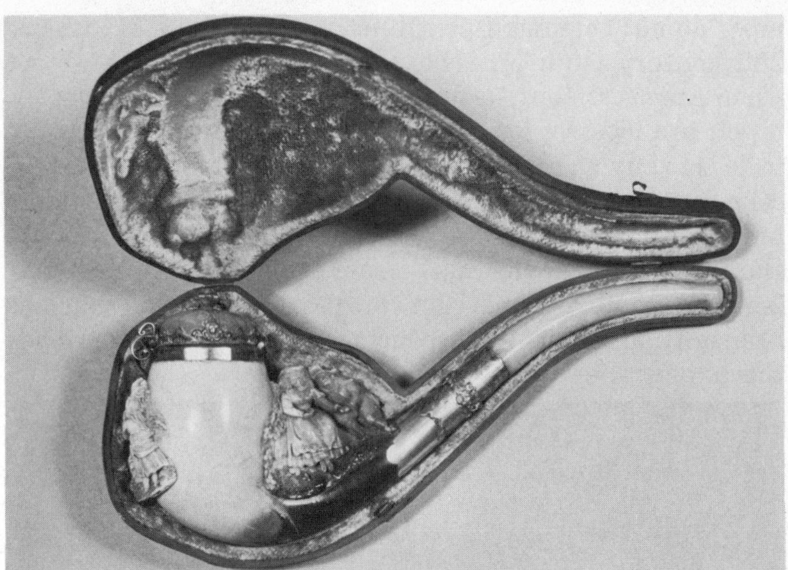

Elegant older pipes came with their own fitted case, which accounts for the survival rate of many of these fragile pipes.

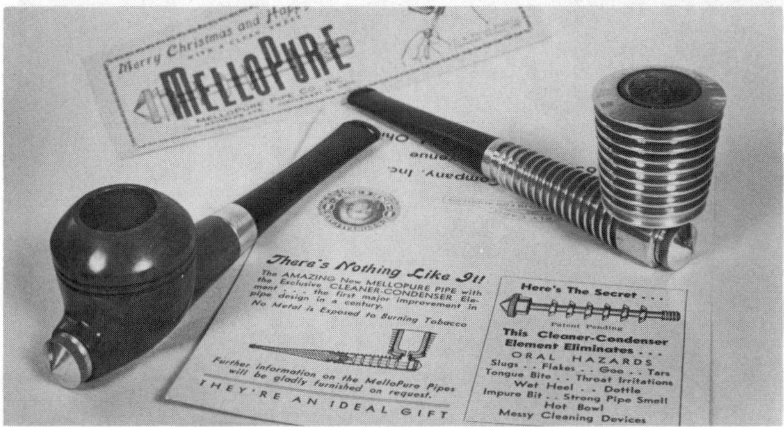

Not all collectible pipes have to be antique. These curious American pipes date from just before World War II and were the brainchild of Dr. Harry Paine, an engineering professor who devised a unique multi-chambered filtration system that unscrewed from the front of the pipe stem for cleaning. Called the MelloPure, the pipes were only marketed briefly before the war broke out. They were stored away for decades until discovered recently in Dr. Paine's garage by his heirs. While relatively unknown, these unique system pipes are part of pipe smoking history and form an interesting link to a chronological collection.

pipes do not command premium prices in the U.S., just as 20th century estate pipes have little value in Europe (except when American tourists buy them, of course!). Consequently, if you are looking for a money-making venture, the thing to do is to buy up all the cheap old smokable pipes in Europe, take them to America and sell them, then use the profits to purchase antique pipes in the U.S. and bring them back to Europe. Whatever the case, please realize that this chapter is written from an American viewpoint, by a writer who has been only slightly influenced by many pipe-smoking friends throughout the world.

A spectacular meerschaum, carved in 1871 to commemorate the marriage of H.R.H. the Princess Louise and the Marquess of Lorne. The silver crowned pipe was patterned after an illustration of the wedding that appeared in the "Illustrated London News". In 1978 it was purchased by the Dunhill museum for £2,200.

Credit: Dunhill Collection

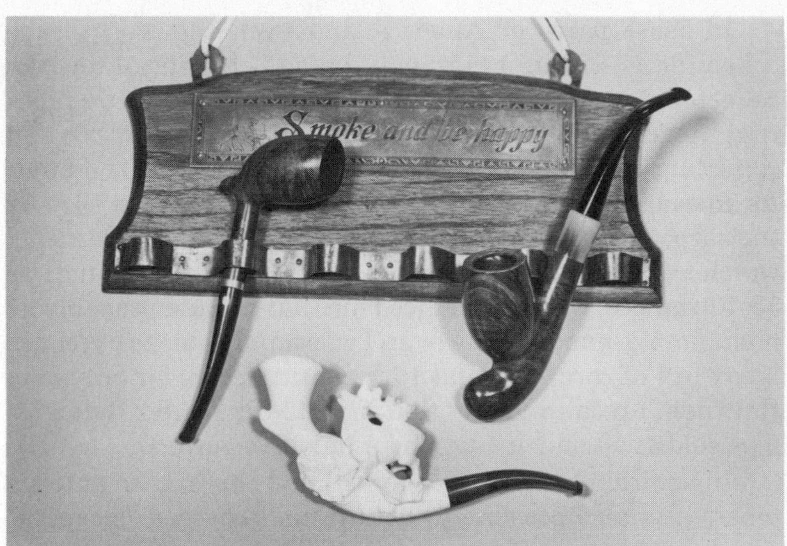

Reproductions of antique pipes are popular today and are as smokable as when these pipe designs were in style during the 1890s. In the rack is (L.) the 19th century Cavalier, made today in Saint-Claude, France and (R.) an 1890s bent reissue made by Gefapip. Interestingly, both briars are made by descendants of the pipemaking families who originally produced them in the last century. Below is one of the antique meerschaum replicas now being imported from Turkey. The pipe comes with an extra, smaller bowl for smoking cheroots. Some Turkish carvers can re-create fairly accurate copies of antique meerschaums for collectors who do not wish to smoke their originals.

A high flying rarity is this 1982 limited edition 14k gold banded Dunhill made to commemorate the space shuttle flight. Yes, the miniature pipe is smokable.

In most parts of America and even the world, pipe collecting is still in its infancy, which is beneficial for new collectors for it makes it possible for them to find rare pipes that are affordable. Even in some of the more sophisticated collecting circles it is possible to stumble across good buys. As an example, during a well-publicized sale held in 1978 by the respected auctioneering firm of Sotheby Park-Bernet, I watched dejectedly as antique pipes fetched as much as $3,400 apiece, which convinced me that I would probably go home empty-handed. However, I was finally able to purchase a box full of rare 18th and 19th century clays for only $10. But then, I recall reading that in 1911 Sir Walter Raleigh's pipe sold at a London auction for only five guineas.

In addition to being able to still find bargains in antique pipes, it is also possible to obtain undiscovered "sleepers" and desirable estate pipes for affordable prices. In fact, I was admonished by one collector *not* to include this chapter in my book for fear that the world would be awakened to the true value of some of the older pipes. Unfortunately, many antique dealers have already convinced themselves that any pipe with a spider web inside its bowl must be valuable, so they price it accordingly and then wonder why it never sells. Obviously, not having enough knowledge can be detrimental. Besides, the guiding purpose of this book is to inform the reader, for only by knowing the facts can one determine the true value of things. The law of supply and demand takes care of the rest.

The simple truth is that not every old pipe is an antique and in fact, may not even be desirable as a collectible, especially if it is poorly made, has been poorly smoked, or badly mistreated. Moreover, many pipes have an intrinsic value all their own; their real worth may be known only to the owner, and the pipe otherwise would not be worth a second glance. Pipes owned by departed relatives or notable smokers fall into this category. It must be remembered that the value of any collectible is based upon three things; in order of importance, they are: 1) desirability, 2) condition, and (as a distinct third) 3) rarity.

As to age, *Pipe Line* editor Jacques Cole considers pipes made before 1920 are *antiques*, those made between the world wars are *classics*, and pipes made since then, but which are at least 20 years old, are *vintage*. In the U.S., nothing is "officially" declared an antique unless it was made prior to 1898. *Vintage* is anything old and a *classic* is something desirable but no longer made. Fortunately, there are no rules to pipe collecting, thank goodness. Some collectors will seek out any high grade, no matter what the brand, while others only covet a single maker's product or one of its variations. Personally, I do not choose to limit myself to any one category of pipe, but instead, prefer to expand my collectible pipes in as broad a range as my interests and finances will permit. Some I smoke; some I display. But all my pipes have one thing in common: I like them!

The collector who chooses 20th century briars usually smokes them, whereas the antique pipe collector normally has his pipes only for display. Of course, there are exceptions to everything and the owner of a mint condition, unsmoked Dunhill ODA (a large-bowled pipe which we will discuss in greater detail later on in this chapter) may elect to keep it that way, while a collector with a rare 19th century Barling might get immense satisfaction from smoking this older briar, which may be made of wood more exquisite than what is commonly found on the market today. As an aside, one interesting thing about collecting antique pipes is that meerschaums are never more than 250 years old while briars must always be less than 200 years old, just by the very nature of the time of their popularity. Thus, if one wanted to collect truly ancient pipes, he would have to concentrate on the earliest of the South American effigy pipes.

Although the pipe collecting mania embraces both dealers and individuals, most true collectors are not in it for any real monetary benefits, a point that most of them, without a moment's hesitation, readily admit. Naturally, a professional tobacconist or pipe broker must plan on making a profit to compensate him for his time, effort and display space in handling these collectibles. However, most private collectors are more intent upon upgrading their collection and would rather trade a pipe than sell it. What then is the motivating force that causes so many to spend time, money and energy on long distance phone calls, postage and shipping, disappointments over "lost deals" and countless hours in written correspondence over mere chunks of meerschaum and briar?

One of the obvious attractions of most collectible pipes is their quality and workmanship. Another factor is the psychological drive to own what is no longer available or is not easy to obtain. Additionally, many collectors simply like smoking older pipes because of the better wood and the fact that not only are they well-broken in, but they have a certain patina to them that a smoker might never be able to achieve in his own lifetime, especially if he has many "favorites" that all detract from the total smoking time he can lavish on any one pipe. But not all pipe collectors are smokers and I know of one Beverly Hills professional who abhors smoking of any kind, but has his office decorated with antique pipes simply because they are "nice to look at." Thus, the collectible pipe strengthens our own ranks by bridging the gap between smoker and non-smoker alike and therein is the main impetus of its attraction: it is the pipe's overall image as a symbol of understanding, knowledge, security and a sense that all is right with the world.

Perhaps it is because of this image that the majority of pipe collectors are, or have been at one time, pipe smokers. Moreover, they usually collect pipes that are smokable and in America, at least, that trend has focused the greatest attention on the high grade briars, many of which are no longer being made, or, due to the scarcity of a certain design, are in extremely short supply.

In the Sourcebook Section (Chapter Ten) I have attempted to list most of the more popular briar manufacturers in the world, giving a brief history of each firm so that the pipe smoker will have a greater appreciation of his hobby. However, because many of these same pipes are enthusiastically collected in either new or "pre-smoked" versions, this information may also be of interest to the collector who may or may not find his favorite briar listed in this chapter, as only the more recognized collectible pipes are discussed here.

In compiling this list, because of my long-term working relationship with the pipe industry, plus the fact that many of these pipemakers are personal acquaintances of mine, I had greater access to information and company records than most individuals. Yet, in spite of these obvious advantages, I have found that there is simply not much factual material to be found regarding some of our most respected pipemakers. Sadly, many of these grand old pipe companies simply have not kept track of their histories. They were merely in business to make quality pipes and, without the benefit of hindsight, were not aware of the interest and importance their pipes would one day have as high grade collectibles. Thus, much of the old knowledge is lost, and while rumors and suppositions abound, I choose to only acknowledge the facts. Fortunately, individuals such as George Cushman and his no longer-existing *Pipe Lovers Magazine* and Jacques Cole with the current *Pipe Line* have done much in chronicling some of our past pipe smoking history. In addition, many of our pipemaking pioneers are still very much with us and I was able to obtain new information and to verify suspected facts on a firsthand basis. Nonetheless, I feel it would be a noble effort on the part of pipemakers today if they would begin to document not only their past histories, but their current achievements while this information is still obtainable. In the interim, I have attempted to gather the mere dottle of material that it was possible to accumulate. If some companies seem to be covered more thoroughly than others, it is simply a reflection upon the amount of information I was able to procure and verify. To my knowledge, this is the first time such a comprehensive list has been put together.

By far the most popular collectible pipe in the U.S. is Dunhill. That prestigious British firm has been indirectly and unknowingly responsible for helping to create the collecting interest in their pipes, as they are the only brand in which the pipes can be accurately dated. For example, up until 1955, all Dunhill pipes had a patent number and a one or two digit year date, whereby a collector could determine the exact year his pipe was made. Since 1955, the patent dates have been omitted and the pipes have been stamped with only the numerical digit. From 1955 until 1960, all Dunhills had a single digit, sometimes underlined, denoting the last number of the year it was made; this digit was half the size of the "D" in "England," which was stamped on the pipe. From 1961 to 1964 this system continued, but without the underlining, and from 1965 to 1970 the number was enlarged to the same size as the "D" in England. All Dunhills made in the 1970s have two digits with a line, starting with the number 11 for 1971, 12 for 1972 and so on. Pipes made in the 1980s have had the first number changed to a 2 and the second digit is the year in which the pipe was made (i.e., 21 for 1981, 22 for 1982, etc.). The origins of this dating system had nothing to do with the collector; it was started because of the firm's one-year guarantee from date of manufacture. Nonetheless, precise dating is a luxury few other brands, with the exception of some one-year-only limited editions, are able to offer the collector. Patent number Dunhills are highly sought after, as are the larger sizes.

Alfred Dunhill opened his pipe shop in 1907 but did not make his first pipe until 1910. Interestingly, following the trend of the times, these first pipes had a metal filter (which he felt was an improvement over the glass filters so common back then). Up until 1919, all Dunhill bowls were made in France and then finished by Dunhill workers in London. The famous "white dot" on the Dunhill stems first appeared in 1912 and was put there to show which end was "up."

All currently made Dunhill pipes come in one of the following finishes: the original dark reddish-brown "Bruyere", introduced around 1910, when Dunhill began selling his own brand; the "Shell", a black sandblast that appeared in 1917; "Root Briar", introduced in 1931 and one of the most sought-after finishes, because the natural blond color of the briar shows off the grain the best; a light tan sandblast called "Tanshell", first offered around 1952; "Redbark", a sandblast with a reddish finish that was brought out in 1972; a smooth "Black Briar" dress pipe introduced in 1973; Cumberland, brought out in 1979 as a dark brown sandblasted pipe with the bowl rim polished smooth and offered with a two-tone marbleized mouthpiece reminiscent of the vulcanite used during the 1930s (and erroneously called "bowling ball pipes" by American collectors); Chestnut, similar to the Cumberland but without the polished rim and introduced in 1982 to commemorate the closing of the

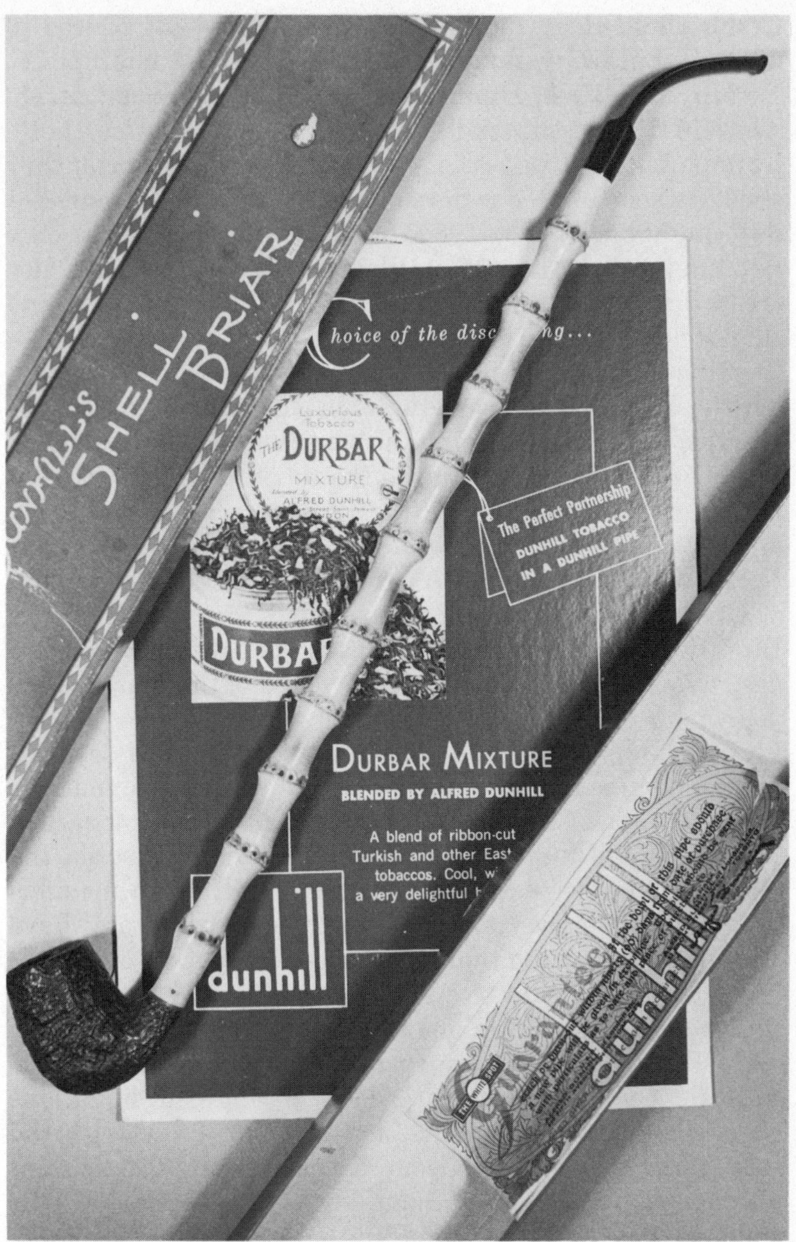

An extremely rare Dunhill black shell bamboo churchwarden which was made in 1960. All Dunhills are collectible, but unique pieces such as this bring a premium, as few of them were produced.

Cumberland Road factory; and the County, introduced in 1986 as a pale tan sandblast with a Cumberland mouthpiece.

Up until 1960, Dunhill had a double sandblast finish, wherein they would sandblast their Shell pipes twice, thereby imparting a strong craggy character to the fine briar they used. As soon as it was discontinued, smokers demanded it be brought back and in 1980 Dunhill resumed the style, only now they call it their Deep Blast finish. In 1986 they also created a Ring Grain blast, which costs more in England than it does in America for some reason.

Since 1975, Dunhill has offered six different bowl sizes, which are numerically designated and are referred to as Groups, with Group 1 being the smallest and Group 6 being the largest and rarest, due to the amount of wood that is necessary to create it. Due to the high cost of tobacco, Group 2 and 3 pipes are more popular in Europe, while Americans tend towards larger sizes. A Group 4 or 5 makes an excellent size for a practical smoking pipe, but if one were buying a Dunhill strictly for investment, then the Group 6 would be a desirable acquisition, as there are fewer of them made each year.

Originally, Dunhill only offered bowl sizes in designations of Groups 1, 2, 3, 4 and then used the letter designations ODA, ODB and ODC for sizes larger than a Group 4; each of the Oversized Dunhills carried a shape number, just like the numerical bowl size designations. For years, due to an unfortunate lack of verifiable information, collectors have erroneously assumed that ODA stood for Oversized Dunhill America, ODB meant Oversized Dunhill Bermuda and ODC was Oversized Dunhill Canada. However, a recent discovery in the Dunhill archives has turned up the fact that while OD stood for Oversized Dunhill, the A, B, and C designations were simply letter classifications for bowl sizes, with the ODA being larger than a Group 4. The lettering system went all the way up to ODF although I have only seen two ODBs and one ODC and these pipes in themselves are extremely rare; I suspect few, if any, of the larger ODE and ODF sizes were ever made. It should be noted that the differences in all of Dunhill's bowl sizes only amounts to one or two millimetres in height and diameter, with some deviation being allowed for variances in the carving. Around 1978 Dunhill changed their lettering and numbering system for bowl sizes, but a few ODAs continue to be made and they are a much-coveted item among collectors as well as those who like a long smoke.

Dunhill also used the lettering system for the DR series of select straight grains, with the DR symbol being stamped on the pipe's shank and standing for "Dead Root", a designation for the part of the heath tree from which the briar burl is cut. The DR designation was followed by a letter, beginning with "A" and theoretically going all the way to DRJ, the higher up in the alphabet, the greater the finite perfection of the straight grain. One well-known entertainment celebrity smokes a DRH, which is one of the most remarkable straight grains in any collection today. As an example of the value placed on this DR series, a DRD sold for £725 in 1982 and a DRH fetched £975 in 1987.

Dunhill has now replaced their DR letter series for straight grains with a star stamping, with a single star being equivalent to the older DRA. The stars can go as high as six (after which the old lettering of DRG, DRH, etc. takes over, should such rarified pieces of briar ever be found). I suspect that one has reached an acceptable level of prosperity when he can regularly drink Moet & Chandon White Star champagne, dine in a four-star restaurant, and afterwards, smoke a five-star pipe.

Even though the many categories of Dunhill pipes can be more or less authenticated, there are enough deviations

Certain GBDs, such as the Unique Straight Grain on the left and the two gold banded Milliniums, are highly collectible, especially in America. *Credit: Dr. Ken Coffield Collection*

A comparison of a pre-transitional Ye Olde Wood Barling (bottom) and the current post-transition Guinea Grain Barling (top).

A trio of Sasieni's, showing an early patent number One Dot leaning against the box of a 1979 era gold banded Eight Dot (the last Sasieni to use the old-style stamping on the stem). In the foreground is one of the Sasieni Four Dots produced in 1984. This pipe features the newer, more "upright" Sasieni script stamping.

from "fact" to bewilder the most experienced collector. Nonetheless, any Dunhill pipe, whatever the stamping or group size, is a quality piece for any collection.

Sasieni is another of the great U.S. collectibles, especially because of their Four Dot "firsts," which are actually four blue dots inset in the near (left) side of the pipe stem (on narrow stems, these dots are found on the top of the bit). So enamored are some collectors over the Sasieni blue dots that they actually collect variations of the blue dot colors!

Sasieni pipes have always been more popular in the United States than in Great Britain, where they were made, primarily because the pipes were more aggressively marketed in the U.S. Yet, for all their popularity, there has been a great deal of misinformation circulating among collectors concerning the various One, Four, and Eight Dot Sasieni's and the matter should now be set straight to avoid further confusion. Joel Sasieni first worked for Charatan and later moved to Dunhill in 1910. Around 1918, he left to start his own pipemaking company. He put a single blue dot on all his "firsts", which at that time were only being sold in Europe and other non-U.S. markets. Later, when Sasieni pipes were being exported to the U.S. in ever increasing numbers, some means was necessary to identify these pipes for purposes of the company guarantee. It was decided to put Four Dots on all the U.S. pipes, and retain the One Dot designation for all others. (Up until recently, it has been erroneously assumed by some U.S. collectors that these early One Dot Sasieni's – which all had patent numbers on their shanks – were "rejects", but that is not the case.) The Sasieni pipe had a reputation for being extremely dry smoking, which made it all the more in demand. Yet, only 3% of the pipes were going to Europe, with the rest being eagerly sold in the U.S., where the Sasieni Four Dot had become a mark of desirability. To further add to the pipe's prestige, the U.S. importer talked Joel Sasieni into putting an additional set of four dots on the opposite side of the pipe stem, so that it could be seen by a person standing on either side of the smoker. Thus evolved the mysterious Eight Dot Sasieni that is now so eagerly sought after by U.S. collectors. It doesn't exist in Europe; only in America. And it only lasted until just after World War II. By then Joel's son Alfred had taken over the company and with post war shortages of material, it was decided that doubling the four dot logo took too much time, equipment and money. As a result, the company went back to the Four Dot system on all their "firsts", a tradition which Sasieni continued until 1979, when he sold the company. In addition, in the 1960s, a Two Dot Sasieni "first" was introduced to denote pipes made with wood of less character than the Four Dots. During this period Sasieni also produced "rejects" which only bore the company name and no dots. Late in the 1970s Sasieni again began using a single blue dot on their pipes, only this time it was on specific U.S. lower priced "seconds" such as the Claret.

In 1979, when the company was sold, the new owners commemorated the event by reissuing a limited run of Sasieni Eight Dots, each of which bore a blue string running from the mouthpiece and around through the bowl and affixed with a lead seal and a paper tab which was signed by Alfred Sasieni, signifying that he had personally inspected each of the pipes. Each pipe was stamped with a serial number, as was the blue velvet-lined box that came with it. There were only to be 100 pipes in this series although I have talked with two collectors who claim to have seen a Sasieni reissue Eight Dot stamped #119; pipe #33 is in my personal collection and it came in a box stamped #93, so I strongly suspect there were some numbering discrepancies and perhaps a few overruns at the factory. When new, the reissue Eight Dot sold for $400 and an even rarer version came with a gold band and sold for $550.

Most collectors are aware of the fact that the pre-World War II Sasieni's were stamped with patent numbers and when found on the walnut or smooth-finished pipes, are a guarantee that they are early products of the company. However, the patent numbers were retained on the plum finished pipes up until 1970, so extra caution should be exercised when considering these pipes for purchase, as the earlier pipes always bring a premium.

Other desirable Sasieni's are the King Size (larger pipes of all high grades are always attractive to collectors, due to the scarcity of obtaining the bigger chunks of quality briar) and any of the Four Dot Canadians and larger bowled pipes of unusual shape. Virtually any early 1946–1979 Four Dot or pre-World War II Eight Dot is desirable, with the short-lived 1920s Four Dot being the most difficult to find. Although many of the early (patent number) European One Dot Sasieni's are desirable, they can often be purchased by knowledgeable collectors at prices far below their actual worth, as many sellers, looking at the dot and not the wood, have mistakenly assumed that these pipes were "seconds".

After Alfred Sasieni sold his company, he remained on briefly as a director and the firm continued to produce the Four Dot series in Natural, Walnut, Rustic (carved) and Ruff Root (sandblast). Alfred Sasieni is no longer involved with the pipe world and the pipes are made by a totally different firm, primarily for export to the U.S. However, the collector's interest is only in the older family-made pipes, whose various dot configurations still conjure up a certain mystique. While some may chuckle at this fascination over the number of dots that can fit on the stem of a Sasieni, the fact that many One Dots are still being smoked in Europe gives ample testimony to the pipe's value.

There has always been a certain romantic purity connected with the smoking quality of the Barling pipe and this image has no doubt been responsible for it being one of the most sought after collectibles by the true briar connoisseur.

Pipes can be a part of history, such as the commonly seen carved Boer War pipe and a unique BBB inlaid with a silver RAF emblem. The metal match covers are from WW II.

The Barling name itself is one of the oldest of all the collectible pipes. The family started business in the late 1700s as silversmiths. In 1812 Benjamin Barling began making meerschaum pipes, fitting them with his own hall-marked silverwork. The meerschaum Barling pipes won an award of recognition during London's Great Exhibition in 1851, but the Barling name did not really come into its own until 1854, when the family began making briar pipes. Although not the first of the briar pipemakers, they were certainly one of the earliest.

As far as the pipe historian and collector is concerned, there are three classifications of Barling pipes: pre-transition, transition and post-transition. It is the pre-transition Barlings which are by far the most collectible and which are the most eagerly sought after. These are the pipes that were actually made by the Barling family and which have become one of the most coveted smoking pipes to be found on the collector's market today. Barlings are prized for their use of very old, finely figured briar, even though very few straight grains were actually produced. It is the quality and age of the briar that has made the pre-transition Barlings so desirable. Additionally, these early Barlings were known for their extremely comfortable bits, in which the vulcanite was handcarved into wide fish-tail designs that made holding them in your mouth seem almost effortless. Many of the bowl designs themselves, such as the Barling Brandy Glass, were unique to the firm. In short, the pre-transitional Barlings were a pipe smoker's dream come true.

In 1960, the family sold their respected pipemaking company to the Imperial Tobacco Company. From 1960 up until 1967 or '68 (the facts become hazy during this period), the Barling pipe went through a sort of identity crisis and lost favor with pipe smokers and dealers alike. The briar quality was changed, the bowls were made by a number of different manufacturers, the numbering and classification systems stamped on the stems were modified and even the stylings were eventually altered. It was simply no longer the same pipe it used to be. This 1960–68 period constitutes the transition period and has little interest to collectors.

The post-transition period is probably the most intriguing, for it started in 1969 and is still going on, which means we may be witnessing a part of pipe collecting history. By the 1970s the Barling name had completely died out, in spite of several attempts to revive it. Finally, Imperial sold the company to an English investor group, which reorganized the firm under the name of Barling Pipes Limited, located on the Isle of Man, off the coast of England. The new company, though no longer affiliated with any of the original Barling family and using entirely new machinery, started remaking Barling pipes in the old tradition, going back to the original shapes and limiting their initial production to the United Kingdom. By 1979 Barling felt confident enough to expand their marketing operations to West Germany. Finally, in 1984 Barling pipes were once again exported to the United States. Today, thirty different shapes are offered, including many of the old Barling traditional styles, which were copied directly from pre-transition pipes in private U.S. collections, and included a return to the flat saddle bits that were so popular with American smokers back in the 1930s. In England, Barling pipes have found a modern market of their own and the factory even produces a great number of own brands for stores such as Harrod's. But in the U.S., it is the fascination with the old Barling Ye Olde Wood smokability and the family name that excites collectors' interest; so much so that in 1987 Barling produced a long-awaited run of 150 silver mounted Christmas pipes just for American smokers; needless to say, the pipes were immediately sold out. Still, if one is to collect (or at least appreciate) Barling pipes, it is important to identify the three classifications.

One of the most obvious means of identification is the Barling logo and numbering system that was stamped on the shank of each pipe, yet this tricky combination has already tripped up more than a few experienced Barling collectors. Both the pre-transition and the early transition Barlings have the name stamped BARLING'S MAKE in block lettering, arranged in a semi-circle. However, only the pre-transition Barlings used a *three-digit* numbering system stamped on the shank, denoting the pipe shape. The transitional Barlings kept the block lettering but changed to a *four*-digit numbering system stamped on the shank and these 1962–68 era pipes have often been confused for the more desirable pre-transition versions, so check your pipe carefully. Hopefully, the appearance of this information in print will save many a Barling collector from future calamity and will help clear up some of the mystery surrounding these pipe stampings. After 1968, the Barling logo was changed to a script design, and these pipes have no collector value. Only the three digit number and the block Barling letters identify the pipe as a true pre-transition collectible. However, it should be noted that the Barling family stamped their pipes which were sold in Europe with a four digit number (which only went from #1 to #1999) but fortunately these pipes are rarely encountered in the U.S. To further confuse matters, although the 1979–84 Barlings continued to be stamped with the post-transition script and four digits, in the latter part of '84 the Barling stamp on some of the pipes was changed back to the older block lettering style, while the higher grades, such as the Ye Olde Wood, still used the script logo. Fortunately, the four-digit numbering system has been retained throughout the new post-transitional line.

Barling pipes came in a number of finishes, which were stamped Special, Ye Olde Wood, Guinea Grain, Fossil (sandblast) and Specimen Straight Grain. There was also a Quaint finish which featured exquisite tiny carvings on the pipe bowl; it was rumored that all of these carvings were done by just one man in the Barling factory; because of the time-consuming and expensive handwork involved, Barling Quaints are quite rare. The most often encountered Barling

Lady's pewter jewellery pipe with amber stem c.1840.
Credit: Frank Burla Collection

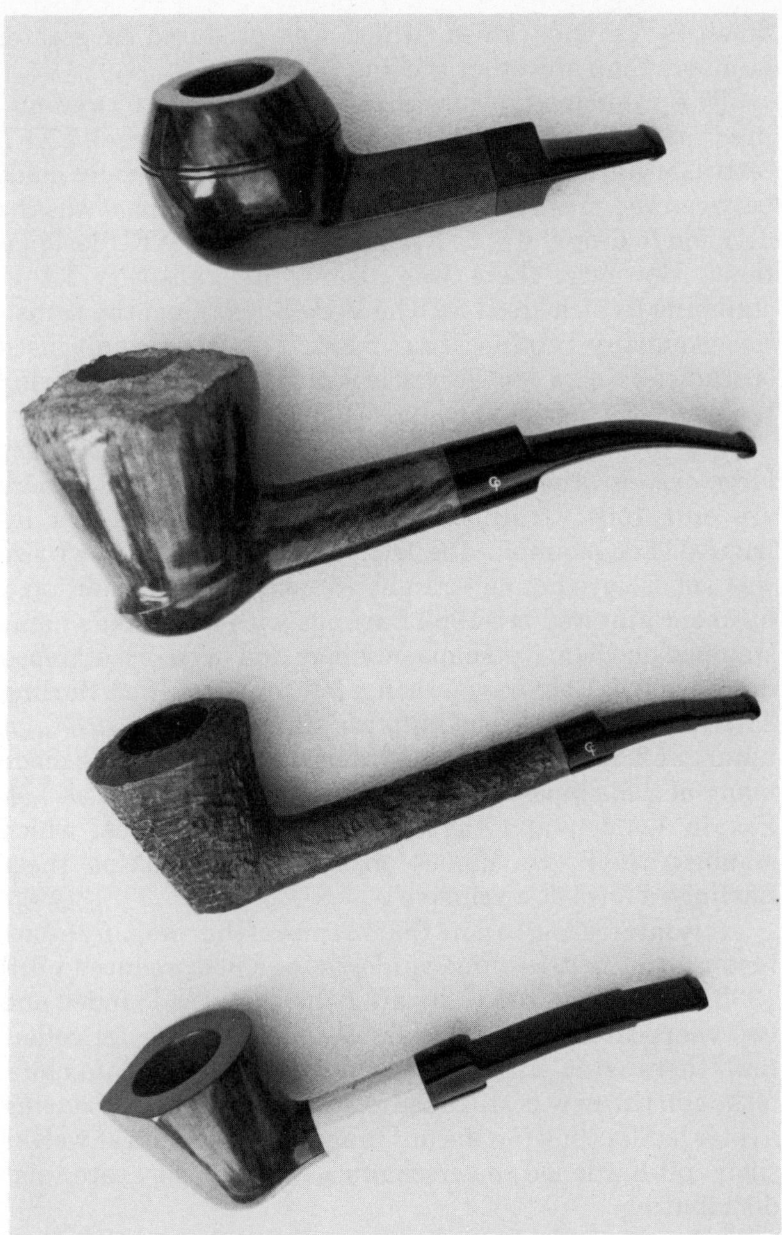

The many characteristics of Charatan (top to bottom): Selected, stamped FH (freehand); Executive, stamped Extra Large in script; Free Hand Relief, extra-large; Executive After-Hours, a style featuring a white shank and designed by Reuben Charatan after seeing an ivory-shanked Victorian briar.

finish is Ye Olde Wood, which was produced in greater numbers than any other Barling.

The pre-transition bowl sizes were identified by a stamping that included S (small), L (medium), EL (large), EXEL (extra large), and EXEXEL (giant). One of the changes made between the pre-transition and transition Barlings was the decision to drop the S, E, EL, EXEL, and EXEXEL designations. However, there was also a pre-transition T.V.F. stamping (which stood for The Very Finest) and the transition company retained that mark, but it was only used sporadically on a few very select pipes encountered during the transition period.

The pre-transition Barling pipe factory was never a very large organization and like many handmade objects, there are numerous variations that will keep the collector intrigued. For example, the letter designation for bowl size was not always put on straight grained pipes. In addition, I have encountered pre-1960 Barlings with no maker's name stamped on them, no shape numbers and even one stamped upside down! I have even seen a few pre-transition Barling EXEXEL Ye Olde Wood billiards stamped with a *two*-digit number 52. Prior to the sale of their company, Barling made many of their pipes for individual pipe dealers such as J. J. Fox in London and the Army and Navy stores, which stamped their own names on the briars, making these Barlings a form of "exclusive".

It is interesting to note that in spite of the company's long history, the first Barling catalogue was not produced until 1962, coming out 150 years after the firm was founded and two years after the Barling family sold it. Thus, for collectors, there is no such thing as a pre-transition catalogue, although the new post-transition company is now producing a color leaflet showing the full range of their briars as well as their oil-hardened meerschaums, which they are also distributing.

Like the early Barlings, the collectibility of Charatan pipes can be attributed to the high quality of their briar, most notably their freehands, which were stamped FH, a designation used for any Charatan that was not a standard shape. Of special interest were the many briar pipes such as the Newmarket, Lonsdale, and Artist, which were inspired from old clay shapes. Many of these exquisite early Charatan freehands were carved by the skilled hands of Dan Tennison, who was employed by the firm for over fifty years. In addition to their large freehands, during the 1950s Charatan also made Giant Billiards, Giant Dublins and Giant Bents, all of which came in Selected or Supreme quality briar.

Charatan was the first pipe company to break the retail price barrier of the $100 mark in the early 1960s, when they came out with their Supreme (designated S100 for Supreme $100), the top of the line at that time. Later came the S200 and the S250 and it does not take a calculator to guess what they each originally sold for. The single most expensive briar pipe in the world is the Charatan Summa Cum Laude, a large straight grain, wedge-shaped pipe with a square shank. When introduced in 1976 the pipe sold for $2,500. The rarity of the wood is such that only three of these pipes have been made and each one is currently rumored to be valued in excess of $10,000.

The collector of Charatan's, especially those made during the 1950s and 60s, will find a great fascination with superb wood and craftsmanship, but a great deal of frustration with trying to make any assemblage of facts out of the stampings and gradings, as there are many inconsistencies. For example, not all freehands were stamped FH and some high grade Supremes have been encountered that are not as finely figured as a lower grade Select. In addition, in their 1951 catalogue, Charatan advertised that they would custom-make any pipe to a customer's specifications. Thus, it may be possible to encounter a Charatan pipe that is not shown on any shape chart. The pipe firm's numbering system is also hard to fathom for many collectors, although Charatan uses a numerical designation for bowl size, similar to Dunhill, with the Group 3 and 4 being the most often encountered in America. Any large size Charatan high grade is desirable for a collector, as they are quite rare and the growing difficulty in obtaining the exquisite pieces of briar for these giant pipes, especially the freehands, means that there will be fewer of them made each year.

All early Charatan's are superb-smoking pipes and one of my favorite estate briars is a Charatan Group 4 black sandblast Canadian, which I purchased for $35 back in the mid-70s.

Savinelli is an extremely popular brand both in the U.S. and in Europe and is one of the few Italian pipes that is regularly available in Great Britain. Of specific interest to collectors, however, is their top-of-the-line Autograph pipes, which are all handmade of large, quality briar. The first Autograph was made in 1962 and the series now ranges from sandblasted panels all the way up to a perfect three star straight grain smooth, of which only about one or two are produced every few years.

Of particular note to collectors is the Savinelli Linea '76, a special one year offering put out by Achille Savinelli to commemorate the centennial of his family's pipemaking firm. There were six different shapes in the Linea '76 series, four straights and two bents, each made from top quality briar with a modern styling that had not been in the line before and which were not seen again for eight years. (Some of these same shapes appeared in the Savinelli line in 1984, as they were some of the limited edition bowls left over from the 1976 offering.) The Linea '76 pipes were all high grade "firsts" and sold for £50 each. Each of the six shapes came in either a smooth or a sandblast finish. The pipes were packaged in two-pipe sets, with each set consisting of a smooth and sandblast pipe of the same shape, and packaged in a wood and cane-covered round canister. Thus, in order to obtain the complete set, you would have to buy six cannisters and would end up with twelve pipes. It is a unique set and one that is not often seen today.

As the oldest continually operating briar pipe firm in the world, and one of the first to establish itself in London, the firm of Comoy is of special interest to the collector who also has a penchant for pipemaking history. The Comoy story is recounted in both Chapters One and Ten.

There are a number of highly collectible pipes in the Comoy line, which starts at the very top with the Specimen Straight Grain, a flawless, large sized "first" that is so rare, the last one was made in 1980. Next on down comes the

Selected Straight Grain, which oddly enough, exhibits some minor imperfections in the briar but is of usually fine grain configuration. The third designation in the Comoy line is their famous Blue Riband, the most popularly collected pipe of all the Comoy's.

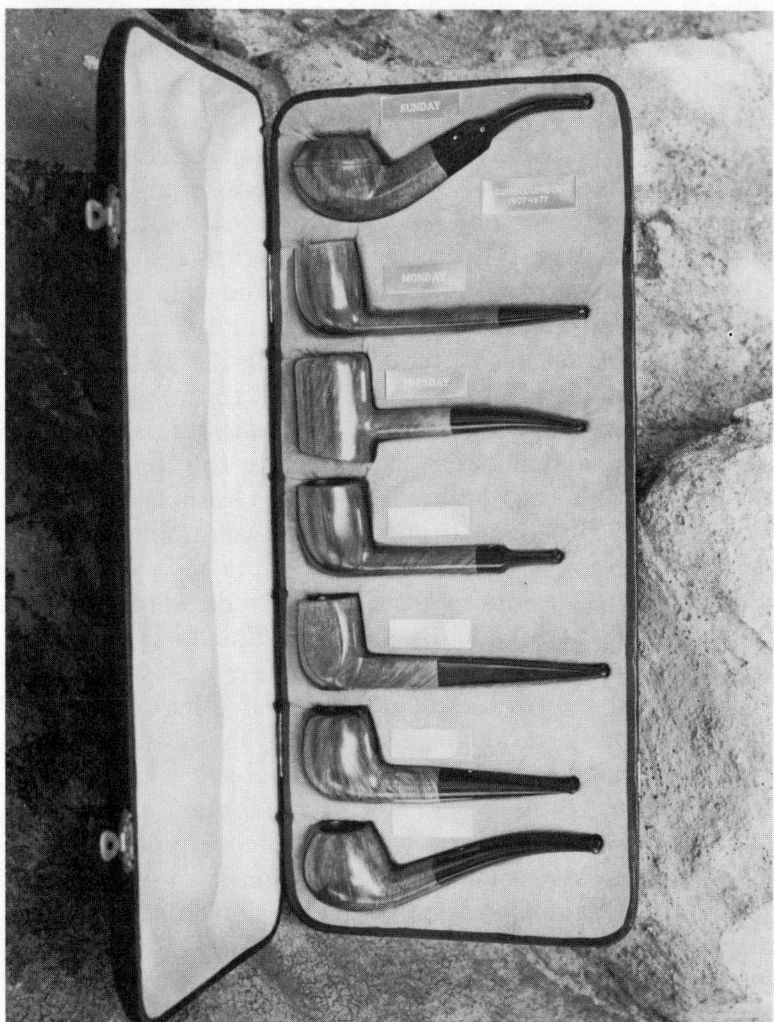

One of the epitomes of pipe collecting is owning a seven-day set of perfectly matched briars, the theory being that you would have a different pipe to smoke each day of the week. These sets are extremely expensive, such as this set of Dunhill Root Briars made in 1977 to commemorate the 70th anniversary of Alfred Dunhill's first pipe shop.

The naming of the Blue Riband pipe is a story in royal elegance itself. Originally, the Blue Riband was a term used to describe the blue silk ribbon signifying the Order of the Garter, the highest order of British Knighthood. (As a sidelight, from that terminology came our popular phrase, "blue ribbon.") In addition, a miniature version of any awarded medal was also known as a *riband*. However, the real significance of the Blue Riband nomenclature is taken from the fact that, as early as 1909, it was the title of an award given to the fastest of the ocean-crossing passenger ships travelling from Europe to the U.S. Although occasionally awarded to American, French and German liners, it was the British who usually won. Thus, besides knighthood, the Blue Riband signifies speed in delivering Comoy's finely-crafted pipes to American shores.

The pipe was first introduced during the 1932 World's Fair and is still in the line, a statement that may surprise most collectors, who might have assumed that it is no longer being made. The fact is that the briar for the Blue Riband, less figured than the Specimen Straight Grain, is equally as flawless, and consequently only a very few numbers of these pipes are ever imported into the U.S. during any one year. As an example, in 1986 only 12 Blue Ribands were made by Comoy. The Blue Riband has a natural finish and the grain pattern can be either straight or bird's eye. It was called ". . . our most beautiful pipe in regular production", according to company catalogues, although those same pages stated that approximately only 40 out of every 1,000 pipes could ever make the grade. Nothing "regular" about that! The Blue Riband pipe has never been officially put on a price list (which is why collectors cannot find it in any Comoy catalogue) and the pipe is sold by allocation only. There is a mistaken belief by some collectors that in 1979 Comoy made a reissue of their Blue Riband, but that is not true; in that year, however, Comoy actually made twelve Blue Ribands, the most that had ever been shipped to the U.S. at any one time, and this may have started the rumor of a reissue. Thirty to forty years ago the Blue Riband was far easier to find, as quality briar was more plentiful and, consequently, more of the high grade pipes could be fashioned. But such is not the case today; in fact, during the past decade, less than 120 Blue Ribands have been made by Comoy.

Another highly collectible pipe by Comoy is their Extraordinaire, which actually has nothing to do with bowl size or grain pattern, but rather, is a designation reserved for any pipe that is out-of-the-ordinary, such as having an extra long shank or a taller-than-average bowl shape. There was, however, an 800 series of Comoy Extraordinaires that were unusually large in bowl size, and came in smooth and sand-blast finishes. On the other end of the scale, Comoy at one time had a Monogram series of miniature pipes, which are no longer being made today.

In 1975, Comoy came out with a special 150th Anniversary pipe to commemorate the founding of the firm. This exquisite briar had a gold band and a Lucite stem and originally sold for £85. Each pipe came with a certificate, which permitted the owner to register his pipe in the City of London. A limited number of 250 of these pipes were distributed worldwide and I have only encountered one, which, not surprisingly, was missing the certificate.

Although certainly not as "collectible" as some of the Comoy high grades, I am fascinated by the existence of the Grand Slam, a filter pipe that originally appeared in 1933. Believe it or not, this pipe is still in the Comoy line, although it is now called the Air-Dry. While I personally do not smoke a filter pipe, it is still unique to be able to buy a piece of living (burning?) pipe history, new and in-the-box.

Of all the Italian pipes, the Castello is by far the most collectible in the U.S., as it is hard to find (even more so in the U.K., where it is not even imported), although the Carlo Scotti family is still making his famous pipes. Castello collectors may be interested to know that, because of the international acclaim he has brought to Italian pipemaking, his country made him a Cavaleri, which is similar to being knighted in Britain. He originally worked for Savinelli, but left in 1946 to start his own factory. His original run of pipes was stamped "Mi Reserva" and dated 1948. They had a small bowl and came in classical shapes with a white bar or line inset within the black Lucite stem. This is the European logo; in America, a "diamond" is used instead, giving the pipe a dual identity that causes some Americans to pay a premium for the "White Bar". Here's the little-known story:

In 1952, Wally Frank, a famous U.S. pipe importer, was on a buying trip in Italy and came across Scotti's pipes. He liked them and wanted to import them into the U.S. Unfortunately, there was a problem: Scotti's "white line" trademark looked almost identical to the trademark Frank was using for his "White Bar" line of pipes. The solution was obvious. Scotti would simply change his logo. The two men sat down in the warm Italian sun and came up with the idea of drilling a hole in the "near side" of the stem, inserting a small piece of crumpled up silver foil, and sealing it over with clear Lucite. Voila! A legend was born and even today some collectors insist that every Castello pipe has a diamond in it . . . or at worst, a rhinestone. But perhaps it is best to leave both the clear Lucite and the image intact, for the superb craftsmanship and smokability of the Castello is really what constitutes the true value of the pipe.

Another highly sought-after Italian pipe is the Caminetto, a brand originally started in 1968 by Gianni Davoli, Peppino Ascorti and Luigi Radice. Caminetto ceased to exist as a brand in 1980 and, although a few continue to show up as estate pipes, they usually command a premium price. This is somewhat ironic, as Ascorti and Radice are still making basically the same pipes today (see Chapter Three).

Originally, the Caminetto name was owned jointly by Davoli, Ascorti and Radice. The firm was located in Cucciago, in the province of Como, Italy. The Tinder Box was the first to import these pipes into the United States and later, the pipe was also imported by Peterson's Ltd. prior to its purchase by Associated Imports. At its height, Caminetto only produced about 4,500 pipes a year.

In 1980 the three partners decided to split up and each go their own way, with the mutual understanding that none of them would ever use the Caminetto name again. Davoli retired, but Ascorti and Radice each started their own pipemaking firms, using their own names. Thus ended the Caminetto brand and its unique gold-stamped logo of Johnny Davoli's thick, upturned moustache, but fortunately, the actual pipe continues to this day with only minor variations in designs that reflect the different personalities of the two carvers, Ascorti and Radice.

After my scathing dissertation on mass-market pipes, the reader might wonder why I am including Kaywoodie in so exalted a chapter on collectibles. However, during the 1920s and 30s, Kaywoodie, although very much a filter pipe, actually turned out some extremely high quality briars which they dubbed their Flame Grain series. These pipes came singly or in beautiful sets consisting of two, seven, twelve and fourteen pipes of matching wood and all snuggled together in leather cases. They have since become highly collectible although until now, the complete Kaywoodie story was largely unknown.

The company was originally started in 1851 in New York by two brothers named Kaufman, who sold meerschaums and clays that a third brother sent them from Vienna. Business thrived and in 1854 the Kaufmans took in a partner named Bondy. Kaufman Brothers and Bondy kept expanding their business, selling mail order pipes throughout the U.S., including sending them by Pony Express to miners

In the 1970s Dunhill began creating a very limited series of ornate, gold-embellished pipes for the collector's market. These three Root Briars are typical of a very untypical rarity. From L. to R. they feature: 18kt gold bowl mounting with a detachable engraved golden umbrella; 18kt Crown windscreen embellished with tiger's eye; bowl mount and pennant made of 18kt gold. And to think, someone will eventually put a match to all this!

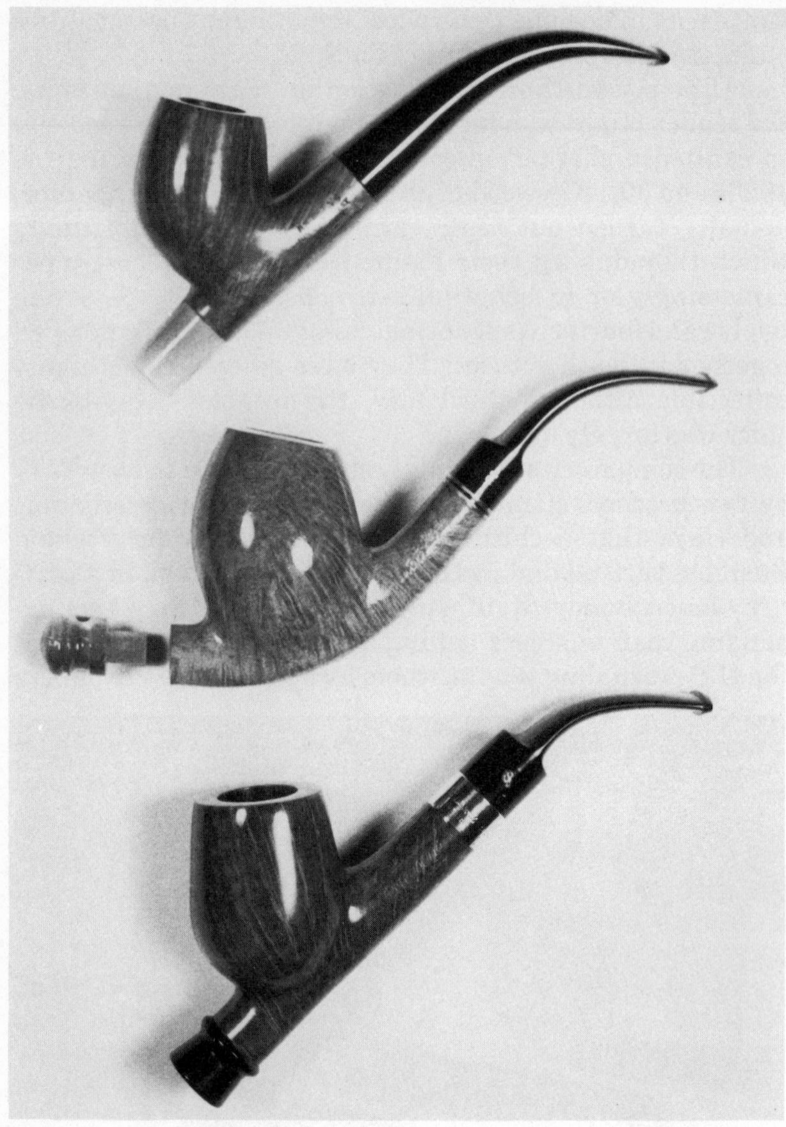

Not to be confused with the Three Musketeers, these three cavaliers represent an old but highly practical pipe design, in which the bottom plug is removed for cleaning and to keep the pipe dry. Pictured from top to bottom are: an Astley's "own brand" straight grain with horn plug, made years ago in the old Charatan factory; a currently-produced Butz-Choquin D'Artagnon inspired by an 1890s French design, and a handsome handmade silver-banded Peterson.

in the California gold fields. The three partners retired in 1898, but their relatives continued on with the firm, which had begun to manufacturer their own briar pipes under the KB&B (Kaufman Brothers and Bondy) trademark. In 1915 the Kaywoodie brand was created as a marketing umbrella for a new briar pipe which the KB&B company introduced and exhibited at the Museum of Modern Art in New York, the Baltimore Museum of Art, the Chicago School of Design and the College of William and Mary.

The KB&B briar pipe brand existed from 1900 until just after World War I (with some overlapping with the Kaywoodie from 1915–1917), and collectors refer to the KB&B as a Kaywoodie transition pipe. During the early years of the 20th century a number of filter systems were designed by the KB&B firm and incorporated into their Kaywoodie pipes under the names of Synchro-Stem and Kaywoodie Drinkless filters. During the late 1920s and throughout the 30s the Kaywoodie became a highly respected pipe in spite of its filter system (which was popular among many smokers of the era) primarily due to the fine quality of the straight grain and the flame grain models. Unfortunately, the hard-to-get-briar years of World War II marked the decline of the Kaywoodie pipe in America, a plummet from which it has never recovered as far as collectors are concerned. Fortunately, the loss of smokability is not shared by Kaywoodie's London-made cousin (see Chapter Ten), while in the U.S. the earlier pipes are still highly regarded.

Freehand pipes are attractive to collectors because of their unique, unbridled designs and, in the case of pipes such as the Charatans discussed earlier, due to their larger size, which requires more exquisite wood, therefore making each pipe somewhat of a rarity. Freehands are generally perceived to be Danish in nature, although the term is often applied to any pipe that is not a standard shape. Freehands are not as popular in America as they once were and that certainly is the case in England. Some of the very first freehands to be imported into the U.S. included the early Larsens, Criswells, Knute and those sold by Pipe Dan.

Today, high grade collectible and smokable freehand

These three Sherlock Holmes commemoratives are anything but elementary. (L. to R.): A silver capped limited edition of 221 pipes and case designed by the author in 1978, a current Peterson Sherlock Holmes Centennial silver band briar calabash, and a limited edition of 250 silver mounted Sherlock Holmes commemoratives with book-case produced by Dunhill in 1987 to mark the 100th anniversary of "A Study in Scarlet," the first Holmes story.

Collecting and smoking estate pipes is like taking a puff of nostalgia.

This pair of carved briar pipes with horn bits are superb examples of 19th century French craftsmanship. Both pipes are signed "Vincent". *Credit: Lennie Weinrib Collection*

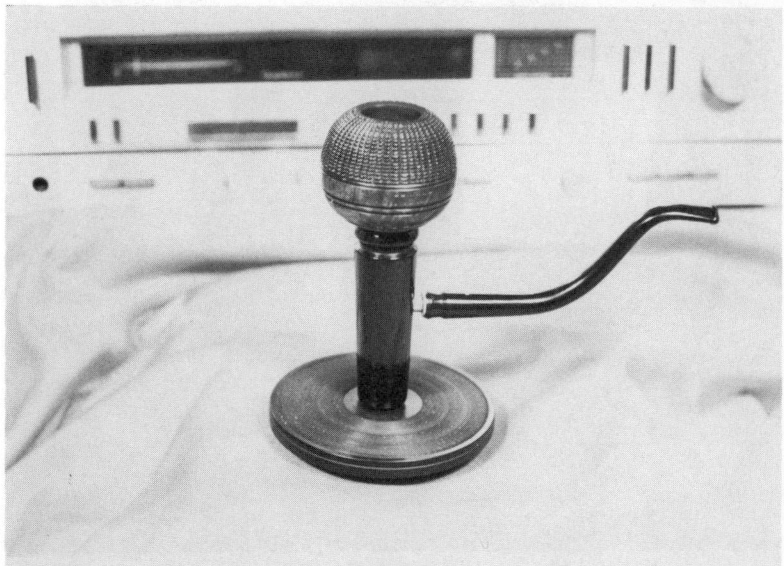

The Show Biz pipe, shaped like a microphone sitting on a vulcanite record, was made by Dunhill to honor disc jockey Dave Lee Travis, Britain's Pipesmoker of the Year for 1982. Only 50 pipes were produced for the collector's market.

This meerschaum is listed in the Guinness Book of World Records as the world's most valuable pipe, and is valued at £8,500.

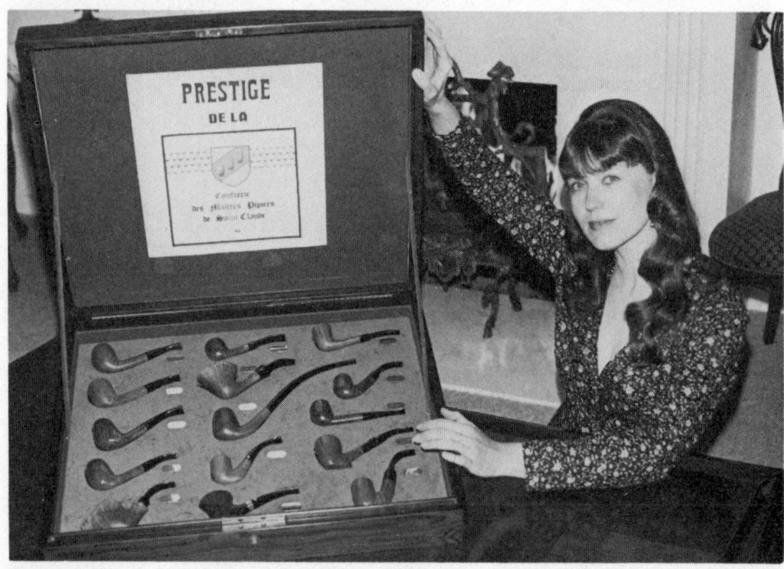

Occasionally, the 15 members of the Confrèrie des Maîtres Pipiers de Saint-Claude create a special set of pipes, with one representative briar "first" from each of the companies placed in a special French fitted case. This 15-pipe Confrèrie set was valued at £17,000 in 1982.

pipes are made by respected firms such as Erik Nørding, W. Ø. Larsen and Karl Erik, just to name a few which have a large following in America. During the early 1970s Preben Holm, under the Ben Wade stamping, produced a series of "hand models," which were numbered from 100 up to 800 based upon grain quality, with the higher numbers denoting the better grade of briar. Only a few 800 numbers are known to exist. Around this time, there was also a Ben Wade Nobel Prize pipe produced, which was an unusually large and finely grained freehand model. Later on in the 70s, Preben Holm began stamping his own name on some of the "Private Collection" freehands his firm created. They were extremely high quality pieces of briar and the "Private Collection" pipes are still being made, but less than two dozen are brought into the world each year due to the growing difficulty in obtaining fine briar.

Although there are very few acknowledged freehand collectors around, the better quality pipes are still very much in demand by pipe smokers in general, and the extra care and handworkmanship that a freehand design requires all help to keep the prices high. In addition, some makers have created certain deluxe models, such as Erik Nørding's gold-banded series, which is aimed at the high grade pipe smoker who wants to add precious metal to his perfect briar "first" for a true masterpiece. In 1979 Nørding also produced

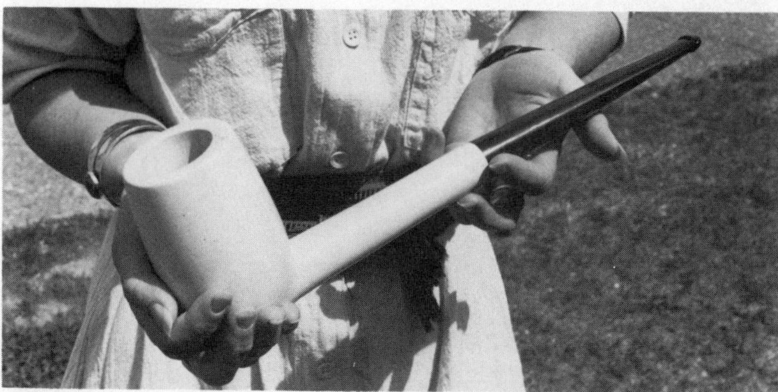

This pipe is not being held by a small woman. It is actually a huge meerschaum with red amber mouthpiece. Made in the 1890s as a tobacconist's display piece, the pipe has at one time been smoked!
Credit: Frank Burla Collection

a one-of-a-kind gold banded seven-day set that sold in the USA for $5,000, indicating that *free*form is strictly a design terminology as far as collectibles are concerned.

Because Christmas is the biggest pipe selling season of the year, it is only natural that Christmas commemoratives (or Year Pipes, as they are called in Europe) would eventually establish their own niche among collectors. Yet surprisingly few varieties existed until recently. Still, it is one of my favorite categories of pipe collecting, for it combines one of my most enjoyable times of the year with one of my most enjoyable pastimes. An open hearth, a full glass, and a loving wife nearby while I light a specially purchased Christmas pipe embodies the best of the Yuletide for me. It is no wonder I have almost enough Year Pipes for each day in December and every Christmas it becomes a chore as to which one will be smoked first.

The brand that holds the record for being the longest continuously-produced Christmas pipe is BBB, which has more than three decades of Yuletide celebration behind it. Sadly, none of these limited edition briars have been ex-

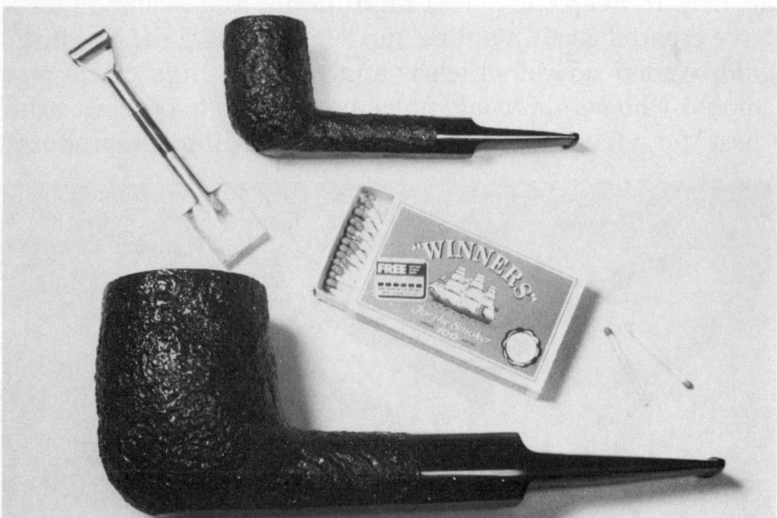

Continuing with the "bigger is better" theme, the pipe on the bottom is the largest standard-shape Ashton ever made. Part of the Magnum series, it is shown with a large XX-size billiard of similar proportions for comparison. The silver shovel with briar handle was made by Les Wood for loading the huge pipe with tobacco.

ported to the U.S. since 1980, although they are sold throughout the rest of Europe. In the antiques field, we must acknowledge the Victorian Father Christmas clays, even though they are no longer readily available. One of the most popular Christmas pipes is the yearly offering by Comoy's, of which 1,800 are shipped out annually and a number of collectors have amassed a complete collection of these pipes, including the rare six-pipe cased set made in 1981, of which only 150 issues are known to exist. Comoy's made their first Christmas pipe in 1976. Three years later Stanwell started their Year Pipe series, although it is not widely available in the U.S. The most expensive Christmas pipes in existence are, quite naturally, made by Dunhill, who started their annual series in 1980. The pipes are attractively cased, usually limited to approximately 250 in number, and consequently are among the most sought after and least-obtained of all the Yuletide offerings; because of their price and scarcity, less than 30 complete sets are known to exist worldwide. Other brands, such as England's Barling, Holland's Zenith, France's Butz-Choquin, Denmark's W. Ø. Larsen, Nørding and Jensen, and Italy's Savinelli all produce Year Pipes, proving that pipe smoking and Christmas are universal combinations.

Starting a collection of Christmas (Year) pipes is one way to insure that you will have a new pipe to smoke each year and it makes gift-giving so much easier for family and friends. It is the least you could do for them!

Besides buying ready-made collectibles, it is also possible to commission your own one-of-a-kind collectible, which then becomes a very personal statement about you and about the ability of the pipemaker. A pipe smoker/collector with specialized interests can provide a great challenge to a custom pipemaker. (You'll find some of these carvers listed in the Sourcebook section of this book.) It seems that pipes just lend themselves naturally to expressions of individual interests and appreciation. As an inspirational example, the Emperor Napoleon once gave his Marshal Oudinot a diamond-encrusted meerschaum that was carved in the shape of a mortar and valued at 30,000 francs at the time of its presentation.

Creating a collectible for an individual is one thing, but very often, inadvertently creating a collectible for the mass market by a major pipe company is not always good business, for in many cases, such as the older Dunhills, Charatans and even the Barlings, the existence of their collectible briars can sometimes interfere with the sale of new pipes. On the other hand, certain limited editions and commemoratives often sell out rather quickly and at prices that are usually much higher than the same pipe in a non-commemorative configuration.

I've always felt that packaging was an interesting part of buying collectible pipes and it is a nice added feature if a limited edition pipe comes with its original box, but it

Pipe collector shows can be a good place to exchange information, meet new friends, and of course, pick up new pipes!

normally should not affect the price, unless the box is part of the overall presentation, as in the case of the Dunhill Christmas pipe or the Sherlock Holmes Commemorative (see illustration), in which case the box alone, at one collector show, fetched almost as much as the pipe!

I have often wondered if a collectible pipe's value is affected by the fact that it was smoked, and I have received an equal number of opinions on the subject both pro and con, so I now feel qualified (having smoked my share of collectibles) to comment for the record. If a pipe is desirable, and is being purchased by a smoker/collector, it actually does not make one bit of difference whether or not it has been smoked. In fact, in the case of a really well-smoked pipe such as a meerschaum or an old briar, the pipe's physical appearance and patina may actually be enhanced by smoking it. To my mind, there is nothing worse than a well crafted pipe whose maker fully intended it for tobacco and match, yet whose destiny has never been fulfilled. I remember once buying a very unusually shaped Sasieni Four Dot that had never been smoked. As I drove home with that pipe on the front seat of my car, I kept thinking of the briar and how it would feel with the smoke curling up out of its bowl and the wax heating up on the wood for the very first time. Well, it felt *great* and it has since become one of my favorite pipes. On the other hand, I know of an owner of a large Dunhill Magnum that has never been smoked and probably never will be, because the pipe is too big for him, he doesn't like the shape, and he merely wanted it for his collection because of its rarity. So the final rule is, if you can identify with the pipe and feel that it is a part of you (and why would you buy a pipe that isn't?) then smoke it. You will actually be getting double value out of your investment by physically enjoying it as well as by owning it.

Smoking an antique pipe, however, is another matter, as extreme heat from a dry tobacco can damage a 100 year-old bowl beyond repair. In addition, many of these pipes have amber mouthpieces. Amber is petrified mineralized resin, solidified under pressure in the ground for centuries. It is quite fragile, like glass and is flammable. Although it was once the favored material for pipe mouthpieces, the number of antique pipes found with broken amber stems indicates why a replacement material was found as quickly as possible. An interesting sidelight that I discovered quite by accident is the fact that many of the new "super glues" will completely dissolve an amber stem. That is why one of my favorite antique meerschaums no longer has a stem. Old pipes are traditionally made of old material, and as the world spins on towards the 21st century, it becomes increasingly more difficult to replace things such as amber, Redolite and silver filagree. Moreover, I have actually seen old meerschaums crack from excessive heat, thereby instantly ruining a costly pipe. It is interesting to speculate what kindred spirit once puffed on the pipe we now possess, but sometimes the imagination must take up where reality leaves off.

It is best not to try and clean an antique pipe unless a professional museum-type restoration can be done. There are experts who specialize in this service and a few of them are listed in Chapter Ten. However, one of the best instructions on this touchy subject can be found in Ben Rapaport's book, *A Complete Guide To Collecting Antique Pipes*, listed in the bibliography section. There are a number of commercially made products available for cleaning or refurbishing briar pipes, such as Briarwipe and the Comoy and Dunhill pipe polishing compounds which can be acquired through your local pipe shop. However, for minor touch-up briar, I recommend shoe dye of the proper color and carnuba wax for the exterior wood. Also, the inside of clear plastic bits can be polished bright by coating a pipe cleaner with abrasive toothpaste, but be sure to polish out all the residue or your next bowlful will make your Latakia taste like fluoride.

Psychology plays a big role in pipe collecting and whether or not we are aware of it, it affects us nonetheless. For example, in addition to their workmanship and wood, most collectible pipes, even the currently made briars, are desirable simply because they are difficult to obtain. That is why an eight-sided Dunhill panel or a Charatan freehand will command premium prices in America, simply because they are rarely, if ever, brought into that country. Added knowledge also affects the pipe collector and patent number Dunhills were never as popular as the day pipe smokers found out they were not being made any more. Whether the newer Sasieni or Barling pipes will ever reach collector status is open to question, but some of the newer pipemakers, such as Ashton and Becker, for example, are already taking advantage of this predominantly American phenomenon. After all, the facts of merchandising dictate that almost anything can be recreated to meet the demands of the purchasing public, although for most collectors and even a few non-collectors, there will always be the fascination for the old, the rare, the unobtainable.

To start on the road to collecting, the first step is to learn all you can. Unfortunately, there is not much to read on the subject of collecting 20th century pipes. Antique pipe collectors have a slightly better choice and visiting museums and private collections is perhaps one of the best ways to learn. You should also try and find a tobacconist who deals in collectible pipes or at least knows something about the market. I strongly recommend getting some friends together and organizing your own pipe collecting and smoking club, learning from each other, perhaps trading a few items back and forth and generally enjoying the camaraderie of mutual interests. Remember, pipe collecting is like pipe smoking. There are no strict rules; it should be fun. Nor do you have to specialize in any one brand or item, although many collectors do. I don't, preferring to buy only those pipes that I like or that have a certain personal interest for me. Interior designers call it "eclectic taste." I prefer to call it "buying what I like." But when purchasing used pipes – just as in new pipes – buy the very best that you can afford. No one ever got hurt buying quality.

Finally, no matter what type of collectible pipe you are buying, whether it be an old Kaywoodie or a rare Dunhill or an attractive Christmas pipe, the best advice I can offer is to admonish you not to buy a pipe to make money. That is a purchase best reserved for stocks and bonds. Buy a pipe because you like it, because you want to smoke it, or just because it stirs up some fond memory hidden back in the deep shadowy recesses of your mind. That way, you can never lose on a pipe purchase, for you will always have a pipe that you like. And if it increases in value, then just consider it a bonus for following your emotions and not your wallet. After all, pipe collecting should be one investment we wouldn't mind seeing go up in smoke!

Chapter Ten

Pipe Smoker's Sourcebook (Of Pipes, Places and People)

"Mortals say their heart is light
When the clouds around disperse
Clouds together, thick as night,
Is the smoker's universe."

– from the German of Bauernfield

Briar Pipe Manufacturers and Brands

The following list is by no means an attempt to identify every major briar pipe manufacturer; to do so would be an exercise in failure, for most assuredly one company would be going out of business just as another was coming in while this book was either being written, printed or read. Moreover, the Law of Probability guarantees that somebody is going to be left out, so I am admitting it right from the start. This is merely an attempt to list some of the better-known (as well as a few of the lesser-known; after all, this is The "Ultimate" Pipe Book!) pipemakers today, giving a brief – and in some cases, where the situation warrants it, a not-so-brief – background on the company's history. Additional details on a few of the more popular pipes will be found elsewhere throughout this book. If any reader is familiar with information on pipes not contained in this section, I would welcome such addendum (as long as it can be authenticated), for updating future editions; all such material should be sent for my attention, care of the publisher. I have not listed any "exclusive" or "own label" brands, for to do so would require as many pages as there are pipe shops throughout the world. However, in addition to listing most of the pipes available in the U.K., I also decided to add a great number of other European pipemakers who have been brought to my attention since the U.S. edition of this book was published, even though many of these pipes are not readily available in the British Isles except by special order. By the same token, I have also included some companies that are no longer in the pipemaking business, merely because their pipes remain popular and are still being smoked. In fact, this entire section of the book exists simply because it occurred to me that all of us might like to know a little bit about the companies and craftsmen who make our pipes, so that we may enjoy the pleasures of their products even more. Moreover, it is hoped that this expanded chapter of the Pipe Smoker's Sourcebook will give us all a greater sense of pride as we pursue our pipe smoking hobby, secure in the knowledge that the Brotherhood of the Briar is not confined by any geographic or ideological boundaries.

Aerosphere

A popular English briar, of which approximately 2,000 are made annually.

Alpha

This is the U.S. brand name for the Israeli-made "Shalom" pipes.

Amorelli

Having started making pipes in 1986, Italy's Salvatore Amorelli is indicative of the recent pipemaking renaissance that is occurring throughout the world, especially by briar artisans concentrating on fewer numbers of high quality pipes. Amorelli's pipes are graded with asterisks, ranging from one to five, stamped into the left side of the shank. Of special interest is the gold bar he insets in both the stem and the shank, so that the two pieces must line up perfectly to indicate that the pipe is properly assembled.

Ardor

Handmade in Italy by the father and son team of Angelo and Dorelio Rovera, the name of their pipe is said to be taken from a compilation of their two names, but I have never quite been able to figure it out.

Armellini

Mauro Armellini operates a very small factory in the Cucciago area of Italy, which has become the pipemaking centre of that country and home for other Italian pipemaking firms such as Lorenzo, Rossi, Savinelli, etc. Armellini started working for Nino Rossi, who at one time ran the largest briar pipe factory in the world. Armellini's forte has always been creating machinery for pipemaking. In America he got his start by creating a popular line of "own brand" pipes such as Verona and Napoli for the large U.S. tobacco chain, Tinder Box. The pipes immediately became good traditional sellers in the low to medium price ranges. In an effort to upgrade his pipes, Armellini began making high grade handmades, such as the Direttore and various "controlled shape" freehands. He has since developed a unique knack for creating both machine-made and handmade pipes of special designs. In addition to his U.S. market, which has shrunk somewhat, Armellini sells to pipe shops in England, Italy, and Germany. At one time he turned out approximately 20,000 pipes a year for both the American and European markets.

Ascorti

One of the three partners who comprised the now defunct but highly regarded Caminetto pipemaking firm, Peppino Ascorti made an identical pipe, first brought out in 1978 and introduced to U.S. smokers in 1980 (the same year that the Caminetto company was dissolved). The Ascorti, like the old Caminetto, is a lightweight, extremely dry and cool smoking briar – one of the best to come out of Italy today. Peppino passed away in October, 1984, and the pipes are now being made just as skilfully by his sons Roberto and Pierangelo. About 6,000 pipes are produced annually, the majority of which are shipped to the U.S.

Ashton

William Ashton Taylor is indicative of a new breed of pipemaker coming out of England who belies his youth by making high grade pipes using old-fashioned techniques of hand turning, hot oil curing of bowls, and boiling the raw vulcanite that will be used for mouthpieces to remove much of the sulfur that causes oxidation. As a result, his Ashton brand pipes have become one of the British-made pipes most sought-after by American smokers. Taylor began making his classically shaped briars in 1984, but export demand was so strong it was not until 1985 that the high grade Ashton pipes were available for the Home Trade. All Ashton pipes are completely handmade one at a time, by Bill or one of the other three workers in his small factory, a situation which naturally limits production; approximately 3,000 pipes are produced annually, of which 90% are exported to the U.S. Ashton is extremely conscious of the collector's market in America and stamps his pipes accordingly with the date each one is produced. The company produces three finishes: a deeply sandblasted "Pebble Grain," a patented "Pebble Shell" which involves hand-rusticating and then sandblasting (usually reserved for pipes with extremely dense wood), and the very scarce smooth "Sovereign", which often exhibits some exquisite straight grain patterns. Only "firsts" bear the Ashton hand stamp. The "seconds" are sold in the U.K. under the Briarwoods brand and a few of these were introduced to the U.S. market in August, 1987.

BBB Pipes

Despite other claims to the contrary, BBB is unquestionably the oldest registered briar pipemaking name in England, having been first recorded as a British trademark in 1876, the year the Registration of Trade Marks Act became law. The pipes, in fact, had been made many years prior to that, possibly as early as 1847. Although many smokers think that BBB stands for "Britain's Best Briars", the initials originally represented "Blumfeld's Best Briars", after Louis Blumfeld, who was head of the company for many years. The pipes were awarded top honors during the Franco-British

Exhibition of 1908 and at the Brussels Exhibition of 1910. These well-respected pipes are still being made in England. However, none of the London-made BBB's have been imported into the U.S. since 1980, where BBB is now a "private label" brand and made in the same factory as the Jobey. With the exception of its U.S. alter-ego, however, the British BBB pipe is sold worldwide.

Baldo Baldi

An architect by training, Baldo Baldi lives in Genoa, where he makes extremely high quality pipes costing hundreds of dollars and aimed at the high grade collector/smoker. A total of about 250 pipes are produced a year, of which approximately 75 are shipped to the United States, making this a very limited pipe indeed.

Bang

No, this is not the sound your extraordinarily dry tobacco makes when you light it with a match; it is the brand name of Sven Bang, one of Denmark's most exclusive individual pipemakers.

Barling

A great name in pipes among smokers and collectors alike. The original Barling family were silversmiths in England during the latter part of the 1700s. In 1812, Benjamin Barling began fitting his hallmarked silver mountings to his own carved meerschaum pipes, which later received an award at London's Great Exhibition of 1851. Around 1854 Barling began making briar pipes, which soon became quite coveted due to their smokability and unique shapes. Many pipes featured a comfortable saddlebit and bowl designs unique to the firm, such as the "brandy glass". The Barling family sold their company in 1960 and for the next 20 years Barling pipes suffered a severe and sad loss of identity. Barling was reorganized in 1979 and in 1984 the pipe was finally reintroduced to smokers (although the new Barlings had been sold to the U.S. and European markets on a trial basis previously). Today, Barling pipes are made on the Isle of Man and over 30 different shapes are produced, including some of the old classics. The firm also makes a number of private brands for tobacco specialists and department stores.

Becker

A native of Austria, Fritz Becker has lived in Rome for the past forty years. A master designer of houses and furniture, he began making pipes around 1982. Today Becker and his son Paulo make a wide variety of uniquely designed neo-classical pipes. Completely handmade and expensively priced, each pipe is graded according to the suits of cards, with a Royal Flush being the highest quality obtainable. About 800 pipes are produced a year, which does not leave much room for dealing off the bottom of the pack.

Benson & Hedges

A popularly priced pipe introduced to the British market in the latter part of 1985 and made in the same factory as Comoy's. It is only available in England. As for the well-known brand name itself, it originated in 1873, when Richard Benson & William Hedges opened their tobacco shop at 13 Old Bond Street (how's that for trivia?).

Big Ben

A popular brand name manufactured in the Gubbels factory in Holland. A wide variety of briar pipes and a lesser number of non-briar pipes, such as the calabash, are sold under the Big Ben name throughout Europe.

Brebbia

One of the many Italian pipe companies that came into existence after World War II, Enea Brebbia began making pipes in 1948. However, it was not until the mid-1980s that Brebbia pipes were introduced to most of Europe and the United States. They have since gained a favorable reputation, whenever they can be found, primarily due to the fact that so many different styles and price ranges are offered. The high grade pipes have lucite mouthpieces, while the lower grades are fitted with vulcanite. The company shows a unique flair for marketing, creating specific lines in pipes for specific countries. For example, the filter-system Serie pipes are aimed at West Germany, the Classical is for England and the U.S., and the handmade Collection is for the high grade collector. All of the pipes have a unique "smoke dispersing device" in the mouthpiece, which breaks up the stream of smoke, allegedly cooling it as it reaches the tongue. Approximately 25,000 pipes are produced annually.

Butz-Choquin

(Pronounced Boots-Show-Can) One of the fifteen great French pipemaking firms of the Maîtres-Pipiers de Saint-Claude, France. Founded in 1858, today the company is operated by Jean-Paul Berrod and his cousin Jacques Berrod. "B.C." is now the largest of all the remaining briar pipe factories in Saint-Claude and is one of the few that still turns its own bowls. This respected firm makes a complete range of medium-to-high-grade briars with classic French craftsmanship, creating pipes under its own name and fashioning pipes for other well-known pipe companies as well.

Buckingham

A popular and economically priced London-made briar introduced to British pipesmokers by the John Redman company.

Colin Byford

An old English pipe brand that was eventually taken over by the Orlik pipemaking firm. There was also a Colin Byford tobacco marketed in the U.K. from 1957 until the 1960s, but neither pipe nor tobacco are made any longer.

Caminetto

In the U.S., older versions of this pipe are highly sought-after by pipe smokers and collectors. The Caminetto was the first pipe of the "new" Italian renaissance to be brought into the U.S. in any appreciable numbers. It was introduced to American pipe smokers in 1968 and the last of the "old"

Caminetto pipes was produced in 1980. During this 12-year reign, it was one of the finest smoking Italian briars available, due to the unique finish and curing process that made for an unbelievably dry smoke. The pipe is once again being made, although it is expensive and the styles have changed from the originals. For more interesting revelations on Caminetto, see Chapters Three and Nine.

Castello

The all-time classic Italian pipe that has been credited with starting the Italian pipemaking renaissance in the smoking world. The Castello (which means "castle") was originated by Carlo Scotti in Cantu, Italy, who began carving his pipes in the 1950s. Today the operation is supervised by his son-in-law and daughter, Franco and Savina Coppo. The Castello pipe was first "discovered" by U.S. tobacco retailer Wally Frank and it gradually caught on in America, which remains its biggest market. By the 1960s, it was highly acclaimed by the more sophisticated smokers, and the limited number of pipes that have come into America each year tend to keep the pipe something of a secret to the mass market. The Castello pipe was the first Italian brand to incorporate smooth, carved, and sandblast finishes of the same bowl designs and set a trend for popularizing the unique lightweight, dry, and airy smoking qualities that has become a characteristic of today's better quality Italian pipes. Adding to the mystique of the Castello, especially for U.S. collectors, is the use of two different trademarks on the stem. All Castello pipes exported to the U.S. have a tiny "diamond" that Scotti puts into the left side of all his stems. The pipes sold in Europe, however, feature an inlaid white plexiglass bar on the stem instead. Because of its scarcity in America, many U.S. collectors pay a slight premium for the European trademark and a "white bar" Castello is one of the first things they look for when travelling overseas! No matter what trademark they have, all Castello's are highly desirable and make a worthy addition (when they can be found) to anyone's pipe collection. For more on this legendary pipe, see Chapters Three and Nine.

Cesare

Italian pipes made by Cesare (pronounced Chez-are-ay) Barontini, whose father was a briar merchant. Cesare pipes are made in one of the most modern pipe factories in Italy. Like his father, Reno (as he likes to be called) is also a briar merchant. Thus he literally has the pick of the current crop – or at least *his* current crop – of fine wood. Like Armellini, Cesare builds his own pipemaking machinery, which he uses to create classically shaped pipes with a distinctively heavy masculine character.

Chacom

Brand name of the pipes produced by Chapuis-Comoy in Saint-Claude for the American market. An extremely fine pipe offering a wide variety of styles and prices.

Chapuis-Comoy

Originally known as La Bruyère, this pipemaking firm could be called the French cousin to Comoy's of London, as it is literally a close relation. Yves Grenard, a descendant of the original Comoy family, was working in the London factory of Comoy when the decision was made to close the Chapuis-Comoy plant in Saint-Claude due to lagging sales. Yves volunteered to try and save the family firm and successfully negotiated with Comoy's to buy the French factory. He has since succeeded in turning Chapuis-Comoy into one of France's best known pipemaking firms and one of the few who still turn their own bowls. The company is now the headquarters for a cartel of Saint-Claude's premier names in pipemaking. Chapuis-Comoy is also one of the 15 prestigious members of the Confrèrie des Maîtres-Pipiers de Saint-Claude.

Charatan

Frederick Charatan, a Russian emigré with a tobacco industry background, founded his pipemaking firm in the City of London in 1863 and the company never moved more than a few blocks from the original site. Charatan was the first of the London pipemakers to actually import briar ebauchons and turn the briar bowls within his own factory, as opposed to purchasing already-turned bowls from France and then finishing them in England by company workers (as was the practice in those early years). The original Charatan factory had a large window which overlooked the Tower of London and passers-by could see the workers hand-turning Charatan bowls, a process which soon became a Charatan trademark and also was responsible for creating many of the special shapes and freehand designs that became a speciality of the CP brand. Unfortunately, much of Charatan's early history is unknown, as the factory archives were destroyed during an air raid on London during World War II. For a while, Charatan operated two retail shops in London (one in Whitcombe Street and the other in Jermyn Street, which only recently closed its doors). Rueben Charatan took over the business from his father, but his two sons decided not to enter the pipemaking industry and the family's involvement with Charatan pipes ceased when Rueben's widow sold the company (along with the Ben Wade trademark which Charatan had used for its "seconds"). Charatan has always been a highly respected pipe and was one of the favorites of British royalty. In 1960, Charatan was one of the first pipes to sell for over $100. In the early 1980s, Charatan's Prescott Street factory in London was closed and the pipes are now made in the same location as others in the Dunhill Group.

Clairmont

Aside from the well-known Ropp cherrywood, this is the only pipe in this section that is not made of briar. Conceived in the 1970s by legendary Italian pipe personality Alberto Paronelli, the pipes are actually carved out of Sardinian olivewood. The grain is dark and threadlike and stands out dramatically against the blond-colored wood. As the pipe is smoked over a period of time, the wood gradually changes into a darkish matte-brown hue. The olivewood imparts a rather unique taste to the tobacco, but if you want to be less adventurous, the Paronelli family also makes a version of the Clairmont pipe out of Sardinian briar. Both types are sold throughout Europe and the U.S. And in case you are wondering, the name of the pipe is taken from the Italian town of Clairamonte, where the olivewood and the briar used for these pipes are harvested.

Comoy's

The oldest, continuously operating manufacturer of briar pipes in the world. François Comoy began making clay pipes in France in 1825. In 1848 his son Louis was one of the first to adopt briar for his pipemaking artistry (see Chapter One for the complete story). In 1879 Louis' son Henri moved the family briar-making business to London, thereby establishing Comoy's as one of the premier briar pipemakers of that city. Today, more than 150 years and five generations later, Comoy's continues in the tradition of excellent medium-to-high grade pipes, and many of their products have been quite collectible.

Davidoff

Long recognized by connoisseurs of Havana cigars, the Davidoff name entered the pipe smoker's world in 1974, when their pipes were first introduced in England. The Davidoff pipe reached American shores a few years later. The pipes are all high grades and are priced accordingly. They are definitely not for the man who is timid about reaching for his credit card! Available in 14 of the most traditional styles, the Davidoff pipe is readily identified by a semi-saddleback scalloped underside of the bit, which also exhibits a dramatically swirled "D". Three finishes are offered; in ascending price ranges, they are: black sandblast, a double stained "red", and a polished natural "matte". The Switzerland-based company also offers a complete range of tobaccos and an elegant line of humidors and accessories, some of which are stratospherically priced. The Davidoff line is sold through their London store and a few other selected tobacco specialists in that city, as well as in Manchester, Edinburgh and Birmingham.

Dr. Max

A popular, economically priced pipe made by John Redman Ltd. and sold throughout England, as well as other countries, including some of those behind the Iron Curtain. First introduced in 1945, the pipe was named after the firm's sales agent in South Africa, Max Cunard, who wanted an exclusive pipe of his own. He got it!

Dr. Plumb

One of England's most popular pipes, primarily with the filter system, both in the Home Market and abroad, although these pipes are not normally available in the U.S. The "Plumb" does not refer to "plumbing," but was actually the name of a jovial, mustachioed factory manager who invented the pipe system, and who was therefore given the honorary title of "Doctor" by the company.

Duncan Briars

Originally started in 1899 by John Louis Duncan, who was then succeeded by his son Robert, the firm is currently headed up by a third generation of the family, John Duncan, grandson of the founder. Perhaps best known for their Duncan Dental bits, the original John Duncan invented the Pipesmoker's Friend combination tool and the Duncan Delta spare bowl system, both of which are still in the line. In addition to their pipes, Duncan Briars also market a variety of smokers' accessories under their name.

Dunhill

One of the most prestigious pipemakers in the world today and also one of the most expensive, as this firm makes only "firsts" and removes any "seconds" that they may discover during their 80 different inspections along each step of the pipemaking route. The company was started in London in 1907 by Alfred Dunhill. In 1912 he began incorporating the "white spot" to enable workers to tell quickly which end was "up" when the handcarved vulcanite mouthpiece was hand-fitted to the pipe shank. This "white spot" has since become a classic Dunhill trademark. Today, the London-based company continues to use only Premium Grade AA briar for their bowls and produces pipes that range from classical shapes to special order items that may take a year or more to complete. Dunhill is presently personified in Richard, grandson of the founder, who continues with Alfred's ideals of perfection. The firm has always had its own line of "My Mixture" tobaccos, but under "Mr. Richard's" guidance has recently branched out into jewellery, fragrances, leather goods, and designer clothes, lending their elegant name to fashions now as well as to pipes.

Falcon

One of the most popular pipes in England, if not the world, although it is snubbed by many pipe smokers in the U.S., the country where it was invented by an American engineer named Kenley Bugg. Nonetheless, the Falcon is the favored pipe of 1987 Pipeman of the Year (and BBC TV critic) Barry Norman, so who can argue with that? The Falcon is a system pipe, but what makes it unique is its interchangeable bowls and metal stems (although some recent models in the U.K. have a much more traditional look to them). The pipe was first introduced to American smokers in 1940 and by 1954 more than six million pipes had been sold in the U.S. Due to its amazing popularity at the time, arrangements were made by a British concern to manufacture and sell the pipes in the U.K. Although test marketed a few years earlier, the pipe was officially introduced to British pipe smokers in 1958 and 30,000 pipes were sold in that year alone. Today the British-made Falcon is unquestionably one of the best-selling pipes of all time, with approximately one million pipes being sold in 92 different countries annually. With seven different stem styles and 48 types of bowls, quick calculations indicate that 13,680 individual pipe variations are possible! And you only need one pipe rack.

Ferndown

See L. & J. S. Briars.

Wally Frank Ltd.

A well known New York pipe firm selling pipes since 1930. Its imported and private label briars and clays were often sold under a variety of names. Still very much in business.

GBD

The initials stand for the names of the three 19th century French founders, Ganeval, Bondier and Donninger. Founded in Paris in 1850, they began their enterprise by making meerschaums, the most popular "high grade" of the day. Eventually the GBD brand became known for its French briars and in 1903 the firm established a factory in England to be closer to the booming briar pipe trade that was starting to use London as a nucleus (although French-made GBD's had sales offices in London as early as 1870). The GBD London branch was operated by the historic English firm of Oppenheimer. Although the three original partners were no longer associated with the company, by then their trademark, the GBD initials surrounded by an oval, was so well known for quality briar, it has been retained on the stem of all GBD pipes to this very day. In 1952 the entire GBD factory was transferred from Paris to Saint-Claude, and for many years the GBD name could be found on both English and French made pipes. Since 1981, however, virtually all GBD pipes have been made in England.

Hardcastle

Edmund Hardcastle began making pipes in 1908 and for a while the pipes were made in the old Jack O'London factory in Walthamstow. The firm has since been acquired by Dunhill, where it eventually became part of the Parker-Hardcastle operation. Hardcastle pipes are still being produced for the U.K. and the Continent, although they are not as available in the U.S. as they once were. A tremendous number of variations and price ranges exist.

Preben Holm

Excellent high grade Danish freehands, each of which is

personally inspected by Preben Holm prior to being shipped from his factory in Denmark. Production of Preben Holm pipes ceased temporarily in 1986 due to a variety of economic factors, but the pipes are again being made, albeit on a very limited basis, and most are exported to the United States.

Il Ceppo

A finely crafted Italian pipe made by former architect Giorgio Imperatori, whose stylings range from the classic to the radical. And in case you were wondering, "il ceppo" is Italian for "the root", referring to the part of the briar from which all good pipes come.

Israeli Pipes

There are numerous small pipemaking companies, but there has been only one large pipemaking firm in Israel, known as Shalom. Unfortunately, this firm curtailed operations in 1987. Their pipes can be found in Europe under a variety of names, including the Hebraically spelled Shalom. Ever since 1971, however, they have used the Alpha brand for those pipes which are imported into the U.S.

Jack O'London

A popular pipe from the past which eventually became part of the Parker-Hardcastle family.

Georg Jensen

The Georg Jensen family began making their Danish pipes in 1954. The pipes are primarily traditional in design, although a few freeform models are produced. Many Jensen pipes feature silver bands or inlaid panels which are suitable for engraving. Like most Danish pipes, the Jensen briars are superbly finished and may be found, albeit not plentifully, throughout Europe and occasionally in the United States.

Jobey

Over the years, this popular U.S. pipe has existed in both freehand and traditional stylings, and while many smokers assumed it was a Danish brand, the pipe actually originated in England, before it "emigrated" to America. The Jobey pipe holds the distinction of being one of the last of the mass-produced, medium priced quality pipes to be made in the United States. In June 1987, however, Jobey production was moved to Saint-Claude, in France. It still retains its popularity, even though it must now be imported to the country it once called home. At one time the firm was owned by Carl Weber, author of *The Pleasures of Pipe Smoking* (one of the books listed in our Bibliography).

Kaywoodie

Ironically, the Kaywoodie brand has much more respect in England than it does in its American homeland, where the once-popular U.S. made pipes are now being imported from Italy as a low grade mass-market variety. All Kaywoodies sold throughout Europe, however, are made near London and their quality has helped preserve some of the tradition of yesteryear. Their "Synchro Stem" and "Drinkless" fitment has made the London Kaywoodie especially popular on the Continent. For a complete history of the original American-made pipe, see Chapter Nine.

Keyser Hygienic Pipe

An aluminium system pipe that does not use a separate filter. The pipe was invented in the 1940s by Peter Keyser. Designed and manufactured in England of French briar, the Keyser is available in a variety of standard styles; one of the features is that the mouthpieces are interchangeable (and replaceable) from pipe to pipe, with no hand-fitting necessary.

L. & J. S. Briars

One of England's "new generation" of quality pipemakers. L. & J. S. Briars is really a pseudonym for Les and Dolly Wood, a husband and wife team who produce a wide spectrum of pipes, primarily for the U.S. market. Although they make numerous brand label pipes for Europe, their premium product is the Ferndown pipe (which gets its name from Wood's house), an oil-cured high grade made from Grecian plateau. About 90% of the Ferndowns (which are marketed in Germany under the name Ellwood – for L. Wood – get it?) are made in a rusticated "Bark" finish and the balance are a smooth "Root" finish. Especially unusual is the fact that a full 50% of all Ferndown pipes are mounted in silver or gold. The reason for all this precious metallurgy is that Les Wood is England's premier silver mounter of briar pipes and is the only pipemaker in Britain with engine turning/mounting facilities in his workshop. From personal experience I can tell you Les can create a silver cap or gold engraved band for virtually any pipe. The Ferndown came into existence in 1983 and approximately 1,500 are produced annually, with about 80% of these going to the U.S. trade, where the sparkle of silver combined with superb smoking qualities has made the Ferndown very much in demand. The balance of the pipes are sold in the U.K. and in West Germany, where a special filter version is available.

Loewe

Founded by Emile Loewe, a French pipemaker who settled in London, Loewe & Company Ltd. started life as a pipe shop in the Haymarket in 1856. As the years went on, Loewe briars gained an enviable reputation. They were noted for their wide variety of pipe styles, such as silver mounted, multi-stemmed cased traveling sets. Sadly, with the redevelopment of the Haymarket area, the old shop, showroom and offices are now gone. Although no longer located in London's West End, the famed Loewe brand is still being manufactured in England and this high grade enjoys a following of dedicated pipe smokers throughout Europe as well as in Australia and Korea. In 1988, the Loewe pipe was exported to the United States for the first time in its long history.

W. Ø. Larsen

W. Ø. "Ole" Larsen is one of Denmark's most highly respected high grade pipe designers, and is the fourth generation of the family's firm, which was founded in 1864. His handmade pipes exhibit an elegance of form and perfection which makes them very popular with knowledgeable smokers and collectors. The Larsen firm also markets four different types of pipe tobaccos under the name Larsen's Choice. Ole's son Neils is now the fifth generation of the family to carry on the business, and has gained his own personal prominence in the field of hand-making carved horn and silver pipe tampers.

Lorenzo Pipes

Until his death in July 1987, Lorenzo Tagliabue was one of two pipemakers in Italy with the same last name, so he used his first name on all his pipes. Comoy's acts as the U.S. agent for Lorenzo, which is why Americans see these pipes in the Comoy's catalogue. Lorenzo made a wide range of high quality pipes and brand label briars and even had a line of Italian-styled Lorenzo pipes made under the Comoy's brand. The firm was founded in 1900.

Mastro de Paja

One of the largest of the Italian handmade pipe carving companies.

Merchant Service

Originally sold by Londoner Herbert Merchant, the Merchant Service Special was a long straight stemmed, long shanked briar that gained fame and glory when it became the preferred pipe of American singer Bing Crosby in the 1950s. So many fans would steal Crosby's pipes whenever he laid them down, that he began importing Merchant Service pipes to America by the boxful. Fortunately, they were never very expensive, but they had an elegant look to them that has rarely been duplicated. Available with and without a silver band and also known to exist with leather covering, the pipe is – alas! – no longer made. But in honor of the celebrity who helped make it famous, its shape is often referred to as "The Crosby" when it occasionally appears in various pipemakers' catalogues.

Millville

Another of England's "newer" pipemakers, the Millville brand was established in 1980 with a nucleus of workers from the old Charatan factory. Primarily run as a small family business by Dennis Marshall and his son John, Millville pipes are high grade, hand turned "firsts" in a variety of classic and freeform shapes. A bit difficult to find in many areas of the U.K., a few are exported to the Continent. In addition to their Millville brand, the family also makes less expensive pipes for various tobacco specialists.

Masta

Made by Parker-Hardcastle, primarily for the Norwegian market.

Mountbatten

A Parker-Hardcastle pipe produced for Switzerland.

Munalli

An Italian brand with non-traditional styling, Munalli pipes gained distinction by being in the collection of former Italian President Pertini.

Nørding

Maker of some of the world's most sought-after and respected Danish freehands as well as a superb line of high grade traditionally-styled briars, many with silver or gold bands. The versatile Nørding also produces a number of private label pipes for individual tobacconists. A former blacksmith and engineer as well as a world-famous sportsman, Erik Nørding began making pipes in 1967 and today his elegantly styled and cool smoking pipes are showpieces in literally hundreds and thousands of collections throughout the world. They are classics of design, and the high grade briars are especially known for their smooth,.glass-like finishes and their tremendous variety of shapes and design innovations.

Orlik

The Orlik pipe factory was established in London in 1899 by Louis Orlik, whose family continued the operation until 1980, when the firm was sold to Cadogan. Today, a wide variety of briar and meerschaum pipes are still produced in England under the Orlik banner, although their tobaccos are now being blended in Denmark. In the 1960s the Orlik pipe was exported to the U.S., where it proved to be a popular economical pipe, but it is no longer widely available in that country. The Orlik trademark of a robed judge peering out sagely from behind his pipe and the motto, "Smoked by all shrewd judges", has become part of British pipe smoking history.

Parker-Hardcastle

A compilation of names which occurred in 1967, arising from the amalgamation of the Parker Pipe Company, which was started in 1922 as a subsidiary of Dunhill, with the Hardcastle pipe company. Today the Parker is a well-made, popular pipe sold under the auspices of the Dunhill company in London.

Peterson

A somewhat controversial pipe that has a great number of highly devoted followers both in America and Europe. The "Peterson System", as it is called by the company, consists of a rather unique hollowed-out chamber bored into the briar directly underneath the pipe bowl and channeled into the airhole of the stem. As the pipe is smoked, the tobacco in the bowl stays dry, as all of the moisture enters the "reservoir" underneath. A more complete description is given in Chapter Three. Charles Peterson began making pipes in Ireland in 1875 and first invented his system somewhere around 1890. His pipes won two gold medals in the London International Tobacco Trade Exhibition of 1895. The pipe is still made in Ireland and has not changed appreciably in design, although the company has changed dramatically since its origin. The Peterson pipe was a favorite of American author

Mark Twain and Basil Rathbone often smoked them in his motion picture roles as Sherlock Holmes. It is a good-smoking nostalgic 19th century design and a number of variations, including meerschaums and briars ranging from plain to gold mounted, are offered today.

Pipe Dan

Pipe Dan was one of the earliest forces that helped popularize the Danish style of freeform pipe design. No longer just a pipemaker, today Pipe Dan is one of Copenhagen's most popular pipe shops and has become a veritable showcase for some of Denmark's most talented (and sometimes elusive) pipemakers. In addition to the maker's mark, every pipe sold in the shop is imprinted with the Pipe Dan name, the date the pipe was purchased and even the customer's initials . . . if there is still enough room left on the shank!

Porsche

If you can't drive the car, you might at least consider smoking the pipe. Ferdinand Alexander Porsche, the man who designed the 904 and the 911, is also a pipe smoker, so it should come as no surprise that he would eventually design a sleek pipe made of briar with an aluminium-shrouded bowl which incorporates an external cooling technology inspired by the cylinder ribs of an aeroplane engine. Introduced in 1984 and sold throughout the U.S. and Europe, the pipe is made in the Henrich Oldencott factory in West Germany. Although not inexpensive, owning the pipe is substantially cheaper than buying the car and might be worth it just for the thrill of inviting some friends over to see your "new Porsche"!

Radice

(Pronounced Rad-ee-chay.) Luigi Radice was one of the two carvers who made Caminetto pipes (along with Peppino Ascorti) before starting his own company in 1981. A former pipemaker for Castello, his designs are a bit more pronounced than the old Caminetto stylings, but his finishes and wood curing are of the same fine and characteristic quality. He produces less than 6,000 pipes a year.

Redman

John Redman started his pipemaking firm in 1933 and has been continuously producing a wide variety of London-made briars ever since. His speciality is popularly priced models, gift sets and "own brand" pipes, for tobacco specialists.

Ropp

Eugene Ropp started his company in 1869, making it the oldest French pipe trademark. Today the famous name is found on both briar and meerschaum pipes but Ropp is still best known for its distinctive cherrywood pipes.

Sasieni

Another one of the great collectible and smokable pipes of England's recent past. Today they are no longer produced by the original company. Joel Sasieni began his career working as an apprentice pipemaker for Charatan and left to manage the "new" pipemaking operation for Alfred Dunhill in 1910. He left Dunhill in 1918 to start his own London pipemaking firm. His son Alfred took over the company reins after World War II. The majority of the pipes were exported to the United States, where they were renowned for their famous eight-dot and four-dot series of "firsts". Ironically, these same pipes were sold in the U.K. and other European countries with a one-dot configuration on the stem and for years U.S. tourists passed them up as "rejects", rather than as the high grade "firsts" they really were. Now that the truth is out, however, all that has changed. The company was sold in 1979 and today the pipes are produced by a completely different firm, primarily for sale in the U.S.

Savinelli

In 1876 Achille Savinelli first opened his pipe shop in Milan. His two brothers opened a similar pipe shop in Genoa. Over the years their name became well known among Italian pipe smokers in these areas and in 1920 Achille's son Carlo entered the business and also began making pipes. In 1948 his son, Achille, started a pipe factory in Varasso, and was the first to begin producing pipes that were stamped with the Savinelli trademark that we know today. Savinelli became one of Italy's earliest large-scale pipemakers and the company remains a highly respected name worldwide. Its high grades are extremely popular with American smokers and collectors. Of all the Italian pipes, it is one of the few that can be found in Great Britain with any regularity. Interestingly, the original Savinelli pipe shop in Milan is still in existence and is still operated by the family. Achille Savinelli passed away in March 1987, and now his daughter, Marisetta, supervises the pipemaking activities.

Ser Jacopo

Another of the new, high quality, nontraditionally-shaped pipes being exported out of Italy and destined primarily for the lucrative U.S. smoker/collector market.

Stanwell

Paul Stanwell can be credited with making the Danish pipe popular throughout Europe and the United States. He started his pipemaking company in 1942 under the name Kyringe. However, in 1948 he began stamping his pipes with his surname to make post-war pipe smokers think that his pipes were British! Stanwells were the first of the Danish freehands to be sold in any quantity in the U.S., beginning in the early 1960s. Although there were other Danish freehands before Stanwell, less than 100 a year were usually exported. Stanwell changed all that. He created one of the most automated pipe factories in Europe, which today turns out 150,000 pipes a year, primarily for Germany, the U.S. and Denmark. The company makes "firsts" under the Stanwell line but also exports "seconds" under other trade names, such as Royal Danish, Royal Guard, Soverain, etc. Paul Stanwell died in 1982 and his company was subsequently purchased by another firm. Today this pioneer Danish pipemaking operation continues to produce a wide variety of popular pipes for the world market.

Stokkebye

Conceived by noted Danish tobacconist Peter Stokkebye, the pipes bearing his name are actually made by Jorgen Larsen, who used to be factory manager for Stanwell. There are two eras to the Danish Stokkebye pipe. The first pipes were created from 1975 to 1978 and each featured a 24 kt. gold "family crest" in the stem. Many had ivory mountings. Then there was a hiatus until 1986, at which time Larsen made 12 new Stokkebye pipes, all of which were sold in the U.S. The pipes are again being made, at the rate of about six a month. Most of the pipes are straight grains, and are graded by letters of the alphabet, according to quality, with A being the best.

Talamona

A talented Italian pipemaking family, headed by Cesare Talamona. Noted for their straight grains, the pipes were initially introduced in the U.S. in 1983 and are also sold in Italy, Belgium, Switzerland and Canada.

Tilshead

Made of top grade Grecian plateau briar, these pipes are the Upshall "rejects". As such, they represent one of the best smoking values in England. These pipes, of course, are named after the small town in England where they are manufactured. About 5,000 Tilshead pipes are produced each year and they are available in either a "Red" or "Natural" finish.

James Upshall

Until it was first publicized in the U.S. edition of this book, the Upshall brand was one of the "sleepers" in the high grade pipe world. It has now become one of the most respected of all the English briars and the small five-person factory has a difficult time keeping up with demand. The company was formed in 1977 by Colonel Kenneth Barnes, who had been the former managing director of Charatan for 16 years. He and his son Kennedy had started a pipe shop in Salisbury in

Wiltshire, and decided to put out their own line of high grades. Soon the demand became more than the shop could produce and a separate factory was set up under the name of the Tilshead Pipe Company Ltd. The high grade pipes were christened James Upshall, as the Colonel's full ancestral family name was Kenneth James Upshall-Barnes. When Colonel Barnes died, his son Kennedy took over operation of the firm. In the manner of master pipemakers decades ago, all of the briars are individually hand turned and made only from the finest Grade AA plateau. The company is known for producing primarily smooths and due to Barnes' penchant for quality, only "firsts" are stamped with the James Upshall name. Consequently, less than 6,000 pipes are turned out each year, with about 40% going to the U.S., where they were first introduced in 1979. The rest of the Upshalls find their way into various British pipe shops, especially around London, as well as on the Continent, Malaysia and Canada. Considering their quality, the Upshall pipe is very competitively priced.

Ben Wade

A English pipemaking firm dating from the 1860s and originally located in Leeds, Yorkshire, where it remained for over a century. Ben Wade was a well respected high grade, and most of the pipes were sold in the Midlands and northern England, along with the Dr. McQuade pipe, which the company also made. The company's operation passed from the original family's hands in 1965, when the factory shut down and the name was sold to Charatan, who used the brand to market their "rejects". Such is no longer the case and Ben Wade is once again a highly respected pipe made by the Charatan factory that occasionally seems to have a difficult time deciding whether it should be English or Danish in design; at one time the brand was used for the less extravagant versions of Preben Holm's pipes that were imported into the U.S. The craftsmanship and smokability, however, have always been superb and remain so to this day.

Willmer

Although this London firm makes some pipes under its own name for both Great Britain and the U.S., it is primarily known for the vast number of private label pipes it produces for England's tobacco specialists.

Clay Pipe Manufacturers

Ayto (Old & New Designs)

Eric Ayto (12 Green Lane, Clansfield, Portsmouth, PO8 0JU) is not one of the biggest, but is one of the most versatile in terms of both historic and custom designs. He makes cutties and colored pipes as well as traditionally styled 17th century reproductions.

Lepeltier

Georges and Rosalie Lepeltier (Box 61, East Fairfield, VT 05448, USA) are the only manufacturers of double walled-clay pipes in the United States. They are also one of the few pipe companies to sell direct to the consumer. The company started business in the U.S. in 1978 and currently produces 5,000 pipes a year. The double-walled clay, which is glazed on the outside but left absorbent on the inside of the bowl, permits the exterior walls of the pipe to remain cool as it is smoked. An additional feature is the design possibilities of the glazed bowls, which range in concept from Currier & Ives prints to fraternal crests and hand-painted initials, and the Lepeltiers welcome such customized orders.

John Pollock & Co.

Founded in 1879, this firm (2, Scott Street, Manchester M11 3EW) is virtually the last of the Victorian English clay pipe factories still in operation. Gordon Pollock, grandson of the firm's founder, still makes clays from their original moulds, which include many facial portraits of Victorian celebrities. Pollock clays are not reproductions, but actually a continuation of a historic pipe that has not changed in over a century.

Zenith

The oldest continuously operating pipemaker in the world, this firm began making clays back in 1749 and is still producing the same pipes today, using many of the same moulds. They are especially noted for their long clay churchwardens. In addition, Zenith pioneered the double wall clay pipe around the turn of the century and today produce a variety of glazed models in various colors, including a series of "mystery pipes", in which a hidden object gradually appears on the bowl as the pipe is smoked. Up until 1987 the Zenith factory had been operated continuously by eight successive generations of the same founding family. Located in the city of Gouda in Holland (the same place where the cheese is made), Zenith continues to turn out over seven million clays a year and their Delft china pipes are especially sought after as collectibles, even by non-smokers.

Meerschaum Pipes – Manufacturers

Bauer

Andreas Bauer was one of the best known of the recent (1960s) pre-Turkish meerschaum carvers. This Austrian firm continues to produce the classic "Holmesian" calabash as well as figural and traditionally shaped models.

Laxey Pipe Ltd.

The Quay – Old Laxey,
Isle of Man.
Manufacturers of calcinated "Manx" meerschaum pipes.

London Meershaum Ltd. (Jambo)

64 Eastgate
P.O. Box 1
Cowbridge
South Glamorgan
Wales, CF7 7AB.
The largest manufacturer of block meerschaum pipes in

England. In addition, this firm also manufactures stylish calabash pipes of both horn and gourd, and specializes in mounting their pipes in silver and occasionally gold.

Corncob Pipes – Manufacturers

Missouri Meerschaum Co.
P.O. Box 226
Washington, MO 63090
USA.
The world's oldest corncob pipemaking firm, currently turning out approximately 30,000 pipes a year worldwide. The complete history of this picturesque American company can be found in Chapter One.

Custom Pipemakers

There are literally hundreds of talented individual pipe carvers throughout the world, and as many are known only in their town or region, it would be virtually impossible to list them all. The majority of these carvers seem to be in Denmark and in the United States, where a pipe carving renaissance has been taking place ever since the first U.S. edition of *The Ultimate Pipe Book* was published in 1984. In Europe, many of these carvers are nomadic and tend to change their addresses almost daily. Therefore, their limited edition handiwork can only be viewed in pipe shops which display the best of the lot, of which Copenhagen's Pipe Dan is perhaps the best known on the Continent. At the risk of offending many talented craftsmen but as a more important service to the reader who might not appreciate sitting with an enormously heavy book on his lap, I have only listed a few of the world's top quality pipe carvers, utilizing as a criterion those whose work is personally known to me and who pursue the art of pipe carving as a profession, rather than as a hobby. Although many of their briars can be obtained through your tobacco specialist, some custom pipe carvers, especially those in the United States, may be contacted directly concerning their work.

A Special Note Concerning American Pipe Carvers

There are over 300 pipe carvers in the United States. Some of their exquisite workmanship can be seen in Chapter Two. However, to list them all would require a separate booklet. Fortunately, just such a publication exists, complete with photographs of many U.S. carvers and their handiwork. It is entitled the *Directory of American Pipemakers* and is obtainable for $3 (U.S. funds; be sure to add extra money for international postage) by writing to:
Pipe Collectors International
P.O. Box 22085
Chattanooga, TN 37422
USA.

. . . And now, here are a few carvers from the rest of the world:

Pierre and Robert Blatter
Blatter & Blatter
365 President Kennedy Avenue
Montreal, P.Q. H3A 1J5
Canada.
The Blatter family began making pipes in Cape Town, South Africa, in 1900 and were noted for producing perhaps some of the very first calabash pipes, which earned them a gold medal in 1905 for their handiwork. The Blatter family moved to Montreal shortly after that, and by 1907 had established a chain of pipe shops and a pipe factory. Today the family pipemaking tradition is kept very much alive by brothers Pierre and Robert, who specialize in creating large handmade pipes of various designs, which are displayed and sold through their well-known retail store.

Alberto Bonfigliolo
Via Piella 8/A–3/C
Bologna
Italy.
A dedicated craftsman who produces about 800 pipes a year in a variety of non-traditional shapes, using sun-cured Calabrian and Sardinian briar.

Ingo Garbe
Havnegade 94
DK-9950 Vestero
Denmark.
A superb craftsman who makes classical and semi-traditionally styled pipes that have been exhibited as works of art.

Julius Vesz
Royal York Hotel
Toronto, Ontario M5J 1E3
Canada.
Perhaps one of North America's most stylish pipesmiths, the Hungarian-born Vesz is capable of creating a vast array of styles, ranging from the traditional billiard all the way up to horn-shanked, silver mounted deep bents with precious metal embellishments of owls, buffalo or flowers gracing the bowls and even sculpted into windcaps.

Repairs/Reconditioning

Practically all tobacconists can handle basic pipe rejuvenation or repair. However, there are some specialists for hard-to-get materials, antiques restorations, etc. Try your tobacconist first; if he is unable to perform the required services himself, have him contact one of the individuals listed below.

General Repairs/Rejuvenation

Jim Benjamin
3818 Royal Woods Drive
Sherman Oaks, CA 91403
USA.
The chances of your going to the States to have your pipe retrofitted are pretty remote; the only reason Jim is listed is that he is the only person in America, other than myself, whom I ever let restore my pipes. He can take the shoddiest briar and completely transform it to "like new" condition, including bit polishing and bowl staining to original factory specifications.

Invicta Briars of England
King Street
Chatham
Kent.

Antique Pipe Repair

Ashton Pipes
1 Old Church Rise
Romford
Essex RM 7 0AD.
Bill Taylor has one of the U.K.'s few remaining supplies of quality amber and, with the turning equipment in his factory, can repair many older briar and meerschaum pipes. He also has vulcanite rods should you wish to have your tobacco specialist fit your pipe with a new bit.

Astleys Ltd.
109 Jermyn Street
London, SW1Y 6HB.
Established in 1862, this shop maintains a more than adequate supply of antique pipes for sale and display and, as such, is a good source for antique pipe repair. Although no work is done on the premises, they will send your pipe out to the proper source to be restored correctly.

John W. Bromage Ltd.
The Ferns, Eskdale Green
Holrook
W. Cumbria CA19 1UA.
A specialist in antique meerschaum repairs, but a craftsman who can also bring modern 20th century briars back to life as well.

Bowl/Bit Replacement

James Upshall
19–20 Candown Road
Tilshead
Wiltshire.
Should you have a case which has lost its pipe, Ken Barnes

can use his handturning skills to fashion a briar pipe that will fit it perfectly. He can also perform other bowl turning and staining operations, in addition to replacing broken vulcanite bits.

Gold & Silver Mounting

L. & J. S. Briars
4 Jubilee Industrial Estate
Stickling Green Road
Clavering
Essex.
Les Wood is England's specialist in creating or repairing military mounts, making elegant gold or silver bands for pipes with cracked shanks, and fashioning precious metal caps for briars.

Miscellaneous Accessories

Most of the pipe smoking accessories mentioned or shown in this book can be found in or ordered through your local tobacco specialist. However, there are a few unusual American items I have illustrated that may be difficult to find in Europe. Thus, I have listed them here as speciality items under their respective company names.

Cash Manufacturing Co.
816 So. Division Street
Waunakee, WI 53597
USA.
Early 18th and 19th century tobacco boxes made of brass, steel and German silver; patterned from the American colonial and fur trade eras.

Dixie Gun Works
Gunpowder Lane
Union City, TN 38261
USA.
Early American tobacco and snuff boxes; flint and steel fire starters and reproduction tinder lighters.

PipeKing
Bellinghieri Enterprises
75 North Union Street
Arlington, MA 02174
USA.
Electronic pipe cleaning machine that can also be used for breaking in new briar pipes and for coloring meerschaum pipes naturally. Because this noisy but effective device runs on American voltage (120V), you will have to use a converter to operate it. Be sure to adjust the air intake value carefully to avoid overheating and burning out your pipe.

Pipe Clubs

Australia

The Pipe Club of Australia, Ltd.
Box 4702, G.P.O. Sydney 2001.

Belgium

Belgische Pijpclub
c/o Sels Pol
Piervenshoek 20
2850 Keerbergen.

Europipe Club Bruxelles
c/o J. C. Dubois
rue du Champion, 25
1070 Bruxelles.

British Isles

Due to the constantly fluctuating number of pipe clubs in Great Britain, it is suggested that you write to the following address to find a current club that is near you. If there isn't one, why not start a club yourself?
The Pipesmoker's Council, c/o Michael Butler
19 Elrington Road
London E8 3BJ.

Canada

Club des Fumeurs de Pipes de Quebec
c/o Michel Sawyer
Case postale 910
Succursale Desjardins
Montreal, QC H5B 1C1.

Denmark

The Nordic Smokers Guild
c/o Leif Slot
Ellekrattet 18
2950 Vedbaek.

France

Le Pipe Club de France
c/o Andre-Paul Bastien
9 rue Saint-Fiacre
75002 Paris.

Poland

Polish Pipe Club Council
c/o Janusz K. Molski, Chairman
Aleje WP 68/20
62-805 Kalisz.

Portugal

Cachimo Clube de Portugal
R. Infante D. Henrique 162
8500 Portimao.

South Africa

M. B. Ussher (Founder)
Pipe and Tobacco Club of Southern Africa
P.O. Box 85082
2029 Emmarentia.

Spain

Barcelona Pipa Club
Placa Reial, 3 Principal
08002 Barcelona.

Pipa Club de Espana
Avenida Argentina, 22, 1o,1a
Palma de Mallorca.

Switzerland

Pipe-Club Swisse
c/o Jonathan Lussy, President
C.P. 3874
CH 4002 Basel.

United States of America

International Association of Pipe Smoking Clubs
c/o Paul Spaniola
Paul's Pipe Shop
647 S. Saginaw Street
Flint, MI 48502.
Organized in 1949, most of the clubs that comprise membership are concentrated in the U.S. The IAPSC is noted for conducting an annual World Champion Pipe Smoking Contest, which is held in the United States and is hosted by a different pipe club each year. The IAPSC pipe smoking championship adheres to a strict set of rules that deviate somewhat from those followed by European contests, the main difference being that only cube cut Burley tobacco is permitted.

Pipe Collectors International
P.O. Box 22085
Chattanooga, TN 37422.
Not the oldest, but certainly the most organized club in the U.S. Formed in 1983, PCI is run primarily for the pipe collector, but as most collectors in America are also pipe smokers, there is much information for everyone in their

interesting four-color magazine, which is published six times a year. The magazine provides a good way to learn of the benefits and values of many new and used pipe brands as well as to find out about local U.S. pipe clubs and collectors' organizations. An annual PCI convention is held in the Spring of each year, where pipe collectors come from all over the world to buy, sell and visit. Write to PCI for full particulars as to dues and benefits.

The Universal Coterie of Pipe Smokers
c/o Tom Dunn
20–37 120th Street
College Point, NY 11356.
An informational and widely spread international assemblage of pipe smokers, hobbiests, collectors and manufacturers, all linked together by an "irregular quarterly" (which means it is usually published once every year or so, much to the chagrin of its readers), edited and published by Tom Dunn, one of the most devoted hobbiests of the century. His publication, *The Pipe Smoker's Ephemeris*, is a pipe smoker's treasure chest of information on current activities throughout the world. To receive this unique 40-plus page communiqué, simply write to Tom and tell him you want to join the Coterie. There are no dues, but inasmuch as Dunn finances the entire operation himself, contributions are always welcome, be they money, tobacco, or pipes. I even think he takes wooden matches!

Honorary Associations

Académie Internationale de la Pipe
Via del Chiostro 1/3
21026 Gravirate
Italy.
Formed on October 12, 1985, this is one of the newest and certainly one of the most prestigious organizations that has ever been devoted to the pipe. Membership in the Académie is limited to just 30 specially selected individuals (although Associate Memberships are possible), each of whom has been nominated from the world's most renowned writers, journal-

ists, and historians who have dedicated their lives in various ways to the proliferation of the pipe. Thus, the Académie is an international cartel of information and source material, and is pledged to the ongoing preservation and perpetuation of the pipe on a worldwide basis.

Confrèrie des Maîtres Pipiers de Saint-Claude
45, Rue de Pré
39200 Saint-Claude
France.
A prestigious 200-year-old society composed of fifteen of the top pipemakers of France who are dedicated to the promotion of Saint-Claude made briars throughout the smoking world. Membership is worldwide but is by invitation only and nominees must travel to Saint-Claude to participate in the ancient pipe ritual that results in their induction as a member of this honorary group.

Trade Organizations

British Isles

Association of Independent Tobacco Specialists
Craftsman House, Worcester Road
Hartlebury, Kidderminster
Worcestershire DY11 7XD.
Organized in 1976, this dedicated group strives to preserve those elements of professionalism among tobacconists that make England's pipe shops unique. The AITS are also publishers of the invaluable *Tobacco Index*, which gives the names and descriptions of every pipe tobacco found in Great Britain.

Briar Pipe Trade Association
c/o John Barber Pipes Ltd.
133 Bletchingley Road
Merstham, Redhill
Surrey RH1 3QQ.
A professional organization concerned with export and taxation as they relate to Britain's briar pipe industry.

The Pipesmoker's Council, c/o Michael Butler
19 Elrington Road
London E8 3BJ.
Formed in 1978, this organization has become the "guardian angel", so to speak, of all British pipe smokers. The council's sole purpose in life is to publicize the finer aspects of pipe smoking through a mixture of publicity, marketing knowledge and various pipe-oriented promotional activities. One of the Pipesmokers' Council's more celebrated activities is the annual selection of Britain's Pipesmoker of the Year award, an event that spotlights some of the nation's more newsworthy pipe smokers.

Wholesale Tobacco Trade Association
15 Tooks Court
London EC4A 1LA.

Worshipful Company of Tobacco Pipemakers and Tobacco Blenders
Bouverie House
154 Fleet Street
London EC4A 2HX.
A distinguished organization, made up of notable members of the tobacco trade, and known for its charitable activities.

Publications for Pipe Smokers – International

British Isles

PIPE LINE
J. P. Cole, Editor
Hill Park Publications
18 Kay Avenue
Meadowlands Park
Weybridge Road, Addlestone
Surrey KT15 2RE.
A true labor of love by the editor and a worthy magazine for all dedicated pipe people, containing news featurettes on pipe clubs, pipe personalities, pipe manufacturers, products in the U.K. and other pertinent items. Jacques Cole has

more than enough credentials to put such a publication together and it should be on the reading list of anyone owning more than one pipe. Published quarterly; write for current subscription rates. Two other Pipe Line efforts worthy of note are *Pipe and Pen International Circle*, and the *International Register of Pipe Smokers*.

Denmark

PIBER & TOBAK
Leif Slot, Editor
Ellekrattet 18
2950 Vedbaek.
A colorful journal on pipe smoking, made even more colorful if you happen to read Danish. Even so, the photography on products and events is fascinating.

France

REVUE DES TABACS
9 Rue Saint-Fiacre
75002 Paris.
Gérald Bastien's bi-monthly publication with beautiful color covers and much news, in French, of the world situation as it pertains to tobacco. In addition to the magazine, a highly informative quarterly newsletter is also published.

Italy

AMICI DELLA PIPA
Casella Postale 10734
Roma.
A bi-monthly publication with much news, photography and advertisements concerning pipes and pipemakers.

EXTRA-EXTRA
Corse Vittorio Emanuelle 37/b
20211 Milano.
Published by Luciano Colombi, this magazine even features a centrefold . . . of pipes!

LA PIPA
Museo Italiano Della Pipa
Via Del Chiostro 5
21026 Gavirate (Varese).
A fantastic quarterly publication put out entirely by Alberto Paronelli, a legend in the pipe world. Although only printed in one color, the drawings of pipes are superb, especially when one realizes that Paronelli does all the artwork himself. There is also a compendium of articles, letters and graphics from around the world, some written in French, some in English and some in Italian, or whatever nationality the writer happens to be.

SMOKING
Via della Farnesina, 224
00194 Roma.
A superbly produced four-color magazine with photographs that make you want to light a pipe whenever you pick this magazine up. This is a quarterly publication worth having even if you don't read Italian.

Netherlands

ROOKSIGNALEN
Stichting Pijp van Pijprokersclubs
(Dutch National Organization of Pipe Clubs)
Postbus 40
Oudewater.

United States of America

ANTIQUARIAN TOBACCIANA
11505 Turnbridge Lane
Reston, VA 22094.
A quarterly newsletter put out by Ben Rapaport, one of the true deans of the authoritative pipe smoking world. Contains news of what is happening in the field of tobacco collecting and a listing of out-of-print, rare, and current books and related items of tobacciana for sale. Write for current subscription rates.

Pipe Smoker
P.O. Box 22085
Chattanooga, TN 37422.
The official publication of the Pipe Collectors International. This interesting four-color publication comes out six times a year and is an excellent source of pipe collecting information as well as providing news of local pipe shows and clubs in various areas of the U.S. (See PCI under Pipe Clubs listing.) Write for overseas subscription rates.

The Pipe Smoker's Ephemeris
20–37 120th Street
College Point, NY 11356.
The original international newsletter of casual, relaxing informative reading for pipe smokers. A thick "irregular quarterly" that comes out once or twice a year at best and is eagerly awaited by a vast, worldwide audience of readers who are interested in pipes, smoking, tobacco, Sherlock Holmes and virtually anything else directly or even remotely connected with pipes. (See the Universal Coterie of Pipe Smokers under Pipe Clubs listing.)

Sir Walter Raleigh Pipe Smokers Club Newsletter
P.O. Box 35340
Louisville, KY 40232.
A bi-monthly publication of pipe-worthy news from all over the U.S. Subscription is only a dollar a year and the occasional special offers on pipes and tobaccos make it well worth the price.

West Germany

Die Tabak Zietung
P.O. Box 3120
D-6500 Mainz 1
Federal Republic of West Germany.

Tobak Journal International
P.O. Box 3120
D-6500 Mainz 1
Federal Republic of West Germany.

British Trade Publications

TOBACCO MAGAZINE
Queensway House
2 Queensway
Redhill
Surrey RH1 1QS.

WORLD TOBACCO
Queensway House
2 Queensway
Redhill
Surrey RH1 1QS.

Museums

Many large and small museums throughout the world feature pipes as a part of their overall presentation, but the ones listed here are just a few of those that devote themselves predominantly to historical display of the pipe in its many forms. Not all these museums keep regular hours and if planning to visit, it pays to check with them ahead of time to avoid disappointment.

Austria

Jagd Museum
Hotel Schloss Fuschl
A-5322 Hof bei Salzburg.

Museum der Austria Tabakwerke
Porzellangasse 51
Postfach 14
A-1091, Vienna.

Österr Tobak Museum
1070 Wien
Mariahilfer Strasse 2
Vienna.

Belgium

Musée du Tabac et du Folklore
Musée de Damme
Vresse-sur Semois 6869.

British Isles

Alfred Dunhill Ltd. Museum
30 Duke Street, St James's
London SW1Y 6DL.
Some of the finest, earliest and rarest pipes in England are on display in this pipe smoker's landmark. The various items are rotated periodically, so that different items from the Dunhill Archives are on display at different times of the year. Strategically located near the stairway between the pipe showroom and the cigar cabinet. Open during regular business hours.

The House of Pipes
Bramber, Steyning
Sussex BN4 3WE.
If ever a museum could be called "entertaining", this one is it. Originated in 1973 by curator-showman Anthony Irving, the House of Pipes contains more than 38,000 pipe-related miscellanea, including advertisements, toys, carvings, cartoons, trade tokens, fire prevention items . . . and of course, pipes, pipes, pipes! Open every day except Christmas.

The Sherlock Holmes
10 Northumberland Street
London WC2N 5DA.
Yes, I know this is a pub but some of my greatest pipe research has been conducted in British pubs (especially my classical study on Pipe Smoking and Beer Drinking, which analyzed how long one could go without the other). Besides, this pub houses an excellent collection of memorabilia belonging to the greatest pipe smoker in literature. In addition, a lifesize recreation of the famous sitting room at 221B Baker Street has been encased in a corner of the

upstairs restaurant and gazing at it while eating can help the digestion almost as much as a good pipe afterwards.

Canada

Ontario Tobacco Museum
200 Talbot Road (Highway 3)
Box 182
Delhi, Ontario N4B 2WG.

The Borkum Riff Collection
Imperial Tobacco Products, Ltd.
3860 St. Antoine Street
Montreal, Quebec H4C 1B5.

Denmark

W. Ø. Larsen Museum and Library
9 Amagertorv
DK 1160
Copenhagen.
Located in the centre of Copenhagen in the Pedestrian (Walking) Street, this well-known and well-stocked museum is right next to the original Larsen pipe shop, which first opened its doors in 1864. Inside, one may browse (smoking is permitted!) among the hundreds of artefacts, pipes, books, tins, snuff boxes and related paraphernalia that the Larsen family has been collecting for five generations. If you are lucky, Ole might just be in the building to give you a personal guided tour. Be sure to show him a copy of this book and ask if he ever found the pipe that the author left on his tobacco counter a few years ago.

King Frederik VII's Foundation
Jaegerspris Palace
3630 Jaegerspris.
This is the palace of Denmark's King Frederik VII, who was a dedicated pipe smoker and pipe collector. Here, in addition to many of the king's possessions, you will find his elegant smoking chair (on which he sat, smoked and fished, all at the same time) and Frederik the Great's fantastic collection of

85 pipes, including exquisite meerschaums and silver capped clays. He was known for presenting many favored acquaintances with some of his finest pipes. Even for those of us who regret never having met the king, the palace is well worth the visit.

France

La Confrèrie des Maîtres Pipiers de Saint-Claude
45, Rue de Pré
39200 Saint-Claude.
You do not have to be a member of the Confrèrie to be able to visit this excellent museum that is dedicated to the history and art of pipe smoking.

Fabrique de Pipes
9, Passage des Panoramas
75002, Paris.

Musée Chacom
4, Rue des Etapes
39200 Saint-Claude.

Musée d'Intérêt National du Tabac
Rue Neuve Bergerac
Ville de Bergerac
24100 Bergerac.

Musée de la Seita
12 Rue Surcouf
75007, Paris.
A small museum almost hidden from view on the first floor of an office building, visitors will discover a detailed display of tobacciana, including a surprisingly vast collection of antique pipes.

Japan

Tobacco Trade Monopoly Museum
2-1 Akasaka Aoi-Cho
Mirato-ku, Tokyo.

Italy

Claudio Rebecci Tobacco Museum
P.O. Box 5
41100 Modena, 10.

Musée de la Pipe
via del Chiostro 1/3
21026 Gavirate.
A "must see" collection assembled by master pipe historian Alberto Paronelli.

Netherlands

Douwe-Egberts N.V. kon.Tabaksfabriek
Keulsekade H3, P.O. Box 2
Utrecht.

Niemeyer Nederlands Tabacologisch Museum
Brugstraat 24
9711 HZ Groningen.

Pijpenkabinett Duco
Oude Vest 159a
2312 XW Leiden.
One of the few privately funded pipe museums in existence, this collection provides an extensive research and reference library in addition to more than 10,000 clay pipes of all descriptions, including those excavated from every part of Western Europe, with an emphasis, of course, on Dutch clays. New and old books and clay pipes may be purchased at the museum, which is only open on Sunday or by appointment.

Stedelijke Musea te Gouda
Moriaan (Blackamoor)
Westhwen 29, Gouda.

Sweden

Svenska Tobaksmuseet
Gubbyhyllen, Skansen
Stockholm.

Switzerland

Galerie du Coq Muet
7, rue de l'Academie
1005 Lausanne – Cte.
Opened in 1979 by dedicated collector Jacques Schmied, this museum houses everything from antique firearms to military uniforms, but the best part (to readers of this book) is the pipe museum, which is professionally displayed in the cellar of this 17th century building. More than 2,500 pipes are exhibited, including pipes from Africa, Asia, Europe and the Americas. The pipe museum is also the meeting place for the Swiss Pipe Club and in case you are wondering, the name of the museum is taken from the Coq Muet (silent rooster) pipes which are on display.

United States of America

Half and Half Pipe Collection
Valentine Museum
1015 E. Clay Street
Richmond, VA 23219.

Duke Homestead Historic Site and Tobacco Museum
2828 Duke Homestead Road
Durham, NC 27748.

Phillip Morris Collection
Phillip Morris Manufacturing Center
Operations Center
Commerce Road
Richmond, VA 23234.

Museum of Tobacco Art and History
800 Harrison Street
Nashville, TN 37203.
A superb collection of tobacciana, tracing its origins from the earliest times up through the present. An excellent gift shop with many unusual items, and unique in the fact that it is one of the few remaining establishments in America that does not accept credit cards, so bring cash if you plan to buy something.

National Tobacco-Textile Museum
614 Lynn Street
P.O. Box 541
Danville, VA 24541.

Pioneer's Museum
215 South Tejon Street
Colorado Springs, CO 80903.
Houses the multi-pipe collection of a dedicated Colorado collector.

Pipe Smoker's Hall of Fame
P.O. Box 218
Galveston, IN 46932.
An unusual museum operated by L. E. Lawrence, who only shows his vast collection by appointment, so be sure to write well in advance, as this somewhat eccentric curator is often travelling the world in pursuit of his many interests. More than 1,000 pipes and accessories, collected since 1971, are on display.

West Germany

Deutsche Tabak – und Zigarren Museum
Fünfhausenstrasse 10–12
4980 Bünde Westfalia.

Tabak Museum Husum
Schwermer Schiffbrucke 4 & 6
2251 Husum.

Antique and Estate Pipes – Appraisals, Sales, Brokers

British Isles

Astley's Ltd.
109 Jermyn Street
London, SW14 6WB.
Although actually a tobacco specialist, this store sells and displays a fascinating variety of antique pipes that make it well worth stopping in to browse, if not to buy.

Desmond Sautter Ltd.
106 Mount Street
London W1Y 5HE.
A well known tobacco specialist in Mayfair, the always jovial Desmond Sautter, in addition to his array of excellent modern briars, also has a tantalizing assortment of antique pipes, lighters, and related smoking collectibles for sale.

"The Pipe Shop" Antiquarius
Brian Tipping
139 King's Road
London SW3 5EL.
Located in Chelsea, this small but well stocked shop is crammed full of antique pipes of all descriptions and price ranges, in addition to a wide variety of tools, ashtrays and other vintage accessories.

France

Pipes Anciennes
Denise Corbier
3, Rue de l'Odéon
75006, Paris.

Holland

P. J. G. Tengnagel
P.O. Box 1330-1200 BH
Hilversum.
A mail-order source for clays, tiles, moulds and related items pertaining to the Dutch clay pipe.

United States of America

Ben Rapaport
Antiquarian Tobacciana
11505 Turnbridge Lane
Reston, VA 22094.
Internationally noted authority on antique pipes, literature and related tobacciana.

Barry Levin
Levin Pipes International
RFD 1, Box 83
West Hill Road
Craftsbury, VT 05826.
One of the leading mail order brokers in the U.S. for 20th century pipes of all kinds. Produces a periodic mailing complete with color photos of every pipe.

Bibliography

Pipes and books just seem to go together, whether it be for relaxing reading or to delve deeper into the mysteries of tobacciana. Come to think of it, that's how *this* book got started! Listed here are some of the volumes that may help your next bowlful smoke just a little more mellower than before.

BARRIE, J. M. *My Lady Nicotine*. London: Hodder and Stoughton, 1890.

DUNHILL, ALFRED. *The Pipe Book*. London: A. & C. Black, Ltd.; New York: The Macmillan Co., 1924; revised ed., London: Arthur Barker Limited; New York: The Macmillan Co., 1969.

DUNHILL, ALFRED H. *The Gentle Art of Smoking*. London: Max Reinhardt Ltd.; New York: G. P. Putnam and Sons, 1954.

EHWA, CARL Jr. *The Book of Pipes and Tobacco*. New York: Random House, 1974.

FAIRHOLT, F. W. *Tobacco: Its History and Associations*. London: Chapman and Hall, 1859; reprint ed., Detroit: Singing Tree Press, 1968.

FISHER, ROBERT LEWIS. *The Odyssey of Tobacco*. Hartford: The Case, Lockwood & Brainard Company, 1939.

GRAVES, CHARLES. *A Pipe Smoker's Guide*. London: Icon Books Ltd., 1969.

HACKER, RICHARD CARLETON. *The Christmas Pipe*. Beverly Hills: Autumngold Publishing, 1986.

HAMILTON, A. E. *This Smoking World*. New York: The Century Co., 1927.

HERMENT, GEORGES. *The Pipe*. New York: Simon and Schuster, 1955.

Pipe and Pouch. The Smoker's Own Book of Poetry. Compiled by Joseph Knight. Boston: Joseph Knight Company, 1895.

The Pleasures of Smoking. Compiled by Sylvestre C. Watkins. New York: Henry Schuman, Inc., 1948.

RAM, SIDNEY P. *How to Get More Fun Out of Smoking*. Chicago: Wisconsin Cuneo Press, Inc., 1949.

RAPAPORT, BENJAMIN. *A Complete Guide to Collecting Antique Pipes*. Exton: Schiffer Publishing Limited, 1979.

Tobacco Dictionary. Edited by Raymond Jahn. New York: Philosophical Library, 1954.

WEBER, CARL. *Carl Weber's The Pleasures of Pipe Smoking*. New York: Bantam Books, 1965.

WERNER, CARL AVERY. *Tobaccoland*. New York: The Tobacco Leaf Publishing Company, 1922.

Whifflets. Compiled by A. M. Jenkinson, Pittsburg: R. & W. Jenkinson Co., 1897.

Additional Readings/Reference Works

Tobacco Encyclopedia
c/o Tobak-Journal International
Postfach 3120
6500 Mainz am Rhein
West Germany.
Published in 1984, this is a collection of more than 6,000 tobacco terms and their meanings. In English.

Briar Pipe Shapes & Styles
c/o J. P. Cole
Hill Park Publications
18 Kay Avenue
Meadowlands Park
Weybridge Road, Addlestone
Surrey KT15 2RE.

"The Ultimate Pipe Video" hosted by Richard Carleton Hacker. Beverly Hills: Autumngold Publishing, 1987. VHS; Running time: 60 minutes.

Index

Page numbers in bold type refer to illustrations